BEYOND
ECONOMIC
MAN

BEYOND ECONOMIC MAN

Feminist Theory and Economics

Edited by

Marianne A. Ferber and Julie A. Nelson

THE UNIVERSITY OF CHICAGO PRESS / CHICAGO AND LONDON

The University of Chicago Press, Chicago 60637
The University of Chicago Press, Ltd., London
© 1993 by The University of Chicago
All rights reserved. Published 1993
Printed in the United States of America
02 01 00 99 98 97 96 95 94 93   2 3 4 5

ISBN: 0-226-24200-5 (cloth)
ISBN: 0-226-24201-3 (paper)

Library of Congress Cataloging-in-Publication Data

Beyond economic man: feminist theory and economics / edited by
   Marianne A. Ferber and Julie A. Nelson.
      p.   cm.
   Includes bibliographical references and index.
   1. Feminist theory—Economic aspects. 2. Economics. I. Ferber,
Marianne A., 1923–   II. Nelson, Julie A., 1956–
HQ1190.B48   1993
305.42′01—dc20   92–40149
                                                     CIP

⊗The paper used in this publication meets the minimum requirements of the
American National Standard for Information Sciences—Permanence of Paper for
Printed Library Materials, ANSI Z39.48-1984.

Contents

Preface

What can feminist theory possibly have to say about economics? If economics is practiced correctly, that is, as an objective science, are not its methods and assumptions beyond the reach of social and political movements? Would not openness to influences from interest-group positions like feminism undermine the ideal of impartiality of economic study?

The subtitle of this book, *Feminist Theory and Economics,* may well appear to be an oxymoron to a reader who subscribes to such views. The main title, *Beyond Economic Man* may be equally puzzling, since it seems to suggest that the goal of the book is to replace the study of economics. We intend for the title to be read with the emphasis on the word "man." As economists and social scientists, we want to retain and improve economic analysis by ridding the discipline of the biases created by the centrality of distinctively masculine concerns. Feminists raise questions not because economics is too objective but because it is not objective enough. Too many assumptions and methodological ideals have been exempted from critical scrutiny because existing communities of economists have perceived them as universal and impartial.

Economists today and in the past have filled volumes with discussions of what might be wrong (as well as what may be right) with our profession, but mention of any tie to sexism has been extremely rare. More recently, feminist theories have brought forth a substantial literature on questions of feminism and the pursuit of knowledge, but they have focused largely on the physical sciences and social sciences other than economics. The first discussions of the possible connections between feminist theory and mainstream economic research to achieve high visibility in the economics profession took place at sessions of the 1989 meetings of the Southern Economic Association and the American Economic Association. Plans for the present volume started soon thereafter and were finalized at a small conference following the Midwest Economics Association meetings in April 1990. This book is the first of its kind. We trust that it will serve to expand the discussion of the issues it raises, bring the discussion to the attention of a wider range of scholars, and lead to improvements in economic practice.

Marianne A. Ferber and
Julie A. Nelson

Introduction: The Social Construction of Economics and the Social Construction of Gender

Is the development of the discipline of economics a story of continuous refinement and unidirectional progress, guided only by the internal requirement of logical coherence and the self-evident "nature" of external economic phenomena? If this is so, then social distinctions such as gender and social movements such as feminism are largely irrelevant for the development of economic analysis. If this is so, then, as one of the most influential books on the history of economic thought suggests, the story of economics can be written as "yesterday's blunders now corrected . . . , undiluted by entertaining historical digressions or biographical coloring" (Blaug 1962, ix).

Many feminists find such an ahistorical, disembodied account of the discipline bizarre. In the extreme it suggests that the ideals and definition of economics have been given to humankind through divine intervention, or perhaps dropped from a Friedmanesque helicopter. If we instead recognize that the discipline we call economics has been developed by particular human actors, it is hard to see how it could fail to be critically influenced by the limitations implicit in human cognition and by the social, cultural, economic, and political milieu in which it has been created. Acknowledging the importance of human factors and social influences by no means implies a wholesale rejection of current practices or an abandonment of the pursuit of objectivity. As the chapters show, it can improve the objectivity of practice.

This introduction begins by reviewing how the role of people within economics, and the attention given to their experiences, has differed according to their sex. We then turn to feminist theory, which explores the links between the social construction of scientific disciplines and the social construction of gender, to suggest reasons why such differences in experience should not be dismissed as just "historical digressions or biographical coloring."

Men, Women, and Economics

The most obvious point to be made about gender and the social construction of economics is that historically, and continuing to the present day, men have dominated the community of scholars who have created the discipline. Equally important, gender also affects the construction of the discipline in terms of the standpoint from which the world is perceived, and the way the importance and relevance of questions are evaluated. Certain activities and experiences that are historically of greater concern to women than to men have all too frequently been neglected. Further, even when economists have attempted to understand phenomena from such traditionally feminine realms as the home and family, the results are often judged as unsatisfactory by feminists who believe that the analysis of women's experiences is inadequate or even biased.

Economists Are (Mostly) Male

The small number of women listed in Mark Blaug's *Who's Who in Economics* is one indication of the extent to which women have been absent from the ranks of prestigious economists who have played a significant part in shaping the discipline. A mere thirty-one out of one. thousand entries are women. Only five of these women were born before the turn of the century; seventeen have been born since 1930.[1] Other evidence points in the same direction. No woman has yet received the Nobel Prize in economics. All seven recipients of the Francis A. Walker medal, bestowed by the American Economic Association every five years between 1947 and 1972, have been men, as have the twenty-one recipients of the John Bates Clark medal awarded between 1947 and 1989, and the thirty-seven honorary members from other countries in 1989. Of the forty distinguished fellowships awarded between 1965 and 1989, only one was bestowed on a woman.[2] There has been one woman president of the American Economic Association since it was founded in 1886.[3]

The proportion of economists who are women has increased in recent years, but women continue to be underrepresented among recipients of advanced degrees and among faculties of colleges and universities, particularly

1. Blaug's selections were based on the number of citations each author had during the years 1972–83. The five female economists born before 1900 are Rosa Luxemburg, Jane Marcet, Mary P. Marshall, Harriet Martineau, and Beatrice P. Webb; those born between 1900 and 1930 are Carolyn S. Bell, Barbara R. Bergmann, Mary J. Bowman, Phyllis M. Deane, Selma Mushkin, Barbara R. B. Reagan, Joan Robinson, Anna Schwartz, and Barbara M. Ward. Dorothy Lampen Thomson's *Adam Smith's Daughters* (1973) claims to "fill a void that exists in most treatises on the history of economics" by discussing the contribution of six women: five from Blaug's list, plus Millicent G. Fawcett.

2. Margaret G. Reid

3. Alice M. Rivlin, who was president in 1986.

in senior ranks and at the most prestigious institutions. Between 1949–50 and 1985–86, the share of B.A. degrees in economics awarded to women rose from 8 percent to 34 percent, the share of M.A. degrees rose from 12 percent to 26 percent, and the share of Ph.D. degrees rose from 5 percent to 20 percent (National Center for Education Statistics 1977–78, 1988). The Committee on the Status of Women in the Economics Profession (1990) reports that while women made up 16 percent of the faculty of undergraduate institutions in 1988–89, only 9 percent of the faculty and only 3 percent of the full professors at universities with graduate programs were women.

One frequently suggested explanation for the low number of women majoring in economics is that women are inadequately prepared in mathematics. However, in 1985–86 fully 47 percent of bachelor's degrees and 35 percent of master's degrees in mathematics were awarded to women. (NCES 1977–78, 1988).[4] Assuming that the equivalent of an M.A. in mathematics is currently adequate for an economist, there appears to be little support for this explanation. There is somewhat more reason to believe that a differential by sex in the understanding of undergraduate economics could be part of an explanation: an extensive review of the literature on economic education yielded some evidence that female undergraduate students tend to do less well in economics courses than male students, even though females' overall grade point averages tend to be higher (Siegfried 1979). The reasons for females' poorer performance have been little researched.

Two studies found that when essay questions were used instead of the standard multiple-choice questions, men's and women's scores were no longer significantly different (Ferber, Birnbaum, and Green 1983; Morawetz 1976). In addition, the "classroom climate" may be relatively unfriendly toward women students because of lack of support by predominantly male faculty[5] and because stereotypical or disparaging references to women continue to be found in undergraduate textbooks.[6] Or the construction of economics itself may continue to signal to students its status as a distinctively masculine preserve.

Women who do go on to get doctoral degrees and take jobs in academia advance to associate and full professor levels in lower numbers than would be expected, given the number of female assistant professors (CSWEP 1990). While direct discrimination is one possible explanation, research has focused on the extent to which lower measured productivity may play a role. Far less

4. Even the percentage of women among Ph.D.s has been about as high in mathematics as in economics.

5. Teachers have been found to be more supportive of students of the same sex (Tidball 1976).

6. Feiner and Morgan (1987) cite a number of such stories about women, for example, the story of a female graduate student who has to learn about supply from an old roadside vegetable vendor (Leftwich 1984). Ferber (1990) also discusses the "classroom climate" in undergraduate economics courses.

attention has focused on the question of whether women have equal opportunity to become productive.

Mary Fish and Jean Gibbons (1989) found that in a sample of persons who received Ph.Ds between 1969 and 1984, matched by subfield and year of degree (but not by the quality of the institution at which they were employed), men published more than women. Two studies have compared women's and men's acceptance rates by economics journals with and without double-blind refereeing.[7] The first (Ferber and Teiman 1980) found that women did relatively better under double-blind refereeing, while the second, more recent study found no significant difference (Blank 1991). In addition to quantity of publications, number of citations increasingly has been used as a measure of economists' quality in promotion decisions. Two studies—one that focused specifically on labor economics (Ferber 1986), another that considered five different fields (Ferber 1988)—determined that scholars are more inclined to cite work by authors of the same sex, a clear disadvantage to women as long as the field remains predominantly male.

One very recent study (Dillingham, Ferber, and Hamermesh 1991) has looked at another factor that may be taken into account in promotion decisions: election to offices in professional societies. This examination of a regional economics association found not only that female voters favored women candidates significantly but that male voters also favored them, albeit very slightly. Thus some recent evidence suggests that the situation for women may be improving. But long-term effects of past discrimination, a continuing lack of women mentors, and employment structures that put the highest emphasis on professional achievement during the potential childbearing years may continue to take their toll.[8]

The World of "Economic Man"

Women have been largely absent not only as economic researchers but also as the subjects of economic study. Margaret Reid intensively studied the traditional "women's realm" of household production in the 1930s (e.g.,

7. In single-blind refereeing, the referee knows the author's name, and thus, in most cases, is also likely to know the author's sex. Experimental studies often have shown that if evaluators are told the sex of the author of an article or application, evaluations are lower for women than for men even on identical written work. A review in Wallston and O'Leary (1981) concluded that such "competence biases favoring men are more pronounced when women engage in tasks or seek jobs typically reserved for men" (20).

8. On the importance of mentors, see Berg and Ferber (1983). On the potential problems created by the "clockwork of academic careers" see Hochschild (1975). The effects of family responsibilities, however, should not be overemphasized: not all women economists choose family involvement, and, in spite of continuing inequities in the division of household tasks (and in contradiction of the theory of Becker 1985), there is little evidence that women put forth less effort on the job (Bielby and Bielby 1988). Further, there is no evidence that the productivity of mothers is lower than that of other women (Hamovitch and Morgenstern 1977).

Reid 1934), but such analysis was not given a permanent place in mainstream economics until much later. The first edition of Paul Samuelson's *Economics* (1948) had only two references to "females" and none to "women," both included in a segment on "minorities." Even today, women and families remain strangely absent from many "general" discussions of economic matters.

A few examples will serve to illustrate this point. Consider this recent textbook discussion: "The unit of analysis in economics is the individual . . . [although] individuals group together to form collective organizations such as corporations, labor unions, and governments" (Gwartney, Stroup, and Clark 1985). Somehow the family escaped attention. Or consider this recent argument that consumption is individual while production is social: "If you ask a modern individual who they are, they will usually not tell you about their religion, their hobbies, or the clubs to which they belong. They will first tell you where they work and their occupation. Work is the domain from which one gets esteem in the modern world. . . . We are individual consumers in nuclear families but we are social producers" (Thurow 1988). One must ask whether the "individual" and "we" do not display a distinctively masculine tendency toward identification from work rather than relationships, and whether the notion of "individual consumers in nuclear families" is not fundamentally confused. Such a blind spot when it comes to women's traditional identification through family relations, and disregard of the possibility that the same may be true of men, implies "invisibility" of women and families in the analysis of "human" behavior.

Similarly, little attention is given to the economic value of household work, traditionally done mostly by women. Again taking an example from a textbook, the complete discussion of this issue consists of three sentences: "Many people, particularly leaders of the women's movement, argue that household work should be given a value and included in GNP. This is worth thinking about. Would it be a reasonable thing to do? If so, how would one go about valuing household production?" (Reynolds 1988). Marilyn Waring (1988) and Nancy Folbre (1991) have discussed additional incidents of such neglect and the consequences they have for social statistics and policy. Standard discussions of human capital formation (e.g., Ehrenberg and Smith 1991) start with a discussion of secondary schooling; they ignore the socialization and education processes undertaken at home as well as the care from birth (or even from before birth, as in maternal health and nutrition) devoted to creating and developing a child's capacities.

Even when a topic that is particularly relevant to women is discussed, the gender aspect of the question may be ignored. Lloyd Reynolds (1988), for example, devotes four pages to problems of poverty without ever mentioning the disproportionate representation of women (and particularly women of color) among the ranks of the poor. To the extent that such a tendency to neglect women's issues discourages women students from pursuing study in economics, or to the extent that it goes hand in hand with evaluation of research done on these issues as less important, the patterns of underrepresentation of women discussed in the last section may be reinforced.

Are Women's Experiences Distorted?

Women's rising participation in the paid labor force, and the "women's realm" of the home and family, received noticeably more attention from mainstream economists starting in the mid-1960s. Gary Becker's "A Theory of the Allocation of Time" (1965) and Reuben Gronau's "Leisure, Home Production and Work" (1977) formally introduced work at home as another third alternative in models of individual choice in addition to paid labor and leisure.[9] In "A Theory of Marriage" (1973, 1974), Becker developed a neoclassical model of household behavior that posited a "caring" or "altruistic" household head. A 1974 volume, *Economics of the Family,* edited by Theodore Schultz, included several more papers pursuing these themes. Together, these works laid the foundation for what came to be called the "new home economics."

Directing attention to women and families was certainly a move in the right direction. However, simply adding women as the subjects without changing the tools of analysis has been described as "add women and stir" in the feminist literature. It is interesting to note that the birth of the "new home economics" was accompanied by a contemporaneous, if less well-known, critique by feminist economists. Carolyn Shaw Bell (1974), Marianne Ferber and Bonnie Birnbaum (1977), and Isabel Sawhill (1977) all expressed early reservations about this line of research, in part because such research often served to reinforce outdated assumptions about "natural" male and female behavior. For example, they raised the question "whether economists have done anything more than describe the status quo in a society where sex roles are 'givens'" (Sawhill, 120). They also pointed out the circular reasoning in early arguments, which claimed that, on the one hand, women earn less in the marketplace because of "their" household responsibilities while, on the other hand, women specialize in home production because they earn less in the labor market. Becker's assumption of an "altruistic" household head raised feminist ire, both for its patriarchal bias and because the "heads'" unique capability was ascribed to his altruism rather than his power over household resources.

More fundamentally, these and later authors have suggested that, in general, models of free individual choice are not adequate to analyze behavior fraught with issues of dependence, interdependence, tradition, and power. Tradition, in particular, may be a far more powerful force in determining the allocation of household tasks than rational optimization. Sawhill (1977) sug-

---

9. This was, of course, in some sense a rediscovery and extension of Reid (1934).

gested that "received microeconomic doctrine" may sometimes be a "Procrustean bed," "obliterating" areas of interest such as intrahousehold conflict. Myra Strober (1987) has challenged a number of widely accepted fundamental assumptions of neoclassical economics: "that human beings are rational and maximizing; that efficiency is 'good' because it produces greater welfare; that consumers and workers are hedonistic; that welfare is equivalent to, or at least approximated by, income; and that consumers and workers are atomistic and exhibit constant tastes" (136).

This is not the place for a complete analysis of the "new home economics" in its many varieties, or of the appropriateness of neoclassical tools. More recent criticisms of masculine biases in work on women and families can be found in several works, including those by Nancy Folbre and Heidi Hartmann (1988) and Barbara Bergmann (1986, 1987).[10] Amartya Sen has investigated the applicability of the usual conception of "utility" when women may be socialized to expect little (1990) and has pointed out limitations on the usefulness of bargaining models to examine intrahousehold conflict (1985).

What Is a Feminist to Do?

As we have seen, feminists have noted and commented on the frequent exclusion of women and their experiences, and what they perceive as distortions of women's experiences by mainstream economists.[11] At a minimum, gender ideology can make a difference in what problems are selected for research, how research is operationalized, and how findings are interpreted (Blau 1981). Normative judgments enter even when only measurement of existing relationships appears to be involved. For instance, when investigating whether equally qualified men and women on university faculties receive equal rewards, rank may be used as an independent variable influencing salary or may itself be regarded as one of the rewards to be investigated. Similarly, value judgments enter when interpreting outcomes, since, contrary to general belief, facts do not speak for themselves. For example, the fact that women and men are often found in different occupations may be assumed to be the result of differences in tastes, or the possibility of discrimination may be considered.

In many other disciplines as well as in the cross-disciplinary field of women's studies, a more extensive process of identifying such biases and seeking

10. Bergmann writes that Gary Becker "explains, justifies, and even glorifies role differentiation by sex. . . . To say that the 'new home economists' are not feminist in their orientation would be as much of an understatement as to say that Bengal tigers are not vegetarians" (1987, 132–33).

11. Other published or soon-to-be-published works on feminist perspectives on mainstream economics not cited elsewhere include Barrett (1981), Cohen (1982, 1985), Feiner and Roberts (1990), Ferber and Teiman (1980, 1981), Nelson (1987), and Seiz (1989).

solutions has been going on for a much longer time.[12] Only a thumbnail sketch of some major currents is offered here. Responses to perceived inadequacies in the academic disciplines can be loosely grouped into five, not necessarily mutually exclusive, categories: what we shall call "affirmative action," "feminist empiricism," "feminist 'difference,'" "feminist postmodernism," and "feminist constructionism." The last alternative, being the one most authors in this volume find most congenial, will be described in greater detail.

Four Suggested Alternatives

In the "affirmative action" view, the central problem with the discipline is the underrepresentation of women. The Committee on the Status of Women in the Economics Profession (CSWEP) of the American Economic Association emphasizes this approach. It has taken on the job of monitoring and encouraging women's advancement, publishing regular reports and newsletters and sponsoring sessions at the national and regional meetings. While complementary to several of the other approaches, the affirmative action view need not imply dissatisfaction with the way a discipline is practiced, only with the underrepresentation of women among its practitioners.

Sandra Harding coined the term "feminist empiricism" to refer to the position that "social biases [are] correctable by stricter adherence to the existing methodological norms of scientific inquiry" (1986, 24). Thus, it is not the tools of the discipline that need improvement, only the way they are applied. As the Swedish economist Siv Gustaffson says, for example, "It is not the [neoclassical economic] theory that is patriarchic, but the questions male economists have asked and the conclusions they have drawn and particularly the policy implications based on the research" (1990, 6). Casual conversation suggests that most feminist economists currently adhere to this view.[13]

The next two positions appear to have considerably lower representation among economists. Proponents of "feminist 'difference'" emphasize distinctions between men and women. They often make claims for women's superiority in creating knowledge based on women's experiences, including experiences of oppression or what they call women's "ways of knowing." Some suggest that since the failures and biases of men's past inquiry are the result of their "masculinist" methods, women should use "gynocentric" or women-centered methods in their research. At the extreme, values of objectivity, reason, and analytical inquiry might simply be overthrown in favor of their

12. See, for example, Aiken et al. (1988), Bleier (1986), Eisenstein and Jardine (1980), Farnham (1987), J. Harding (1986), S. Harding (1987), Harding and O'Barr (1987), Jaggar and Bordo (1989), Keller (1985), Lowe and Hubbard (1983), Spender (1981), and Tuana (1989).

13. Given the preponderance of antifeminist and afeminist ("I haven't thought about it") views among economists, including some women economists, espousal of feminist opinions, even of the affirmative action or feminist empiricist sort, may still constitute some risk to professional advancement and hence require courage on the part of the individual.

feminine-identified opposites: subjectivity, emotion, and a holistic approach. There is obviously little common ground for dialogue between those who hold this extreme view and practicing economists and scientists. Indeed there is little likelihood (given self-selection, cognitive dissonance, and professional pressure) that an active economist would subscribe to these views. However, works such as Belenky et al. (1986), Stanley and Wise (1983), Gilligan (1982), and Ruddick (1989), which are sometimes caricatured as taking a radical "difference" stance, contain a more subtle and complex analysis. The extreme "feminist 'difference' " position often serves as a handy *mis*conception in the discussion about science, particularly for those unfamiliar with more sophisticated views. Thus, for instance, Evelyn Fox Keller, a noted writer on the subject of gender and science, recounts with apparent frustration how she has been interpreted as advocating a "female science" (1986, 170).

The intellectual movement of "postmodernism" in general has had little impact on economics; for practical purposes, feminist discussions and uses of postmodernism or deconstructionism are unknown in economics. Associated with the work of Jacques Derrida (1976), Jean-François Lyotard (1984), Michel Foucault (1976), and others in philosophy and literary criticism, this intellectual movement seeks to "deconstruct" traditional understandings. Discussions of feminist postmodernism include Alcoff (1988), Scott (1988), Poovey (1988), and Nicholson (1990). A crucial issue in their discussions is the extent to which gender is a meaningful categorization or whether it also requires deconstruction. As is true of " 'difference' feminism," the majority of economists (who tend to view delving into literary criticism an endeavor of small marginal value) are likely to find little intellectual common ground with feminist postmodernism in its more highbrow forms.

Feminist Constructionism

Studies of the intertwining of the social construction of gender and the social construction of science, sometimes considered "postmodern" in the broader sense of being "after modernism," hold the most appeal for the majority of social scientists writing in this volume. At present, this approach probably provides the best basis for a dialogue between feminist theory and economics. Even here, however, a careful introduction of the central ideas and vocabulary of a feminist and social constructivist view is necessary to provide a foundation for understanding. Let us now briefly explain some of the key concepts of what we call "feminist constructionism." [14]

1. "Gender," as the word is used by many feminists, means something quite different from biological sex. Gender is the *social meaning* given to biological

14. The explanations are derived from a wide range of feminist discussion, although particular aspects of their meaning may remain in dispute. Blame for oversimplification remains with the authors of this chapter.

differences between the sexes; it refers to cultural constructs rather than to biological givens.

2. It is a basic tenet of feminism that many of the characteristics traditionally attributed to either women or men on the basis of biology are more general human characteristics whose identification as "feminine" or "masculine" is a matter of social belief. Patterns of gender attribution are, in fact, subject to considerable historical and cross-cultural variation. Therefore, facile conflation of biological men with constructions of masculinity, or of women with femininity, is condemned as *essentialism*—the mistaken belief that a certain trait is "of the essence" of man or woman instead of socially constructed.

3. Another problem with the word "gender" is that it is often read as "pertaining to women." This confusion arises because it is often assumed that attributes traditionally associated with men are "human," neutral, and universal while only those traits associated with women contain the "contamination" of gender. Such a view is labeled *masculinist* or *androcentric* (i.e., centered about a masculine ideal, with feminine aspects considered marginal and inferior). Feminist discussions of the ideals of science focus, in fact, not so much on the problems created by the absence of women as on the problems created by the power of myths of masculinity.

4. The predominance or *privileging* of masculine ideals is seen as based on an unjust and damaging disparagement of qualities perceived as feminine. In order to remedy the situation, women's experiences and ideals (and at least certain aspects of traditional femininity) must be elevated or *valorized;* in some cases where gender systems used to be different, they must be *revalorized*.

5. Modern Western culture associates masculinity with ideals of *separation* or *separativeness*, femininity with ideals of *connection* or *relation*. In the masculine model, people are perceived primarily as individuals who are separated both from nature and from other humans. In the feminine model, people are regarded as more integrally connected to human and ecological communities. For example, European and American men traditionally have been identified through their individual exploits or their jobs while women have been identified by their relationships as wives and mothers. Many institutions developed under male domination, including science, are likely to display an unjustified affinity with masculine attitudes of detachment and autonomy.

Feminist theory, as applied to science in general and economics in particular, accordingly claims that peculiarly masculine ideals have influenced the formation of science, probably to our benefit but also to our harm. As Sandra Harding writes in *The Science Question in Feminism:*

> Mind vs. nature and the body, reason vs. emotion and social commitment, subject vs. object and objectivity vs. subjectivity, the abstract and the general vs. the concrete and particular—in

each case we are told that the former must dominate the latter lest human life be overwhelmed by irrational and alien forces, forces symbolized in science as the feminine. All these dichotomies play important roles in the intellectual structures of science, and all appear to be associated both historically and in contemporary psyches with distinctively masculine sexual and gender identity projects. (1986, 25)

The issue, then, is whether valorization of some or all of the "feminine" aspects previously excluded would improve the practice of science, and of economics.

An immediate question may be raised about whether the introduction of "feminine" qualities, such as emotion and social commitment, might destroy the objectivity of the scientific enterprise. But this question misses the point. The valorization of feminine-identified qualities discussed here does not imply either the introduction of gender or the creation of a "female science." Gender is already deeply embedded in scientific practice—it just happens to be gender of the masculine kind and hence less noticeable to those who have come to accept masculine values as the only admissible ones. We do not seek to excise all of the values traditionally associated with science but to investigate and remedy the biases that may arise from an unexamined emphasis on masculinity. Objectivity, the search for knowledge that does not reflect particularistic biases, is still a goal. However, it is no longer assumed that objectivity can be reached by the individual researcher, even when he or she follows certain correct methods of investigation. Scholarly work on the social construction of science (e.g., Kuhn 1962, 1970; Feyerabend 1976; works reviewed in Gergen 1985) suggests that objectivity is more of a social than an individual phenomenon. Helen Longino's description of objectivity makes a useful sixth entry to our glossary:

> 6. The *objectivity* of individuals . . . consists in their participation in the collective give-and-take of critical discussion and not in some special relation (of detachment, hardheadedness) they may bear to their observations. Thus understood, objectivity is dependent upon the depth and scope of the transformative interrogation that occurs in any given scientific community. This community-wide process ensures (or can ensure) that the hypotheses ultimately accepted as supported by some set of data do not reflect a single individual's idiosyncratic assumptions about the natural world. To say that a theory or hypothesis was accepted on the basis of objective methods does not entitle us to say it is true but rather that it reflects the critically achieved consensus of the scientific community. In the absence of some form of privileged access to transempirical (unobservable) phenomena it's not clear we should hope for anything better. (1990, 79; emphasis added)

This does not imply that it is acceptable for any group of people to choose to believe any theory they wish; there is a real world, and a scientific approach requires that we seek evidence from that world to support or disprove our hypotheses. However, decisions about whether hypotheses deserve investigation as well as about what constitutes acceptable and convincing evidence are made by scientific communities. From this perspective, the idea that objectivity is individually attainable through rigorous methods, emotional detachment, and "separation" from both the object of study and other researchers itself appears to be an emotionally loaded, culturally created construct. The general devaluation of women and of all things culturally associated with femininity may be partly responsible for resistance to the idea of science as connected to and practiced for the benefit of the community.

Why a Feminist Analysis?

Many of the criticisms of current economic practice that will be voiced in this volume have been voiced elsewhere without feminist identification. Among numerous attempts to move beyond the usual practice are critical discussions of efficiency by Harvey Leibenstein (1969, 1976); of the neglect of social considerations by Robert Frank (1985); of the emphasis on formalism by Nicholas Georgescu-Roegen (1966) and Donald McCloskey (1991); of rationality in a collection edited by Karen Schweers Cook and Margaret Levi (1990); of self-interest in a collection edited by Jane Mansbridge (1990); of the importance of language by Donald McCloskey (1985, 1990); of the neglect of policy by Alan Blinder (1988); of the importance of power by Kenneth Boulding (1989); and of neoclassical labor market theory by Robert Solow (1990). At the same time, no coherent body of new theory has emerged from these piecemeal critiques, no matter how valuable they have been individually.

Further, to a surprising degree these authors have failed to apply their innovative ideas to subjects that have been of special concern to women. Three examples will suffice to make this point. Harvey Leibenstein's "X-efficiency" theory posits that the behavior of interacting individuals is determined by differences in personality and varying conditions rather than by the usual model of autonomous, rationally optimizing agents. While such a theory would seem to have particularly important implications for analysis of households, emphasis has been placed largely on application to firms, and Leibenstein's (1976) own discussion of intrahousehold consumption is curiously gender-free. Robert Solow (1990) has raised the question of how systems of wages may be the result of commonly accepted rules of equity and institutional controls, both of which could constitute substantial hurdles to the operation of equilibrating forces. He even suggests that wages have to be regarded as an independent variable, likely to be important in determining the productivity of labor. Yet he fails to note the relevance of this view to "comparable worth," an issue that has been high on the agenda of many feminists. Donald Mc-Closkey (1985) put great faith in the "body of enlightened scholars" rather than positivist methodological rules to guide economic research. Yet only two of the ninety-two economists and economic historians in the group of scholars he mentions in his acknowledgments are women.

Ironically, the fact that these criticisms have remained piecemeal and have failed to become the new mainstream views may—in spite of their neglect of women's viewpoints—have something to do with sexism. Eliminating androcentrism would involve not merely localized modifications but altering a self-image and a worldview with deep emotional as well as intellectual roots. Is it easier to ignore or to misunderstand these critiques, or merely to label them "interesting" and then forget them, in part because they seem "soft" and "touchy-feely," or "feminine"?

This is not to say, of course, that the feminist analysis presented here pretends to remedy all difficulties in the profession. For one, women have not been the only group historically excluded from the construction of economics. The authors of this volume, while challenging male hegemony in the profession, are all professionals, United States citizens, and, with only one exception, of European descent. Our views are therefore unavoidably partial, and further work from the perspective of women and men of other ethnicities, races, classes, nationalities, and cultures is needed to ensure the sort of objectivity described earlier. An interesting dialogue has, in fact, arisen between the African-American male economist Vernon Dixon (1970, 1976) and the feminist theorist Sandra Harding (1987) regarding similarities and differences between feminist and African-American worldviews. Such discussions are likely to enrich the analysis by revealing previously invisible biases and limitations.

In this book we focus on how economics could be improved by being freed from the straitjacket of masculine mythology. As noted earlier, such a view does not require that all of the methods of scientific investigation developed to date be rejected. Rather, it requires a new conception of where such methods fit in the overall picture of human knowledge and a willingness to consider methods previously rejected, not because they were bad or ineffective but simply because they were perceived as "feminine." One should not infer that this position attributes "feminine" cognitive traits only to women. The point is that while men can think in stereotypically feminine ways and women can think in stereotypically masculine ways, both men and women have become accustomed to regarding the feminine as being of lesser value. For this reason, the simple entry of women into economics is not likely to be sufficient to change economic practice. However, the denial of entry to women is one indicator of the strength and persistence of strong cultural sexism; it indicates the distance that remains to be traveled before economic practice can be freed from its masculine biases.

Elements of a Feminist Analysis of Economics

This volume explores the implications of feminist theories of the construction of science with specific application to economics. Four essays, by Julie A. Nelson, Paula England, Diana Strassmann, and Donald N. Mc-Closkey, focus on mainstream or "neoclassical" economics; Nancy Folbre looks at socialist economic thought; and Ann L. Jennings writes about the institutionalist school of economics. Rebecca M. Blank and Robert M. Solow provide commentary on these main chapters from the point of view of mainstream economics, Rhonda M. Williams offers reflections informed by considerations of postmodernism and race; and Helen E. Longino offers a review from the perspective of a feminist philosopher of science. Within these broad subject categories, many of the themes outlined above emerge and reemerge.

Julie A. Nelson concentrates on controversy about the definition of economics. She argues that economists' overwhelming reliance on mathematical models of individual choice, to the exclusion of other approaches, reflects masculinist biases rooted in Cartesian divisions between rationality and embodiment. She also suggests that the discipline should not be concerned merely with goods and services traded in the market but with all necessities and conveniences that sustain and improve life. She concludes that the discipline would be far richer if it became a fully "human" science that made full use of the tools of "imaginative rationality."

Paula England takes as her subject the androcentric biases in the basic assumptions of neoclassical economics. She points out that three crucial postulates—the impossibility of interpersonal utility comparisons, exogenous and unchanging tastes, and selfish behavior in market transactions—flow from the premise that each economic agent is a "separative self," emotionally disconnected from others. She contrasts these postulates with the opposite assumption that individuals are entirely altruistic in families. She discusses the origin of the separative self assumption and its consequences for economic practice, and argues that these two polarized assumptions together serve to hide women's disadvantage in markets and in their families.

Have the assumptions of self-interested individualism and contractual exchange become dominant in economics because they have won out in a competitive "marketplace of ideas"? Diana Strassmann's chapter challenges such a view, maintaining instead that these core concepts serve as exclusionary devices, insulating the discipline from alternative, and more adequate, perspectives. She discusses four "stories" that serve to exclude issues of values and power—stories of the benevolent patriarch, the woman of leisure, free choice, and the "marketplace of ideas" itself. Because models are by nature incomplete, she argues, a greater openness to alternative perspectives would allow the discipline to capture the complexity of economic activities more successfully.

Unlike the earlier chapters, which tend to focus on gender as a social construct, Donald N. McCloskey takes as his starting point the premise that men and women tend to differ in their approach to economics because they live different lives. In this view, some of the limitations of economics can be traced to the virtual exclusion of the feminine perspective. Nonetheless, he hopes, much as Nelson does, that a "conjective" economics would enlarge and humanize the field, giving its practitioners, male and female alike, a "tolerant confidence" they now often lack.

Nancy Folbre is concerned with the interaction between socialism and feminism in economics. She points out that Marx and Engels downplayed feminist concerns, partly to establish political economy as a science. This distinction between scientific socialism and the utopian socialism of reformers who were more concerned with values and morality for the most part has been uncritically accepted by historians of economic thought. Hence the views of this latter group were largely ignored, and the strongest advocates of women's rights were placed essentially outside the purview of economics. Folbre includes both schools within the broader context of feminist socialism.

Ann L. Jennings examines economics from a perspective that combines feminist and institutionalist approaches. She argues that the way the American-European tradition of institutionalism conceives of "culture" leads to a criticism of dualistic thinking, a criticism that has significant parallels in feminist thought. Yet Thorstein Veblen's recognition of feminist issues at the turn of the century has not been reflected in most later institutionalist work. Jennings uses feminist and institutionalist arguments to challenge dualistic compartmentalization both in knowledge and in social life.

In her commentary, Rebecca M. Blank reflects on the main chapters in the volume from the perspective of a neoclassical economist. Although she defends the use of the neoclassical model, she agrees with several of the other authors that economics would be enriched by a greater diversity of theoretical and methodological approaches. She urges the authors to give more specific examples of how a feminist economics would lead to new insights and questions why the approach they describe should be labeled "feminist."

Rhonda M. Williams's commentary evaluates the main chapters from a postmodernist perspective. She compares feminist and Afrocentrist theories both to each other and to a postmodernist alternative, which deconstructs both gender and race. She suggests that insufficient attention to the complexities of race and class leaves the economic theories outlined in the main chapters regrettably incomplete.

Robert M. Solow, like McCloskey, takes the issue of gender to be largely an issue of differences between men and women. He focuses on the question of whether men and women have different cognitive styles. He suggests that male dominance, in addition to influencing which subjects are considered interesting, may have something to do with the "atmosphere" in which work is done. He is skeptical, however, of the notion that a move away from male dominance would change what he considers to be the substance of the discipline.

In the final commentary, Helen E. Longino reviews what she sees as the main points of the chapters regarding women, households, and economic agents. She finds the arguments regarding the masculine construction of the discipline compelling, but challenges feminist economists to explore the normative influences and purposes of conventional research programs further and to develop new research programs that better represent a diversity of interests.

The authors of the main chapters were not given the opportunity to reply (or to revise) in response to the commentaries. We leave many issues unresolved, with the intention of stimulating further discussion not only among the contributors to this volume but also among a larger community of scholars.

References

Aiken, Susan Hardy, Karen Anderson, Myra Dinnerstein, Judy Nolte Lensink, and Patricia MacCorquodale, eds. 1988. *Changing Our Minds: Feminist Transformations of Knowledge.* Albany: State University of New York Press.

Alcoff, Linda. 1988. "Cultural Feminism versus Post-Structuralism: The Identity Crisis in Feminist Theory." *Signs* 13:405–36.

Barrett, Nancy S. 1981. "How the Study of Women Has Restructured the Discipline of Economics." In *A Feminist Perspective in the Academy: The Difference It Makes,* ed. Elizabeth Langland and Walter Grove, 101–9. Chicago: University of Chicago Press.

Becker, Gary S. 1965. "A Theory of the Allocation of Time." *Economic Journal* 75:493–517.

———. 1973. "A Theory of Marriage: Part I." *Journal of Political Economy* 81:813–46.

———. 1974. "A Theory of Marriage: Part II." *Journal of Political Economy* 82:1063–93.

———. 1985. "Human Capital, Effort, and the Sexual Division of Labor." *Journal of Labor Economics* 3:S33–58.

Belenky, Mary Field, Blythe McVicker Clinchy, Nancy Rule Goldberger, and

Jill Mattuck Tarule. 1986. *Women's Ways of Knowing: The Development of Self, Voice, and Mind.* New York: Basic Books.

Bell, Carolyn Shaw. 1974. "Economics, Sex, and Gender." *Social Science Quarterly* 55 (3): 615–31.

Berg, Helen M., and Marianne A. Ferber. 1983. "Men and Women Graduate Students: Who Succeeds and Why?" *Journal of Higher Education* 54: 629–48.

Bergmann, Barbara R. 1986. *The Economic Emergence of Women.* New York: Basic Books.

————. 1987. "The Task of a Feminist Economics: A More Equitable Future." In *The Impact of Feminist Research in the Academy,* ed. Christie Farnham, 131–47. Bloomington: Indiana University Press.

Bielby, Denise D., and William T. Bielby. 1988. "She Works Hard for the Money: Household Responsibilities and the Allocation of Work Effort." *American Journal of Sociology* 93:1031–59.

Blank, Rebecca. 1991. "The Effects of Double-Blind versus Single-Blind Reviewing: Experimental Evidence from *The American Economic Review.*" *American Economic Review* 81 (5): 1041–67.

Blau, Francine D. 1981. "On the Role of Values in Feminist Scholarship." *Signs* 6:538–40.

Blaug, Mark. 1962. *Economic Theory in Retrospect.* London: Heinemann Educational Books.

————. 1986. *Who's Who in Economics.* Cambridge, Mass.: MIT Press.

Bleier, Ruth, ed. 1986. *Feminist Approaches to Science.* New York: Pergamon Press.

Blinder, Alan S. 1988. "The Challenge of High Unemployment." *American Economic Review* 78:1–15.

Boulding, Kenneth E. 1989. *Three Faces of Power.* Newbury Park, Calif.: Sage Publications.

Cohen, Marjorie. 1982. "The Problem of Studying 'Economic Man.'" In *Feminism in Canada: From Pressure to Politics,* ed. Angel Miles and Geraldine Finn, 89–101. Montreal: Black Rose Books.

————. 1985. "The Razor's Edge Invisible: Feminism's Effect on Economics." *International Journal of Women's Studies* 8 (3): 286–98.

Committee on the Status of Women in the Economics Profession. 1990. "Report." *American Economic Review* 80:486–89.

Cook, Karen Schweers, and Margaret Levi, eds. 1990. *The Limits of Rationality.* Chicago: University of Chicago Press.

Derrida, Jacques. 1976. *Of Grammatology.* Trans. Gayatri Chakravorty Spivak. Baltimore: Johns Hopkins University Press.

Dillingham, Alan E., Marianne A. Ferber, and Daniel S. Hamermesh. 1991. "Sex Discrimination by Sex: Voting in a Professional Society." Manuscript.

Dixon, Vernon J. 1970. "The Di-Unital Approach to 'Black Economics.' " *American Economic Review* 60 (2): 424–29.

———. 1976. "World Views and Research Methodology." In *African Philosophy: Assumptions and Paradigms for Research on Black Persons,* ed. L. M. King, V. Dixon, and W. W. Nobles. Los Angeles: Fanon Center, Charles R. Drew Postgraduate Medical School.

Ehrenberg, Ronald G., and Robert S. Smith. 1991. *Modern Labor Economics: Theory and Public Policy.* New York: HarperCollins Publishers.

Eisenstein, Hester, and Alice Jardine, eds. 1980. *The Future of Difference.* New Brunswick, N.J.: Rutgers University Press.

Farnham, Christie, ed. 1987. *The Impact of Feminist Research in the Academy.* Bloomington: Indiana University Press.

Feiner, Susan F., and Barbara A. Morgan. 1987. "Women and Minorities in Introductory Economics Textbooks: 1974–1984." *Journal of Economic Education* 10:376–92.

———, and Bruce Roberts. 1990. "Hidden by the Invisible Hand: Neoclassical Economic Theory and the Textbook Treatment of Race and Gender." *Gender and Society* 4 (2): 159–81.

Ferber, Marianne A. 1986. "Citations: Are They an Objective Measure of Scholarly Merit?" *Signs* 11:381–89.

———. 1988. "Citations and Networking." *Gender and Society* 2:82–89.

———. 1990. "Gender and the Study of Economics." In *The Principles of Economics Course: A Handbook for Instructors,* ed. Phillip Saunders and William Walstad, 44–60. New York: McGraw-Hill.

———, and Bonnie G. Birnbaum. 1977. "The 'New Home Economics': Retrospects and Prospects." *Journal of Consumer Research* 4:19–28.

———, and Michelle Teiman. 1980. "Are Women Economists at a Disadvantage in Publishing Journal Articles?" *Eastern Economic Journal* 6:189–94.

———, and Michelle L. Teiman. 1981. "The Oldest, the Most Established, the Most Quantitative of the Social Sciences—and the Most Dominated by Men: The Impact of Feminism on Economics." In *Men's Studies Modified: The Impact of Feminism on the Academic Disciplines,* ed. Dale Spender, 125–39. New York: Pergamon Press.

———, Bonnie G. Birnbaum, and Carole A. Green. 1983. "Gender Differences in Economic Knowledge: A Reevaluation of the Evidence." *Journal of Economic Education* 14:182–89.

Feyerabend, Paul. 1976. *Against Method.* New York: Humanities Press.

Fish, Mary, and Jean Gibbons. 1989. "A Comparison of the Publications of Female and Male Economists." *Journal of Economic Education* 20:93–105.

Folbre, Nancy. 1991. "The Unproductive Housewife: Her Evolution in Nineteenth-Century Economic Thought." *Signs* 16:463–84.

———, and Heidi Hartmann. 1988. "The Rhetoric of Self-Interest: Ideology and Gender in Economic Theory." In *The Consequences of Economic Rhetoric,* ed. Arjo Klamer, Donald N. McCloskey, and Robert M. Solow, 184–203. Cambridge: Cambridge University Press.

Foucault, Michel. 1976. *The Archaeology of Knowledge.* Trans. A. M. Sheridan Smith. New York: Harper & Row.

Frank, Robert. 1985. *Choosing the Right Pond.* New York: Oxford University Press.

Georgescu-Roegen, Nicholas. 1966. *Analytical Economics.* Cambridge, Mass.: Harvard University Press.

Gergen, Kenneth J. 1985. "The Social Constructionist Movement in Modern Psychology." *American Psychologist* 40:266–75.

Gilligan, Carol. 1982. *In a Different Voice: Psychological Theory and Women's Development.* Cambridge, Mass.: Harvard University Press.

Gronau, Reuben. 1977. "Leisure, Home Production and Work: The Theory of the Allocation of Time Revisited." *Journal of Political Economy* 85:1099–1123.

Gustaffson, Siv. 1990. "Half the Power, Half the Incomes and Half the Glory: The Use of Microeconomic Theory in Women's Emancipation Research." Inaugural lecture at the official assumption of the Chair of Labour Market Issues with a Special Attention to Women's Emancipation, University of Amsterdam.

Gwartney, James D., Richard Stroup, and J. R. Clark. 1985. *Essentials of Economics.* New York: Academic Press.

Hamovitch, William, and Richard D. Morgenstern. 1977. "Children and the Productivity of Academic Women." *Journal of Higher Education* 6:633–45.

Harding, Jan, ed. 1986. *Perspectives on Gender and Science.* London: Falmer Press.

Harding, Sandra. 1986. *The Science Question in Feminism.* Ithaca, N.Y.: Cornell University Press.

———. 1987. "The Curious Coincidence of Feminine and African Moralities: Challenges for Feminist Theory." In *Women and Moral Theory,* ed. Diana Meyers and Eva Feder Kittay, 296–315. Totowa, N.J.: Rowman and Littlefield.

———, ed. 1987. *Feminism and Methodology: Social Science Issues.* Bloomington: Indiana University Press.

———, and Jean F. O'Barr, eds. 1987. *Sex and Scientific Inquiry.* Chicago: University of Chicago Press.

Hochschild, Arlie Russell. 1975. "Inside the Clockwork of Male Courses." In *Women and the Power to Change,* ed. Florence Howe, 47–80. New York: McGraw-Hill.

Jaggar, Alison M., and Susan R. Bordo, eds. 1989. *Gender/Body/Knowledge:*

Feminist Reconstructions of Being and Knowing. New Brunswick, N.J.: Rutgers University Press.

Keller, Evelyn Fox. 1985. *Reflections on Gender and Science.* New Haven, Conn.: Yale University Press.

———. 1986. "How Gender Matters or, Why It's So Hard for Us to Count Past Two." In *Perspectives on Gender and Science,* ed. Jan Harding, 168–83. London: Falmer Press.

Kuhn, Thomas. 1970 [1962]. *The Structure of Scientific Revolutions.* 2d ed. Chicago: University of Chicago Press.

Leftwich, Richard. 1984. *A Basic Framework for Economics.* Dallas: Business Publications.

Leibenstein, Harvey. 1969. "Organizational or Frictional Equilibria, X-Efficiency and the Role of Innovations." *Quarterly Journal of Economics* 84:600–623.

———. 1976. *Beyond Economic Man: A New Foundation for Microeconomics.* Cambridge, Mass.: Harvard University Press.

Longino, Helen. 1990. *Science as Social Knowledge: Values and Objectivity in Scientific Inquiry.* Princeton, N.J.: Princeton University Press.

Lowe, Marian, and Ruth Hubbard, eds. 1983. *Women's Nature: Rationalizations of Inequality.* New York: Pergamon Press.

Lyotard, Jean-François. 1984. *The Postmodern Condition: A Report on Knowledge.* Trans. Geoff Bennington and Brian Massumi. Minneapolis: University of Minnesota Press.

Mansbridge, Jane J., ed. 1990. *Beyond Self-Interest.* Chicago: University of Chicago Press.

McCloskey, Donald N. 1985. *The Rhetoric of Economics.* Madison: University of Wisconsin Press.

———. 1990. *If You're So Smart: The Rhetoric of Economic Expertise.* Chicago: University of Chicago Press.

———. 1991. "Economic Science: A Search through the Hyperspace of Assumptions?" *Methodus: Bulletin of the International Network for Economic Method* 3:6–16.

Morawetz, David. 1976. "Correlation between Student Performance on Multiple Choice and Essay Type Examinations at the Hebrew University, 1966–74." Research Report No. 93, The Hebrew University of Jerusalem.

National Center for Education Statistics 1977–78. 1988. *Digest of Education Statistics.*

Nelson, Julie A. 1987. "Gender and Economic Thought." Committee on the Status of Women in the Economics Profession *Newsletter,* Fall.

Nicholson, Linda J., ed. 1990. *Feminism/Postmodernism.* London: Routledge.

Poovey, Mary. 1988. "Feminism and Deconstruction." *Feminist Studies* 14:51–65.

Reid, Margaret G. 1934. *Economics of Household Production.* New York: John Wiley & Sons.

Reynolds, Lloyd G. 1988. *Economics: A General Introduction.* Homewood, Ill.: Irwin.

Ruddick, Sara. 1989. *Maternal Thinking: Toward a Politics of Peace.* Boston: Beacon Press.

Samuelson, Paul. 1948. *Economics.* New York: McGraw-Hill.

Sawhill, Isabel V. 1977. "Economic Perspectives on the Family." *Daedalus* 106:115–25.

Schultz, Theodore W., ed. 1974. *Economics of the Family: Marriage, Children and Human Capital.* Chicago: University of Chicago Press and NBER.

Scott, Joan W. 1988. "Deconstructing Equality-Versus-Difference: Or, The Uses of Poststructuralist Theory for Feminism." *Feminist Studies* 14:33–50.

Seiz, Janet A. 1989. "Gender and Economic Language and Research." Manuscript, Department of Economics, Grinnell College.

Sen, Amartya. 1985. "Women, Technology, and Sexual Divisions." *Trade and Development: An UNCTAD Review* 6:195–223.

———. 1990. "Gender and Cooperative Conflicts." In *Persistent Inequalities,* ed. Irene Tinker, 123–49. New York: Oxford University Press.

Siegfried, John. 1979. "Male-Female Differences in Economic Education: A Survey." *Journal of Economic Education* 10:1–11.

Solow, Robert M. 1990. *The Labor Market as a Social Institution.* Cambridge, Mass.: Basil Blackwell.

Spender, Dale, ed. 1981. *Men's Studies Modified: The Impact of Feminism on the Academic Disciplines.* Oxford: Pergamon Press.

Stanley, Liz, and Sue Wise. 1983. " 'Back into the Personal' or: Our Attempt to Construct 'Feminist Research.' " In *Theories of Women's Studies,* ed. Gloria Bowles and Renate Duelli Klien, 192–209. London: Routledge & Kegan Paul.

Strober, Myra. 1987. "The Scope of Microeconomics: Implications for Economic Education." *Journal of Economic Education* 18:135–49.

Thomson, Dorothy Lampen. 1973. *Adam Smith's Daughters.* New York: Exposition Press.

Thurow, Lester C. 1988. "Producer Economics." *Proceedings of the Forty-First Annual Meeting of the Industrial Relations Research Association,* 9–20. Madison, Wis.: IRRA.

Tidball, Elizabeth. 1976. "Of Men and Research: The Dominant Themes in American Higher Education Include Neither Teaching Nor Women." *Journal of Higher Education* 47:373–89.

Tuana, Nancy, ed. 1989. *Feminism and Science.* Bloomington: Indiana University Press.

Wallston, Barbara Strudler, and Virginia E. O'Leary. 1981. "Sex Makes a Difference: Differential Perceptions of Women and Men." In *Review of Personality and Social Psychology: 2,* ed. Ladd Wheeler, 9–41. London: Sage.

Waring, Marilyn. 1988. *If Women Counted: A New Feminist Economics.* San Francisco: Harper & Row.

Julie A. Nelson

1

The Study of Choice or the Study of Provisioning? Gender and the Definition of Economics

Adam Smith . . . saw economics as a two-fold problem, one of which was how society was organized by exchange, the other of which is how society was "provisioned," in what today would be regarded as a more ecological sense. Here again, modern economics has gone wholly towards the view of economic life as society organized by exchange, and has largely lost the sense of it being a process of provisioning of the human race, or even of the whole biosphere.

Kenneth Boulding (1986, 10)

Faculty members from top liberal arts colleges told the Commission that some of their best students have decided against going to graduate school in economics, or have dropped out during their first year, because of the abstract, technical nature of the core curriculum. It is not economics as they know it.

Anne Krueger et al., "Report of the Commission on Graduate Education in Economics" (1991, 1040–41)

So what is economics? This is not an idle question when decisions are being made about publications, promotions, and curricula. Does economics include any study having to do with the creation and distribution of the "necessaries and conveniences of life," as Adam Smith said in 1776? Or is it about goods and services only to the extent that they enter into a process of exchange? Or is the core of economics to be found in mathematical models of individual choice, which sometimes leads to hypothetical exchange? There is no doubt that while room exists around the fringes for other sorts of studies, the last definition of economics is the one that is currently dominant in the most highly regarded research and in the core of graduate study.[1] It is my

Comments on an earlier draft from Paula England, Nancy Folbre, Marianne Ferber, Linda Lucas, Ann Jennings, Julie McCarthy, Don McCloskey, and Diana Strassmann are gratefully acknowledged.
    1. The reader unfamiliar with contemporary mainstream economics may want to scan a recent issue of a prestigious economics journal (such as the *American Economic Review, Journal of*

thesis that this narrowing of the definition of economics reflects particular gender-related biases and that, while significant advances have been made through the mathematical study of exchange, feminist insights can help to reorient the discipline toward a broader and richer economics.

Gender and the Cartesian Ideal

Feminists have used techniques of literary criticism, historical interpretation, and psychoanalysis "to 'read science as a text' in order to reveal the social meanings—the hidden symbolic and structural agendas—of purportedly value-neutral claims and practices" (Harding 1986, 23). There is now a considerable literature that uses such tools to investigate the historical links between social ideals of science and of gender in Western society. Evelyn Fox Keller's *Reflections on Gender and Science* (1985), Carolyn Merchant's *The Death of Nature* (1980), and Susan Bordo's "The Cartesian Masculinization of Thought" (1986) and *The Flight to Objectivity* (1987) have described the radical and gendered change in worldview that occurred during the sixteenth and seventeenth centuries. In this period, the predominant cultural conception of the relationship between humans and nature changed from one in which humans were seen as embedded in a female, living cosmos to one in which men were seen as potentially detached, objective observers and controllers of nature. In this new conception, nature came to be seen as passive and, eventually, as mechanical.

The identification of science with masculinity, detachment, and domination, and of femininity with nature, subjectivity, and submission, is clear in some of the language early seventeenth-century scientists used to define their endeavor. Henry Oldenburg, an early secretary of the Royal Society, stated that the intent of the Society was to "raise a masculine Philosophy . . . whereby the Mind of Man may be ennobled with the knowledge of Solid Truths" (quoted in Keller 1985, 52). Francis Bacon wrote in his *Temporis Partus Masculus* (The Masculine Birth of Time), "I am come in very truth leading to you Nature with all her children to bind her to your service and make her your slave" (quoted in Keller 1985, 39).

Of greater interest for the discussion of the high-status definition of eco-

---

Political Economy, or *Econometrica*) or look at textbooks frequently used in the core graduate curriculum (such as Varian 1984) to get an idea of the importance of the mathematical individual choice model. The degree of agreement on the core model may come as a surprise to other social scientists whose disciplines include a more diverse set of research programs. Rival schools in economics, such as institutionalism, Marxism, and the Austrian and post-Keynesian schools, are so much weaker in numbers and influence than the neoclassical group that many, if not most, academic departments feel no compunction about leaving them entirely out of curriculum and staffing plans.

nomics is the literature on the gendered nature of Cartesian thought. In the Cartesian model of the world, the cosmos is split into a *"res cogitans* (a thinking something which has no spatial extension) and a *res extensa* (a spatial something which has no psychic qualities)" (Stern 1965, 76). Science, and knowledge in general, are a part of the cogito, seen as radically detached from passive matter. And how does the mind gain knowledge? To quote Descartes, "The long concatenations of simple and easy reasoning which geometricians use in achieving their most difficult demonstrations gave me occasion to imagine that all matters which may enter the human mind were interrelated in the same fashion" (quoted in Davis and Hersh 1986, ix). Descartes regarded sensory input from the *res extensa* as deceptive; therefore, he believed that the only true knowledge is that which can be expressed mentally in the form of theorems and proofs. "Cartesianism," write the mathematicians Philip Davis and Reuben Hersh, "calls for the primacy of world mathematization" (1986, 8).

The Cartesian model of objectivity, based on dispassion and detachment, has been interpreted by Susan Bordo and others as related to anxiety created by the loss of the medieval feeling of connection to nature. Karl Stern's book on philosophy beginning with Descartes is entitled *The Flight from Woman.* James Hillman writes in *The Myth of Analysis,* "The specific consciousness we call scientific, Western and modern is the long sharpened tool of the masculine mind that has discarded parts of its own substance, calling it 'Eve,' 'female' and 'inferior' " (quoted in Bordo 1986, 441). The counterpoint to rational, detached "man" is "woman [who] provides his connection with nature; she is the mediating force between man and nature, a reminder of his childhood, a reminder of the body, and a reminder of sexuality, passion, and human connectedness. She is the repository of emotional life and of all the nonrational elements of human experience" (Fee 1983, 12). In the Cartesian view, the abstract, general, detached, emotionless, "masculine" approach taken to represent scientific thinking is radically removed from, and clearly viewed as superior to, the concrete, particular, embodied, passionate, "feminine" reality of material life.

The High-Status Definition of Economics

Economics increasingly has come to be defined not by its subject matter but by a particular way of viewing the world. The phrase "the economic approach to" is commonly used to mean viewing a problem in terms of choices, especially the individual welfare or profit maximizing choices of autonomous rational agents. Lionel Robbins's much-quoted 1935 definition of economics as "the science which studies human behavior as a relationship between ends and scarce means which have alternative uses" (1952 [1935],

16) helped to consolidate this view. "Economic theory" is frequently made synonymous with "choice theory" or "decision theory."

Such a definition is not unrelated to the gendered Cartesian ideal. Defining the subject of economics as individual choice makes the detached cogito, not the material world or real persons in the material world, the center of study. Nature, childhood, bodily needs, and human connectedness, cut off from "masculine" concern in the Cartesian split, remain safely out of the limelight. The emphasis on the "scarcity of means" suggests that nature is static, stingy, and hostile, a view of nature perhaps still based on a conception of man as dominating feminine nature, which, while dominated and passive, is still able to frighten.[2]

While one presumably could attempt to pursue this choice-centered approach in a purely verbal manner, one of the advantages of such an approach is that some aspects are easily expressed in mathematical form. The assumptions of this model and the form the analysis takes have been closely linked ever since economics adopted concepts from eighteenth-century physics (Mirowski 1991). By 1924, W. Stanley Jevons would describe economics as the study of "the mechanics of utility and self-interest" (quoted in Georgescu-Roegen 1971, 40). When economics is assumed to be centered around mathematical models of individual choice, assumptions about human behavior take on the status of axioms (Becker 1976) while nature becomes a mathematical "commodity space" (Debreu 1991).[3] Study of actual markets tends to give way to study of ideal abstract markets or hypothetical games. In fact, the less research has to do with actual economies, the higher its status: purely abstract models are commonly referred to as being "highbrow," "capital T," or "pure" economic theory while models that bring in some institutional detail are only "middlebrow," "small t," economic theory, or "merely applied." Attempts to explain phenomena that do not include a mathematical model of individual choice are not seen as economic theory at all. The "acid test" of articles in economic theory, said Nobel Prize winner Gerard Debreu in his 1990 presidential address to the American Economic Association, comes in "removing all their economic interpretations and letting their mathematical infrastructure stand on its own" (1991, 3). Thus the Cartesian voice echoes down through the centuries.

While the gendered nature of such a definition of economics has not (to my knowledge) been stated as blatantly as in Bacon's and Oldenburg's statements

2. Contrast Robbins's definition with an alternative: "the science which studies how humans satisfy the requirements and enjoy the delights of life using the free gifts of nature." One can appeal to no evidence outside of human prejudice to determine whether this or Robbins's view of the relation of humans to nature is "correct."

3. Debreu's contention that "the concept of the quantity of a commodity has a *natural* linear structure" (1991, 3; emphasis added) has been recently contested by Mirowski (1991, 153–55). In addition, my own research has illustrated the rigidity of the assumptions that must be applied in order to impose such a "linear structure" in empirical studies of actual purchases (Nelson 1991).

about science, "the hidden symbolic and structural agendas" may become apparent when we reread certain texts. For example, the drive toward defining economics in terms of mathematical models of individual choice is institutionally associated with the founding of the Econometric Society in 1930 (Debreu 1991). Consider what sexual imagery may be hidden in this society's statement of purpose (printed inside the back cover of every issue of *Econometrica*):

> The Society shall operate as a completely disinterested, scientific organization, without political, social, financial or nationalistic bias. Its main object shall be to promote studies that aim at the unification of the theoretical-quantitative and the empirical-quantitative approach to economic problems and that are penetrated by constructive and rigorous thinking similar to that which has come to dominate in the natural sciences.

Are the terms "penetration" and "domination" really value-free and gender-neutral, or do they indicate something else about the mind-set of the founders of this school?

Not everyone, of course, is happy with the power this definition holds over the contemporary structure of economics. While some feminist economists have been able to stretch the dominant model to address some of their concerns, others believe that the model is too narrow—that forcing the analysis of such issues as discrimination, comparable worth, inequality within the household, and nonsexist policy reforms into this framework leaves many of the most crucial questions unanswered. But feminists are far from being the only group potentially disturbed by this state of affairs. Debreu himself offers a mild caution in his address, in bringing up the concern that the economist may find "the very choice of the questions to which he [*sic*] tries to find answers is influenced by his [*sic*] mathematical background." Debreu also notes sociological factors that may have contributed to the growth of this form of analysis, including the "reward system of the profession" and the "esoteric character" and "impenetrability" of this type of theory (1991, 5, 6).

Released just a month after Debreu's address, a report by the blue-ribbon Commission on Graduate Education in Economics of the American Economic Association was somewhat more critical. While rejecting the notion that excessive mathematics is a major problem, the commission expressed serious concern that "it is an underemphasis on the 'linkages' between tools, both theory and econometrics, and 'real world problems' that is the weakness of graduate education in economics." The commission also expressed fear that "graduate programs may be turning out a generation with too many idiot savants skilled in technique but innocent of real economic issues" (Krueger et al. 1991, 1039, 1044–45). More vitriolic is Donald McCloskey's paper— "Economic Science: A Search through the Hyperspace of Assumptions?"—

presented at the same meetings as Debreu's address. McCloskey is severely critical of economists who make a "false claim of physics-mimicking scientificity" and who "abandon an economic question in favor of a mathematical one, and then forget to come back to the Department of Economics" (1991, 12–13).

Do these criticisms signal a turning of the tide away from radical detachment from the subject of study? If we can rely on historical evidence as a guide, the answer is probably not. Similar concerns about an overemphasis on mathematical formalism and an underemphasis on relevance to real world issues have been voiced many times before and from equally elevated platforms.[4] Such protests seem to have had no effect on what Debreu called "the seemingly irresistible current" of increasing emphasis on mathematics (1991, 5).

Why has it seemed so irresistible? A feminist psychological analysis suggests that an assumption of masculine superiority, coupled with the association of masculinity with the Cartesian ideal, may continue to make a turn toward increasing mentalism and formalism an appealing choice. If an individual researcher refuses to go along with this current, his or her future work may be considered soft or insufficiently scientific and, by implication, inferior. Recognizing the link between gender and scientific prestige, however, does not itself suggest that an alternative approach would be better. The current situation must be compared with the possibilities that might be opened up if femininity were no longer associated with inferiority.

Thinking about an Alternative to Masculine Economics

When all we know is masculine economics, it is hard to imagine an alternative. The common ways of thinking about gender suggest that the only alternative to macho economics must be emasculated, impotent economics. Given current conceptions of science and masculinity, there is a tendency to think that the only alternative to a definition of economics emphasizing rigor, scientificity, and rationality would be one that gives in to, say, sloppiness, subjectivity, and emotionalism. Or that if economics backs down from an emphasis on theory of individual choice, it would degenerate into a dogmatic theory of sociological determinism or a practice of prosaic, theoryless potato counting. The masculine is good; the feminine (trespassing into science from its proper realm) can only be bad—or so we are accustomed to thinking.

4. See, for example, the American Economic Association presidential addresses by Wassily Leontief (1971) and Robert Gordon (1976), and the Richard T. Ely lectures by Nicholas Georgescu-Roegen (1970) and Alan Blinder (1988)—not to mention addresses by Richard T. Ely, founder of the AEA, himself (e.g., Ely 1936). Nelson (1993) reviews the notions of scientific detachment contained in the various statements of purpose issued by the American Economic Association and the Econometric Society.

Envisioning an alternative that is not simply weak and mushy requires a new view of gender, value, and knowledge.[5] Ideas from feminist theory, recent work in the philosophy and sociology of science, and research on cognition and language all play a role in constructing this view. Starting with the concepts of gender and value, think of sexism as an unjustified association of masculinity with superiority and of femininity with inferiority at the cognitive as well as social level. But instead of substituting for this the idea that "feminine is good, too," or turning the tables to "feminine is good and masculine is bad," think of breaking apart the association of gender with value. If gender and value are thought of as orthogonal dimensions, then it becomes possible to think about good and bad aspects of characteristics cognitively associated with masculinity in our culture, and good and bad characteristics of what we think of as feminine. *At the cognitive level, then, sexism can also be seen as the selective blocking from view of the strengths of femininity and the dangers of unmitigated masculinity.* A better economics would neither be purged of all of its distinctively masculine characteristics nor simply have feminine-associated characteristics tacked on indiscriminately; in a better economics we would choose carefully from both "masculine" and "feminine" approaches those that result in the best science.

Take, as a simple example, the idea that a "hard" economics is preferable to a "soft" economics. This judgment relies on an association of hardness with positively valued, masculine-associated strength and softness with negatively valued, feminine-associated weakness.[6] However, hardness also may also mean rigidity and softness may also imply flexibility. A pursuit of masculine hardness that spurns association with femininity and hence with flexibility can be thought of as leading to rigidity, just as surely as a pursuit of feminine softness without corresponding strength makes us think of weakness. Would not a more balanced and resilient economics be one that is flexible as well as hard?

Alternative Methods

The impression, fostered by the Cartesian view, that only theorems that can be proved (à la geometry) constitute knowledge tends to block from view alternatives kinds of knowledge. The devaluation of language, community, the body, and emotion implied by an emphasis on axiomatic, detached truth has been contested in recent works in feminist theory, the philosophy of science, and studies of cognition and language as well as in economics. These works claim that rationality includes reasoning by analogy, by

5. In what follows, I draw on and expand ideas first presented in Nelson (1992).

6. As has frequently been pointed out, the masculine-hard/feminine-soft association may derive from a metaphor of sexual intercourse.

metaphor, by pattern recognition, by imagination, and by, as Einstein once put it, "intuition, resting on sympathetic understanding of experience" (quoted in Georgescu-Roegen 1966, 14). To denote such a conception of reasoning beyond logic, the economist Nicholas Georgescu-Roegen (1966) chooses the term "dialectical thinking"; Howard Margolis (1987) uses the term "seeing-that"; the linguist George Lakoff and the philosopher Mark Johnson (1980) refer to "imaginative rationality"; and the feminist theorist Evelyn Fox Keller (1985) writes about the search for "dynamic objectivity."

The crucial advantage of this form of reasoning, whatever the term used to describe it, is that it can deal with overlapping, interconnected concepts because it is experientially or contextually based. Georgescu-Roegen distinguishes what he calls "arithmomorphic" concepts, that is, concepts that are "discretely distinct" and suitable for manipulation by the laws of logic, from "dialectical" concepts, which overlap with their opposites "over a contourless penumbra of varying breadth" (1971, 14). Far from being trivial, the latter, he argues, constitute "most of our thoughts."[7] Lakoff and Johnson argue that the elevation of set-theoretic categorization as the basis for objectivist knowledge overlooks important aspects of the way people actually comprehend the world: human categorization is much more flexible, purpose specific, and open-ended, and tends to be based on family resemblances or prototypes (1980, 122–25). Lakoff and Johnson argue that human understanding is based on metaphors, which in turn are based on bodily experience, and that understanding is inseparable from imagination and emotion. This idea of understanding as connected to experience is reiterated in Keller's definition of objectivity: "the pursuit of a maximally authentic, and hence maximally reliable, understanding of the world around oneself. Such a pursuit is dynamic to the extent that it actively draws on the commonality between mind and nature as a resource for understanding. . . . In this, dynamic objectivity is not unlike empathy" (1985, 117). Such reasoning beyond logic makes use of experience and connection rather than suppressing or denying them.

A few examples will illustrate these points. Margolis points out that it is our shared knowledge of language and context that would allow us to make sense of the following statement if heard orally: "Jim Wright, who lives right down the street, to the right of the Kelly's, is a playwright who is studying the Masonic rites, so he will soon have all the rights of qualified members" (1987, 90). In contrast, in formal logic each symbol can have only one meaning, and the very formalism of mathematics makes the reasoning context free. In an example from physics, light corresponds to our understanding of a wave in

7. As another example, Carol Gilligan's *In a Different Voice* (1982) reinterprets the perceived lack of ability of some subjects (largely female in her sample) in studies of ethical development to "appropriately" abstract from the details of hypothetical moral dilemmas in order to apply "logical," "universal" formulas. She suggests that what was perceived as a lack of logic was instead a manifestation of a less rigid and detached, more contextual form of reasoning.

some respects but behaves like a particle in other respects. These two divergent (and metaphorical) understandings of light have been highly fruitful, in spite of the apparent logical contradiction of positing something as simultaneously "A" and "not-A." The experiential, empathetic way in which such reasoning sometimes functions in science is apparent in the words of Nobel Prize-winning biologist Barbara McClintock, who told her biographer of her "feeling for the organism" (Keller 1983).

The point here is not that one way of thinking is peculiar to females and the other to males. Indeed this would be a rather odd conclusion, given the number of males who investigate "imaginative rationality" and the number of females who have worked within disciplines emphasizing formal logic. Rather, gender linkages enter at the level of cultural association: females are stereotypically linked with the intuitive approach, where "intuitive" is taken to mean an effortless, irrational sort of knowledge of mysterious origin. The above analysis suggests that a revaluation of such different-than-logical (not illogical) forms of knowledge, devalued by descendants of Descartes as intuitive and inferior, is in order.

As Donald McCloskey pointed out in his study *The Rhetoric of Economics* (1985), much economic argument already takes this form, although it does so unself-consciously. Even in the most high-tech, abstract economics lectures or seminars, the presenter is usually asked to give the "intuition" behind the model or result, that is, an explanation using analogies or examples that makes the value of the exercise clear. Nevertheless, the formal model is generally considered to be the substance of the talk and the rest merely supplementary material. The broader conception of reasoning outlined above suggests, on the contrary, that the real reasoning comes in the words: the conceptual framework, the applications, the metaphors, and the determination of priorities, within which the role of logic and abstraction is "to facilitate the argument, clarify the results, and so guard against possible faults of reasoning—that is all."[8] This by no means implies the abandonment or neglect of mathematical, analytical argument—as long as it furthers the investigation.

If the neglected strength of feminine-associated knowledge is in "imaginative rationality," what is the unseen danger of unmitigated masculinity? Georgescu-Roegen calls the enthrallment with discrete, arithmomorphic concepts manageable by logic "arithmomania"; he writes that it "ends by giving us mental cramps" (1971, 52, 80). Sound economic reasoning, including (or even especially) about very applied issues and including (or even especially) argument in largely verbal form, should be no reason for apology in economics seminars. The pitfall of empty logic, just as much as of illogic, should be cause for embarrassment.

8. Knut Wicksell (1954), quoted in Georgescu-Roegen (1971, 341).

Alternatives in Subject

For Robbins, Jevons, and their followers, the question of choice between alternative ends, given the means at hand, is at the heart of economics. While economic theory and choice theory have become synonymous in recent decades, there are still substantial echoes of an older definition of economics: the study of the basis of human material welfare. According to the older alternative, in the words of Alfred Marshall, "Economics is a study of mankind [*sic*] in the ordinary business of life; it examines that part of individual and social action which is most closely connected with the attainment and with the use of the material requisites of well-being" (1920, 1). Rather than defining economics as a particular way of looking at human behavior, this definition delineates economics in terms material goods. Of course, as Robbins correctly argued in promoting his definition based on scarcity, the material welfare definition also has its problems. Adam Smith's (and Karl Marx's) distinction between productive labor, which results in the production of a material object, and unproductive labor, which does not, led to interminable and useless debate (Robbins 1952 [1935], 7). Taken literally, the materialist definition implies that nontangibles, even such services as health care, lie outside the scope of economics.

Feminist theory suggests that the definition focusing on choice, which looks at human decisions as radically separated from physical and social constraints, and the definition stressing material well-being, which ignores nonphysical sources of human satisfaction, are not the only alternatives. Such a dichotomy merely reinforces the separation of humans from the world, the *res cogitans* from the *res extensa*. What is needed instead is a definition of economics that considers humans *in relation* to the world.

Focusing economics on the provisioning of human life, that is, on the commodities and processes necessary to human survival, provides such a definition. In contrast to Robbins's view of economics as synonymous with choice, consider the following claim by Georgescu-Roegen: "Apt though we are to lose sight of the fact, the primary objective of economic activity is the self-preservation of the human species. Self-preservation in turn requires the satisfaction of some basic needs—which are nevertheless subject to evolution" (1966, 93). Such a definition is not limited to physical concepts. Georgescu-Roegen points out that "*purposive activity* and *enjoyment of life*," parts of his definition of self-preservation, are not material variables. In addition, when human survival—including survival through childhood—is made the core of economic inquiry, nonmaterial services, such as child care and supervision, as well as attendance to health concerns and the transmission of skills, become just as central as food and shelter. Amartya Sen's (1984) discussion of "capabilities" is also based on such a notion of *relationship* between human needs and the world.

The concept of needs or necessaries is, of course, itself dialectical and fluid. This is not necessarily a disadvantage: recognition of this fact guards against a slide into a too-rigid formalism. It requires a honing of exactly those rational skills that much of the current practice of economics has allowed to atrophy. The line between needs and wants is not distinct, and yet one certainly can say that a Guatemalan orphan needs her daily bowl of soup more than the overfed North American needs a second piece of cake. A refusal to recognize such a distinction on the basis of its logical ambiguity leads to an abdication of human ethical responsibility.

Such a definition of economics need not rule out studies of choice or of exchange, but it does displace them from the core of economics. It does not rule out study of the provision of conveniences or luxuries as well as more basic needs, but it does not give them equal priority. Voluntary exchange is part of the process of provisioning, but so are gift-giving and coercion. Organized, impersonal markets are one locus of economic activity, but so are households, governments, and other more personal or informal human organizations. Issues of the organization of production, of power and poverty, of unemployment and economic duress, of health care and education—in short, the "real economic problems" referred to by the Commission on Graduate Education in Economics—become the raison d'être of the economics profession, not the further elaboration of a particular axiomatic theory of human behavior. The Greek root of both the words "economics" and "ecology" is *oikos,* meaning "house." Economics could be about how we live in our house, the earth.

Conclusion

Feminist theory suggests that the Cartesian divisions between rationality and embodiment, and between man and nature, reflect a peculiarly masculinist and separative view of the world. In this chapter, I have suggested that the Cartesian view underlies the prestige given to mathematical models of individual rational choice in the current definition of economics. A richer economics, while not excluding formal models or the study of choice, would be centered around the study of provisioning and make full use of the tools of "imaginative rationality." Such an economics would be neither masculine nor feminine but would be a human science in the pursuit of human ends.

Lest this be misunderstood, I am not claiming or advocating that men do one kind of economics and women do another. Nor do I believe that the problem can be solved by asking economists who want a richer approach simply to remove themselves to sociology (as has been suggested more than once). While economists and sociologists certainly could learn more from each other, sociology as it stands has its own problems (as feminist sociologists have been quick to point out); moreover, it deals with social phenomena broader than the provision of the necessaries of life. The material side of the provisioning definition of economics has roots reaching back to several of our own, including Adam Smith and Alfred Marshall, and has survived as an undercurrent, if not as the high-prestige current, in economic thought. Rather than keeping high-status economics as it is and pushing all dissidents out, I suggest that the term economics be reclaimed. Let us start by speaking of the mathematical theory of individual choice as "the mathematical theory of individual choice" instead of as "economic theory," of the choice-theoretic approach as "the choice-theoretic approach" instead of as "*the* economic approach."

Does it seem too prosaic or worldly to define economics as centrally concerned with the study of how humans, in interaction with each other and the environment, provide for their own survival and health? If it does, perhaps such a judgment reveals more about how we feel about our own bodily (and gendered) existence than it reveals about the correct level of prestige to be attributed to different definitions of economics.

References

Becker, Gary S. 1976. *The Economic Approach to Human Behavior.* Chicago: University of Chicago Press.

Blinder, Alan S. 1988. "The Challenge of High Unemployment," *American Economic Review* 78:1–15.

Bordo, Susan. 1986. "The Cartesian Masculinization of Thought." *Signs* 11:439–56.

————. 1987. *The Flight to Objectivity: Essays on Cartesianism and Culture.* Albany: State University of New York Press.

Boulding, Kenneth E. 1986. "What Went Wrong with Economics." *American Economist* 30:5–12.

Debreu, Gerard. 1991. "The Mathematization of Economic Theory." *American Economic Review* 81:1–7.

Davis, Philip J., and Reuben Hersh. 1986. *Descartes' Dream: The World According to Mathematics.* New York: Harcourt Brace Jovanovich.

Ely, Richard T. 1936. "The Founding and Early History of the American Economic Association." *American Economic Review* 26 (1): 141–50.

Fee, Elizabeth. 1983. "Womens' Nature and Scientific Objectivity." In *Women's Nature: Rationalizations of Inequality,* ed. Marian Lowe and Ruth Hubbard, 9–27. New York: Pergamon Press.

Georgescu-Roegen, Nicholas. 1966. *Analytical Economics.* Cambridge, Mass.: Harvard University Press.

————. 1970. "The Economics of Production." *American Economic Review* 60:1–9.

————. 1971. *The Entropy Law and the Economic Process.* Cambridge, Mass.: Harvard University Press.

Gilligan, Carol. 1982. *In a Different Voice: Psychological Theory and Women's Development.* Cambridge, Mass.: Harvard University Press.

Gordon, Robert Aaron. 1976. "Rigor and Relevance in a Changing Institutional Setting." *American Economic Review* 66 (1): 1–14.

Harding, Sandra. 1986. *The Science Question in Feminism.* Ithaca, N.Y.: Cornell University Press.

Keller, Evelyn Fox. 1983. *A Feeling for the Organism: The Life and Work of Barbara McClintock.* New York: Freeman.

————. 1985. *Reflections on Gender and Science.* New Haven, Conn.: Yale University Press.

Krueger, Anne O., Kenneth J. Arrow, Olivier Jean Blanchard, Alan S. Blinder, Claudia Goldin, Edward E. Leamer, Robert Lucas, John Panzar, Rudolph G. Penner, T. Paul Schultz, Joseph E. Stiglitz, and Lawrence H. Summers. 1991. "Report of the Commission on Graduate Education in Economics." *Journal of Economic Literature* 24:1035–53.

Lakoff, George, and Mark Johnson. 1980. *Metaphors We Live By.* Chicago: University of Chicago Press.

Leontief, Wassily. 1971. "Theoretical Assumptions and Nonobserved Facts." *American Economic Review* 61:1–7.

Margolis, Howard. 1987. *Patterns, Thinking, and Cognition.* Chicago: University of Chicago Press.

Marshall, Alfred. 1920. *Principles of Economics.* 8th ed. London: Macmillan.

McCloskey, Donald N. 1985. *The Rhetoric of Economics.* Madison: University of Wisconsin Press.

————. 1991. "Economic Science: A Search through the Hyperspace of Assumptions?" *Methodus: Bulletin of the International Network for Economic Method* 3:6–16.

Merchant, Carolyn. 1980. *The Death of Nature.* San Francisco: Harper & Row.

Mirowski, Philip. 1991. "The When, the How and the Why of Mathematical Expression in the History of Economic Analysis." *Journal of Economic Perspectives* 5 (1): 145–57.

Nelson, Julie A. 1991. "Quality Variation and Quantity Aggregation in Consumer Demand for Food." *American Journal of Agricultural Economics* 73 (4): 1204–12.

————. 1992. "Gender, Metaphor, and the Definition of Economics." *Economics and Philosophy* 8 (1): 103–25.

————. 1993. "Value-Free or Valueless? Notes on the Pursuit of Detachment in Economics." *History of Political Economy* 25 (1).

Robbins, Lionel. 1952 [1935]. *An Essay on the Nature and Significance of Economic Science*. 2d ed. London: Macmillan.

Sen, Amartya. 1984. *Resources, Values, and Development*. Cambridge, Mass.: Harvard University Press.

Smith, Adam. 1986 [1776]. *An Inquiry into the Nature and Causes of the Wealth of Nations*. Excerpt in *The Essential Adam Smith*, ed. Robert L. Heilbroner, 159. New York: W. W. Norton.

Stern, Karl. 1965. *The Flight from Woman*. New York: Noonday Press.

Varian, Hal R. 1984. *Microeconomic Analysis*. New York: W. W. Norton.

2 Paula England

The Separative Self: Androcentric Bias in Neoclassical Assumptions

There are androcentric biases in the deep theoretical structure of neoclassical economics. Three of the most basic assumptions underlying economic theory are that interpersonal utility comparisons are impossible, that tastes are exogenous to economic models and unchanging, and that actors are selfish (have independent utilities) in markets. I argue that each of these assumptions flows from a separative model of human nature that has become a focus of criticism by feminists across a number of disciplines. I call the model "separative" because it presumes that humans are autonomous, impervious to social influences, and lack sufficient emotional connection to each other to make empathy possible. This is how they are presumed to behave in "the economy" or the "market."

A fourth, often more implicit, assumption in many neoclassical models is that individuals do *not* behave according to the separative model vis-à-vis their families. In the family, individuals (particularly men) are presumed to be altruistic. Thus, empathic emotional connections between individuals are emphasized in the family whereas they are denied in analyzing markets. I will argue that these assumptions exaggerate both the atomistic, separative nature of behavior in markets and the connective empathy and altruism within families.

These assumptions may be called "androcentric," or male-centered, in part because had the existing system of gender relations not been seen as the only possible or desirable arrangement, these particular assumptions would not have been chosen. In particular, such sharp contrasts between the assumptions thought appropriate to analyze households and those thought appropriate to analyze markets would not have seemed appropriate. These assumptions are also androcentric in the sense of being biased in favor of men's interests. Men's interests are furthered because analyses proceeding from these assumptions direct our attention away from the ways in which typical arrangements between men and women perpetuate women's disadvantage both in their families and in labor markets.

It is quite possible to criticize the major assumptions of neoclassical theory without making reference to feminist scholarship. Many economists and other social scientists have done so.[1] This paper draws upon many of their insights, but it emphasizes something that many criticisms of economic theory ignore: that the way gender has been socially organized has much to do with *which* parts of human experience have been left out of neoclassical models.[2] Contributions typically made by women are often rendered invisible by the theory; men's advantages and power are often rendered invisible as well. Ignoring women's contributions and men's power are important parts of what may be called "androcentric" bias. The reader should bear in mind, however, that all sexism in economic writing cannot be reduced to these criticisms of gender bias in the deep theoretical assumptions of economics. Some analyses suffer from gender bias in the auxiliary assumptions of their particular applications rather than in the most basic assumptions discussed here.

Feminist Critiques of Theoretical Biases

Before applying a feminist critique to economic theory, it is first necessary to clarify what I mean by feminist theory. One result of the entry of women, often feminists, into the academy in the last twenty years has been the allegation that theories in every discipline have been affected by gender bias. Over time, feminist thought has become increasingly diverse and today contains much healthy controversy.[3] What is common to virtually all feminist views, however, is the belief that women are subordinated to men to a degree that is morally wrong and unnecessary. Beyond this, views differ as to the sources of women's disadvantage and the proper remedy.

Two major, though not mutually exclusive, emphases within feminist thinking can be discerned: One body of thought emphasizes the exclusion of women from traditionally male activities and institutions. For example, laws, cultural beliefs, and other discriminatory practices have excluded most women from politics, religious leadership, military positions, and traditionally male crafts and professions within paid employment. These exclusions

1. For critical discussions of the neoclassical assumptions of self-interest, exogenous tastes, and impossibility of interpersonal utility comparisons that do not draw upon feminist theory, see Mansbridge (1990), Etzioni (1988), Sen (1982, 1987), Piore (1974), Hahnel and Albert (1990), Pollak (1976), Frank (1988), and Granovetter (1985, 1988). For critical discussions of the neoclassical rationality assumption (an assumption I do not examine in this paper) that do not draw upon feminist theory, see Hogarth and Reder (1987) and Elster (1979).

2. For other criticisms of economic theory that *do* link the omissions to gender bias, see Folbre and Hartmann (1988) and Nelson (forthcoming) as well as the other papers in this volume.

3. For one excellent review of feminist positions, see Jaggar (1983).

are significant for women since activities traditionally regarded as male are those associated with the largest rewards of honor, power, and money. The mechanisms of exclusion are sometimes so effective that most women do not choose to enter "male" domains, although a minority have always attempted to do so. Here feminists see the corrective to be allowing women to participate in these spheres on an equal basis with men.

A second body of feminist thought emphasizes the devaluation of and low material rewards accorded to activities and traits that traditionally have been deemed appropriate for women. The sexism here is in failing to see how much traditionally female activities or dispositions contribute to the economy, society, or polity. Examples include failing to see how much child rearing, household work, and volunteer work contribute to "the wealth of nations." Another example is failing to see the extent to which work in predominantly female occupations contributes to firms' profits, the issue raised by the movement for "comparable worth" in wage setting (England 1992). Feminists who emphasize this sort of sexism see the remedy to include changing values that deprecate traditionally female activities as well as allocating higher rewards to such activities.[4]

Sometimes these two feminist positions are read as being in conflict: the first is seen as advocating that women enter traditionally male activities while the second is seen to advocate women's continued attention to traditionally female activities. In fact, however, the second position is not inconsistent with a commitment to opening all valued activities to both men and women on an equal basis. It is possible to believe that we should acknowledge the value of traditionally female activities and reward them accordingly without believing that women should continue to do a disproportionate share of these activities. Indeed, a culture that really valorized traditionally female activities would undoubtedly encourage men as well as women to learn these skills and values. In this sense the two feminist positions can be seen as compatible, since together they would encourage that activities traditionally associated with both men and women be open to both men and women, while simultaneously en-

---

4. Nelson (1992) points out that traditionally female and traditionally male qualities each have both a positive and a negative aspect, but our culture has tended to see only the positive side of supposedly masculine qualities and the negative side of supposedly feminine qualities. Consider, for example, the oppositional terms "hard" and "soft" often metaphorically associated with men and women respectively. At least in intellectual or business life, "hard" is seen as positive and "soft" as negative. But Nelson points out that it is more telling to see "hard" as having a positive aspect, strength, and a negative aspect, rigidity, while "soft" has a negative aspect, weakness, as well as a positive aspect, flexibility. The tendency to see the hard-soft distinction as a matter of strong versus weak and to ignore the fact that it is also a matter of flexible versus rigid is an instance of androcentric bias. Nelson's discussion shows that the second feminist emphasis I am discussing here is most defensible when it argues for valorization of the *positive aspects* of traditionally female activities and traits, and when its criticism of androcentric values focuses on the *negative aspects* of traditionally male activities and traits.

courage a more equal valuing and rewarding of both kinds of activities. However, the second feminist emphasis *does* entail disagreement with those feminists who glorify a self for either men or women modeled upon the unconnected, nonempathic self that classical liberalism evoked for men. The second feminist position sees this as a mistaken value for either men or women.

I draw upon the second feminist emphasis here to distinguish between a "separative" self and a self that is emotionally connected to others. Emotional connections, and the skills and work entailed in honoring connections, are an important part of the activities traditionally assigned to women. The focus in this essay is on the theoretical consequences of deprecating and thus ignoring emotional connections. The feminist objection here is as much to the glorification of the separative self as to its link to gender.

The feminist critique of the separative self model has been applied in a number of disciplines other than economics. Seyla Benhabib (1987) traces the ideal of separative autonomy through liberalism in political philosophy. This tradition (whether the version of Hobbes, Locke, Rousseau, Kant, or Rawles) discusses moving from a "state of nature" to the metaphorical "contract" to set up the state. Both before and after the contract, men are presumed to be separative and autonomous; what changes with the contract is the degree of civility or justice achieved by these separative individuals. As these ideas evolved from the seventeenth to the nineteenth century, authors presumed that women would continue to do child-rearing and household work as well as provide emotional comfort and sexual satisfaction for men. They never seriously considered that men would do this sort of work. Nor did they recognize that men are *not* entirely autonomous—that no man would have survived to adulthood but for the altruistic work of a woman, and that every man continues to benefit from such work as an adult. This women's work was taken for granted, seldom discussed, and excluded from political theory, because these authors viewed women and their work as "part of nature" within a metaphysic that denigrated nature. Moreover, women's activities did not count as "moral," since only exercising "autonomy" in the public sphere counted as "moral." Thus the separative self was valued while nurturant connection either was ignored or deprecated.

The emphasis on separation also can be seen in developmental psychology (Keller 1986; Chodorow 1978; Gilligan 1982). Carol Gilligan points out that Freud, Jung, Erikson, Piaget, and Kohlberg, despite their differences, all viewed individuation as synonymous with maturation but viewed connection to others as developmentally regressive. Their views are deeply sexist in that they assumed women would do the emotional work of child-rearing and would provide emotional comfort for men, yet they did not acknowledge learning the capacity for intimacy and nurturance as part of maturation. They presented their theories as generic theories of the human developmental process rather than theories of male development under certain social arrangements.

The separative self is glorified in the philosophy of science as well. Evelyn Fox Keller (1983, 1985) argues that objectivity has been defined in terms of the separation of the subject (the scientist) from the object of study. She believes it is more than coincidental that the men developing science conceived their methodology in terms of what was emphasized as "masculine"—separative autonomy. Emotional connections with one's subject matter were seen as contaminating knowledge. Keller insists, however, that these connections sometimes yield useful insights. Some of our deepest insights come from the ability to empathize with those whose behavior we study. Under the current norms of science, such connections are permitted within the "context of discovery" but not within the "context of justification." Yet scientific articles are written in the language of the context of justification, rendering the context of discovery invisible, rather like housework and child-rearing. As a result, any traces of how empathic connection to the subject provided insights are written out of the record of science, and we do not see how having a connected self in this phase of the research process might contribute to the recognized goals of science. Scientific texts thus deprecate the connective part of the enterprise.

Applying the Feminist Critique of Separative Self Models to Neoclassical Economics

How does the feminist critique of the separative self model apply to neoclassical economic theory? The assumptions to be criticized are: (1) that interpersonal utility comparisons are impossible; (2) that tastes are exogenous and unchanging; and (3) that actors are selfish. These three assumptions are applied to behavior in market transactions—the primary focus of economics. Then, in a dramatic switch, a fourth assumption is invoked when analyzing the family: that altruism is the rule between family members. I will argue that each of the first three assumptions embodies a view of the self that is separative and hence vulnerable to the feminist critique discussed above. The fourth assumption is not discussed in most textbooks, but it is explicit in the one area of economics that has emphasized the household, the "new home economics" (Becker 1981; Pollak 1985). The contrast between the behavior assumed for the family and for markets will reveal how steeped in notions of gender roles these assumptions are.

Interpersonal Utility Comparisons

Neoclassical economists assume that interpersonal utility comparisons are impossible. Since the 1930s, utility has been conceived as the satisfaction of an individual's subjective desires; the concept lacks any dimension of objective, measurable welfare that might form the basis for interpersonal comparison (Cooter and Rappaport 1984). As a result, neoclassical theory tells us that we cannot know which of two persons gained more from a given exchange because the relevant "currency" in which gain or advantage is measured is utility, and utility is conceived as being radically subjective. This is so basic an assumption that it is generally mentioned in undergraduate microeconomic textbooks (e.g., Hirshleifer 1984, 476).

Using Pareto-optimality as the criterion of efficiency derives at least in part from the assumption that interpersonal utility comparisons are impossible. A distributional change is defined as Pareto-superior if at least one party gains utility and no one loses any. For example, voluntary exchange between self-interested individuals produces a Pareto-superior distribution. Each party must have felt that s/he would be made better off by the exchange than by foregoing it or s/he would not have made it. When no more Pareto-superior changes can be made through exchange, the distribution is said to be Pareto-optimal. Thus redistribution requiring some affluent persons to lose utility for the sake of a gain by the poor cannot be Pareto-superior by definition.

How does the feminist critique of separation/connection relate to interpersonal utility comparisons? The assumption that interpersonal utility comparisons are impossible flows from assuming a separative self. To see how this is true, imagine that we started by assuming the sort of emotional connection that facilitates empathy. Such empathy would facilitate making interpersonal utility comparisons, since being able to imagine how someone else feels in a given situation implies the possibility of translating between one's own and another person's metric for utility. Assuming that interpersonal utility comparisons are impossible amounts to assuming a separative self, and to denying the possibility of an empathic, emotionally connected self. But if we assume instead that individuals *can* make interpersonal utility comparisons, then surely we would conclude that as scholars we, too, are capable of making such comparisons. These comparisons would provide information about the relative advantage and disadvantage of individuals under study. We then would view such comparisons as practical measurement problems (analogous to calculating "shadow prices") rather than as impossible in principle.

As long as we accept the principle that utility comparisons between individuals are impossible, we find that the same principle applies to comparisons between groups. To answer questions about groups requires not only measuring utility but also averaging utilities across persons. While some applied economists study inequalities in wealth or income between groups, and discuss their findings in language that seems to imply something about unequal utility between the groups, such interpretations are in fundamental conflict with the theoretical core of neoclassical economics. Hence generalizations such as that women in a particular society are disadvantaged relative to men or that the poor are disadvantaged relative to the rich are moved to the margin of serious research and seldom discussed.

These beliefs also explain why positive neoclassical theories harmonize so well with conservative normative positions on distributional issues. The paradigm denies one the possibility of stating that those at the bottom of hierarchies average less utility than others, which otherwise might provide a basis for questioning the justice of initial unequal distributions of endowments and their consequences. The paradigm also implies that virtually all collectivistic redistribution is non-Pareto-optimal. In sum, it permits no assessments of inequal utility that otherwise might serve as grounds for advocating egalitarian redistribution; rather it criticizes such a redistribution on the grounds of efficiency. To take only one example, this assumption leads one to question the merit of assistance to the large proportion of female-headed families who live in poverty. More generally, it denies us a theoretical basis for saying existing arrangements benefit men more than women.

Tastes: Exogenous and Unchanging

What the utility maximizer of economic theory will do is often indeterminate unless one knows the individual's tastes. Tastes (also called preferences) determine the amount of utility provided by different combinations of goods, services, leisure, working conditions, children, and so forth. They are an input to economic models. Economists do not attempt to explain the origin of these tastes. In a now famous article, George Stigler and Gary Becker (1977) argued that there is little variation in tastes between individuals, so most behavior can be explained by prices or endowments. Other economists disagree and see a role for disciplines such as sociology and psychology in explaining variations in tastes (Hirshleifer 1984). But whether or not they believe that tastes vary across individuals, economists typically see tastes as exogenous to their models.[5] Further, tastes are not expected to change as individuals interact with others in markets or as they experience the consequences of market interaction.

Economists have recently also moved onto the "turf" of other social sciences with models purporting to explain seemingly "nonmarket" areas such as crime (Becker 1968; Witte 1980) and family behavior (Becker 1981; Pollak

---

5. Becker's recent work on addiction is sometimes interpreted as endogenizing tastes (Becker and Murphy 1988). I believe this is a misinterpretation. In Becker's model, called "rational addiction," the actor is presumed to calculate the present value of the future utility that will result from using the drug as well as the future disutility that will ensue from addiction. Then the actor makes a decision based on his/her present tastes about whether or not to begin use of the addictive drug. I see this work as an attempt to show that a model assuming rationality and exogenous tastes can be used to analyze even those phenomena noneconomists see as *most* obviously irrational and *most* obviously involving changes in tastes.

1985). But as they enlarge the scope of their theories and claim that their paradigms can explain not only behavior in what we usually think of as markets but all human behavior, the assumption that tastes are exogenous becomes even more heroic. For example, to retain the assumption in the "new home economics," one must be prepared to argue that tastes are exogenous even to interactions in one's family of origin. But if tastes don't come, at least in part, from the family in which one was raised, where do they come from? Is the implicit assumption that they are freely chosen or biologically determined? Either proposition is highly questionable as a complete explanation.

There is no doubt that assuming fixed and exogenous rather than changing and endogenous preferences radically simplifies neoclassical models. But is the assumption reasonable? To see that it is not, consider the following questions. Are most individuals really so impervious to their surroundings that they can hold a job for years without their preferences being affected by the routines they get used to in this job? Are preferences never influenced by interactions with coworkers? If they are, then results of events in a labor market are affecting tastes. Are consumer tastes never altered by interactions with neighbors? If they are, then events in the housing market (which determine the identity of one's neighbors) are affecting tastes. One needs to assume a misleading degree of emotional separation and atomism to deny the possibility of these effects of market exchanges upon tastes. A model that does not help to elucidate how tastes change through such interactions leaves out too much of human experience. Further, as economists enlarge their scope, the implausibility of the assumption becomes ever clearer. Does anyone really believe that the choice of a spouse in the "marriage market" has no effects on later tastes?

One additional problem with ignoring the endogeneity of tastes is that it obscures some of the processes through which gender inequality is perpetuated. In some of these processes, economic outcomes affect tastes. For example, according to cognitive-developmental psychologists such as Lawrence Kohlberg (1966), childhood socialization is largely a matter of watching what same-sex adults do and forming one's own tastes and values accordingly. Thus, at the societal level discrimination may affect the tastes of the next generation. To take an example from somewhat later in the life cycle, if schools or employers discriminate against women who start out wanting to enter "male" fields, women may adjust their tastes to the available options. In these ways, either market outcomes result from premarket discrimination or market discrimination may create gender-related tastes, thus perpetuating women's lower earnings.[6]

6. There is, however, one sense in which assuming endogenous tastes militates against recognizing gender inequalities in *utilities*. In the extreme, if we believe that people come to desire whatever they are limited to, then no disutility results from discrimination or other types of

Selfishness in Markets

Neoclassical theory assumes self-interested actors. Since it says nothing explicit about what gives people utility, it is not inconsistent with neoclassical assumptions for some individuals to derive satisfaction from being altruistic (Friedman and Diem 1990). That is, self-interest need not imply selfishness in the sense of failing to care for others. Nonetheless, in practice, most economists *do* assume selfishness in markets, as Robert Frank (1988) has pointed out. Sometimes auxiliary assumptions preclude altruism, for instance, the assumption that utilities are independent (Folbre 1993). Since economists generally define A's altruism toward B as the case where whatever gives B utility contributes to A's utility, altruism is precluded by the assumption that actors' utilities are independent.[7]

The assumption that individuals are selfish is related to the separative model of self. Emotional connection often creates empathy, altruism, and a subjective sense of social solidarity. For example, the experience of attending to the needs of a child or of mentoring a student often makes us care more about others' well-being. (Note that this is also an example of changing tastes.) Separative selves would have little basis on which to develop the necessary empathy to practice altruism.[8]

Most labor economists assume selfishness of employers toward employees and vice versa. If employers were altruistic toward some or all of their em-

---

oppression. I believe that this extreme view distorts reality as much as the view that tastes never change as a result of the constraints one encounters.

7. The assumption that each actor's utility is independent of the utility of other actors is distinct from the assumption that one cannot make interpersonal utility comparisons. The assumption of independent utilities is about whether A's utility affects B's; the assumption that interpersonal utility comparisons are impossible concerns whether either the actors or the scientist can measure the amount by which total utilities increased from a particular distributional change. It is the assumption of independent utilities that implies selfishness. One could have a model in which people are capable of making interpersonal utility comparisons but are selfish (i.e., have independent utilities). Even so, the assumptions are related. It is difficult to imagine a model in which people are altruistic (i.e., utilities are not independent) that does not feature actors making interpersonal utility comparisons. To see this, consider how my choice to spend twenty dollars on a gift for my spouse, toward whom I am altruistic, affects my utility. If I buy the gift I forego the utility I would have gained from spending the money on myself, but I gain the utility that comes from seeing my spouse's utility increase upon receiving the gift. A fully specified utility function of the sort economists assume must be able to determine which gain is greater, requiring some common metric. In sum, to assume interdependent utilities may require admitting interpersonal utility comparisons, but admitting the possibility of interpersonal utility comparisons does not necessarily imply interdependent utilities.

8. Of course, empathy can also be used selfishly. As people who have gone through a painful divorce can attest, it is often those who know their utility functions the best who can hurt them the most should they cease to feel altruism (Friedman and Diem 1990).

ployees, they might pay them above-market wages, foregoing some profit. Of course, the *strategic* payment of above-market wages in the new "shirking" models of efficiency wages (Katz 1986; Bulow and Summers 1986) does not violate the assumption of selfishness. In these models, employers are profit maximizing, and thus they pay above-market wages only when such wages increase the productivity of workers, and thus revenue, enough to more than compensate for the costs of the higher wage.[9]

Assuming selfishness in markets is not merely a "male" model of self that may fit women less well; it also fails to account for men's altruism in market behavior, altruism that may work to the disadvantage of women. When people engage in collective action, a kind of *selective* altruism may be at work, at least in the initial stages (Elster 1979; Sen 1987). For example, when male employees collude in order try to keep women out of "their" jobs, they are exhibiting within-sex altruism.[10]

Sometimes selective within-sex altruism also exists between male employers and employees, so that employers are willing to pay male workers more than the contribution of the marginal worker to revenue product. This may be termed pro-male altruistic discrimination as opposed to the more common form of anti-female discrimination in which women are paid less than the (two-sex) market-clearing wage. Matthew Goldberg (1982) has shown that this pro-male altruistic discrimination will not necessarily erode in competitive markets as anti-female discrimination presumably will.[11] The essence of his argument is that a nondiscriminator cannot buy out an altruistic discriminator for a price consistent with the present value of the business to the nondiscriminator. This is because the nonpecuniary utility the pro-male discriminator is getting from indulging his taste for altruism toward male workers

9. By contrast, Akerloff's (1982, 1984) "gift exchange" model of efficiency wages does presume a sort of altruism on the part of employers. In this sense, it is a radical departure from the usual neoclassical assumption of selfishness in markets.

10. Such behavior is documented by Reskin and Roos (1990).

11. For a nontechnical elaboration of Goldberg's argument as well as an explanation of why economists believe most discrimination will eventually disappear in competitive markets, see England (1992, ch. 2). I have taken quite a few liberties in translating Goldberg's technical argument into words. For example, his discussion is about race rather than sex discrimination, and he uses the term "nepotism" rather than "altruism." However, he has stated in a personal communication that he considers my elaboration consistent with the intent of his paper. One qualification is in order: I have characterized "pro-male" discrimination as altruistic toward men because it entails a willingness to pay more than marginal revenue product. It could also be seen as altruistic toward men in the willingness to pay them more than necessary to employ equally productive workers. However, on this latter criterion, anti-female discrimination (paying women less than marginal revenue product) could also be seen as altruistic toward men since it, too, leads to paying men more than the wage for which equally productive women could be employed. Thus, I have not considered discrimination to be altruistic unless it involves a willingness to pay more than marginal revenue product.

makes the business worth more to the discriminator than to the nondiscriminator. By contrast, a nondiscriminator's offer to buy out an anti-female discriminator (who is hiring men for more than he could hire women) will be compelling because the nondiscriminator can make more money than the anti-female discriminator with no sacrifice of nonpecuniary utility. If we assume the absence of altruism in markets, then we cannot recognize the possibility that this selective altruism is a source of sex discrimination that *can* endure in competitive markets. Thus, recognizing selective altruism would revise neoclassical economists' usual assumption that discrimination cannot endure in competitive markets.

Altruism at Home

When it comes to the family, economists generally assume a single family utility function in which the "head" is an altruist. This is clearest in the "new home economics," the application of the neoclassical model to the household, an effort for which Gary Becker (1981) has become famous. From a feminist perspective, the acknowledgment of the importance to the economy of work that goes on in the household must be applauded. However, Becker's assumptions about altruism are in need of a feminist critique. (These same criticisms apply to the more recent 1988 version of Becker's *Treatise on the Family* as well as the 1981 edition.)

Becker's well-known "rotten kid" theorem posits an altruistic family head who takes the utility functions of family members as arguments of "his" own utility function. Becker argues that even a selfish "rotten" spouse or child will be induced to "behave" because of the reinforcement mechanism set up by the altruist. This "rotten kid" theorem doesn't hold without the assumption that the family member who is an altruist *also* controls the resources to be distributed (Ben-Porath 1982; Pollak 1985). Becker refers to the altruistic head as male and to the beneficiaries as women and children, although he claims that he used masculine and feminine pronouns only to distinguish the altruist from the beneficiary (Becker 1981, 173). Since Becker certainly knows that it is generally men who have greater access to money, we must be suspicious of his claim that his choice of the male pronoun to denote the altruist was arbitrary. Yet Becker never discusses the effects of such differential power in the family (England and Farkas 1986, ch. 3), although he does discuss the efficiencies of a division of labor in which men are the primary earners (Becker 1981, ch. 2). Thus his discussion shows us the advantages but none of the disadvantages for women of the conventional sex division of labor. Becker ignores male power and its potentially harmful effects on women while exaggerating male altruism. It is particularly ironic that altruism, in which women seem to specialize more than men (England and Farkas 1986, ch. 3 and 4; England 1989), gets credited to men!

My disagreement is not with the notion that altruism exists in the family, or even with the notion that, on average, people are more altruistic toward family members than toward others. It is rather with the extreme bifurcation of the assumptions about the two spheres.[12] If economic man or woman is so altruistic in the family, might not some altruism be present in market behavior as well? Doesn't this altruism imply an ability to empathize with others that might permit making at least rough interpersonal utility comparisons? Doesn't the susceptibility of an altruist to being influenced by another's joy or pain suggest that s/he also might modify certain tastes through the process of interaction with others? If the answers to these questions are yes, as may well be the case, then the altruistic self assumed for the household is inconsistent with the separative self assumed for market behavior. It is simply not plausible that the altruist who displays an emotionally connective self in the family is the same person who marches out into the market selfish, unable to empathize with others, with utterly rigid tastes.

A second objection to the assumption of extreme altruism in the family is that it conceals the harmful effects of men's selfishness when combined with their greater power within the family. In one of the theoretical traditions within sociology most consistent with neoclassical economic assumptions, exchange theory (Cook 1987), practitioners chose to model the family by characterizing each actor as selfish, or at least as less than completely altruistic. Empirical research in this tradition has examined how relative earnings of husbands and wives affect marital decision-making. The game-theoretic logic of exchange theory suggests that since earnings are resources the earner could withdraw from his/her spouse if the relationship were terminated, we would expect earnings to affect marital power.[13]

When individuals were surveyed, asked to identify areas of disagreement with their spouses, and asked whose wishes prevailed, the general findings showed that men's wishes prevail more often than women's wishes, but that this disparity is less pronounced when women are employed and least pronounced when women's earnings are high relative to their husbands' earnings. (For a review of such studies and a theoretical interpretation, see England and Kilbourne 1990c.) This research makes it clear that men do not use the power they derive from earnings entirely altruistically, as Becker's (1981) model assumes. It also demonstrates that the sex division of labor in the typical household disadvantages women in bargaining within marriage by leaving them with less (or no) earnings to take with them if they left the relationship.[14]

12. Folbre and Hartmann (1988) also make this point.

13. Not all exchange theorists assume that each party is maximizing selfish gain. Some exchange theorists presume that actors also follow norms of equity. Yet those taking the latter view often presume that any existing distribution will tend to acquire an aura of legitimacy and equity over time, regardless of the actual equity of its origins.

14. For a discussion of why a woman's domestic services, which also could be withdrawn if the

The new home economics ignores issues of power when considering consequences of the traditional division of labor and the attendant loss of equity, and instead emphasizes only the efficiency gains from specialization according to comparative advantage (England and Farkas 1986, ch. 4). It also obscures the fact that market discrimination against women results in women's inferior bargaining power within the family.

Conclusion

I have criticized economists' assumptions that, in market behavior, interpersonal utility comparisons are impossible, tastes are exogenous and unchanging, and individuals are selfish (i.e., utilities are independent), but that altruism is the rule in the family. The first three of these assumptions of neoclassical theory contain the "separative-self" bias that feminist theorists have traced in many disciplines. Taken together, this view glorifies men's autonomy outside the family while giving them credit for altruism within the family. Two specific aspects of gender bias were emphasized: unexamined assumptions about gender roles lead to a sharp disjuncture of views about the household and the market, and these assumptions result in an inability to see how conventional arrangements perpetuate women's systematic subordination to men.

But I have not challenged the most "sacred" neoclassical assumption of all, rationality. Clearly, this term has a variety of meanings. Some feminist philosophers argue that the concept of rationality in Western thought has been constructed to be inconsistent with anything associated with traits and activities presumed to be "feminine"—nature, the body, passion, change, emotion—and that this has distorted the concept of rationality (Schott 1988; Bordo 1986; Lloyd 1984). Yet rationality has a rather limited meaning in neoclassical theory. The rational actor has preferences that are both transitive (if I prefer A to B and B to C, I will prefer A to C) and complete (any two outcomes can be compared), and s/he acts on the basis of correct calculations about what means will best maximize utility given these preferences (Varian 1984; Sen 1987). Perhaps this neoclassical concept of rationality is relatively free from gender bias, including the assumption that rationality entails a separative self; perhaps it is not.[15] Resolving this question is beyond the scope of this paper. However, even if we retain the rationality assumption, the neoclassical model

---

marriage broke up, seem not to "count" as heavily in exchange as earnings, see England and Kilbourne (1990c).

15. I have argued elsewhere (England 1989; England and Kilbourne 1990a, 1990b) that the rationality assumption, *in combination with the assumption of exogenous tastes,* does entail an androcentric bias in that it considers emotion and reason to be radically separate phenomena, an idea tied to notions of gender differentiation in the history of Western thought.

needs to be changed substantially in the directions I have indicated above. Relaxing the three assumptions discussed as problematic assertions of a separative self will severely blunt the predictive power of the rationality assumption, even if it is retained. For example, when it comes to wages and discrimination, it is harder to predict what a rational, selectively altruistic employer will do than to predict what a rational, profit-maximizing employer will do. Similarly, it is harder to predict how a rational husband who earns more than his wife will behave in a model of marriage that admits the possibility of both altruism and selfishness than in a model that assumes only one or the other.

Correcting the biases discussed in this paper will generate models in which separation and connection are variable; this variation needs to be explained within both households and markets. Although these new models may entail a loss of deductive certainty, they will illuminate rather than ignore gender inequality in the social and economic world.

References

Akerloff, George A. 1982. "Labor Contracts as Partial Gift Exchange." *Quarterly Journal of Economics* 47:543–69.

———. 1984. "Gift Exchange and Efficiency-Wage Theory: Four Views." *American Economic Review* 74:79–83.

Becker, Gary. 1968. "Crime and Punishment: An Economic Approach." *Journal of Political Economy* 76:169–217.

———. 1981. *A Treatise on the Family.* Cambridge, Mass.: Harvard University Press.

———, and K. M. Murphy. 1988. "A Theory of Rational Addiction." *Journal of Political Economy* 96 (4): 675–700.

Benhabib, Seyla. 1987. "The Generalized and the Concrete Other: The Kohlbert-Gilligan Controversy and Feminist Theory." In *Feminism as Critique: On the Politics of Gender,* ed. Benhabib and Drucilla Cornell, 77–95. Minneapolis: University of Minnesota Press.

Ben-Porath, Yoram. 1982. "Economics and the Family—Match or Mismatch? A Review of Becker's *A Treatise on the Family.*" *Journal of Economic Literature* 20:52–64.

Bordo, Susan. 1986. "The Cartesian Masculinization of Thought." *Signs* 11:439–56.

Bulow, Jeremy I., and Lawrence H. Summers. 1986. "A Theory of Dual Labor Markets with Application to Industrial Policy, Discrimination, and Keynesian Unemployment." *Journal of Labor Economics* 4:376–414.

Chodorow, Nancy. 1978. *The Reproduction of Mothering.* Berkeley: University of California Press.

Cook, Karen, ed. 1987. *Social Exchange Theory.* Newbury Park, Calif.: Sage.

Cooter, Robert, and Peter Rappoport. 1984. "Were the Ordinalists Wrong about Welfare Economics?" *Journal of Economic Literature* 22:507–30.

Elster, Jon. 1979. *Ulysses and the Sirens: Studies in Rationality and Irrationality.* Cambridge, Mass.: Cambridge University Press.

England, Paula. 1989. "A Feminist Critique of Rational-Choice Theories: Implications for Sociology." *American Sociologist* 20:14–28.

———. 1992. *Comparable Worth: Theory and Evidence.* New York: Aldine de Gruyter.

———, and George Farkas. 1986. *Households, Employment, and Gender: A Social, Economic, and Demographic View.* New York: Aldine de Gruyter.

———, and Barbara Stanek Kilbourne. 1990a. "Feminist Critiques of the Separative Model of Self: Implications for Rational Choice Theory." *Rationality and Society* 2:156–72.

———, and Barbara Stanek Kilbourne. 1990b. "Does Rational Choice Theory Assume a Separative Self?" *Rationality and Society* 2:522–26.

———, and Barbara Stanek Kilbourne. 1990c. "Markets, Marriages, and Other Mates: The Problem of Power." In *Beyond the Marketplace: Rethinking Economy and Society,* ed. Roger Friedland and A. F. Robertson, 163–88. New York: Aldine de Gruyter.

Etzioni, Amatai. 1988. *The Moral Dimension.* New York: Free Press.

Folbre, Nancy. 1993. "Micro, Macro, Choice and Structure." In *Theory on Gender/Feminism on Theory,* ed. Paula England, 329–37. New York: Aldine de Gruyter.

———, and Heidi Hartmann. 1988. "The Rhetoric of Self Interest: Ideology and Gender in Economic Theory. In *The Consequences of Economic Rhetoric,* ed. Arjo Klamer, Donald N. McCloskey, and Robert M. Solow, 184–203. New York: Cambridge University Press.

Frank, Robert. 1988. *Passions within Reason: The Strategic Role of the Emotions.* New York: W. W. Norton.

Friedman, Debra, and Carol Diem. 1990. "Comments on England and Kilbourne." *Rationality and Society* 2:517–21.

Gilligan, Carol. 1982. *In a Different Voice: Psychological Theory and Women's Development.* Cambridge, Mass.: Harvard University Press.

Goldberg, Matthew S. 1982. "Discrimination, Nepotism, and Long-Run Wage Differentials." *Quarterly Journal of Economics* 97:308–19.

Granovetter, Mark. 1985. "Economic Action and Social Structure: The Problem of Embeddedness." *American Journal of Sociology* 91:481–510.

———. 1988. "The Sociological and Economic Approaches to Labor Market Analysis: A Social Structural View." In *Industries, Firms, and Jobs: Sociological and Economic Approaches,* ed. George Farkas and Paula England, 187–216. New York: Plenum.

Hahnel, Robin, and Michael Albert. 1990. *Quiet Revolution in Welfare Economics*. Princeton, N.J.: Princeton University Press.

Hirshleifer, Jack. 1984. *Price Theory and Applications*. 3d ed. Englewood Cliffs, N.J.: Prentice-Hall.

Hogarth, Robin M., and Melvin W. Reder, eds. 1987. *Rational Choice: The Contrast between Economics and Psychology*. Chicago: University of Chicago Press.

Jaggar, Alison M. 1983. *Feminist Politics and Human Nature*. Totowa, N.J.: Rowman & Allanheld.

Katz, Lawrence. 1986. "Efficiency Wage Theories: A Partial Evaluation." *Macroeconomic Annual*. Cambridge, Mass.: National Bureau of Economic Research.

Keller, Catherine. 1986. *From a Broken Web: Separation, Sexism, and Self*. Boston: Beacon Press.

Keller, Evelyn Fox. 1983. *A Feeling for the Organism: The Life and Work of Barbara McClintock*. New York: Freeman.

———. 1985. *Reflections on Gender and Science*. New Haven, Conn.: Yale University Press.

Kohlberg, Lawrence. 1966. "A Cognitive Developmental Analysis of Children's Sex-Role Concepts and Attitudes." In *The Development of Sex Differences*, ed. E. E. Maccoby, 82–173. Stanford, Calif.: Stanford University Press.

Lloyd, Genevieve. 1984. *The Man of Reason: "Male" and "Female" in Western Philosophy*. Minneapolis: University of Minnesota Press.

Mansbridge, Jane J., ed. 1990. *Beyond Self-Interest*. Chicago: University of Chicago Press.

Nelson, Julie A. 1992. "Gender, Metaphor, and the Definition of Economics." *Economics and Philosophy* 8:103–25.

Piore, Michael J. 1974. "Comment on Wachter." *Brookings Papers on Economic Activity* 3:684–88.

Pollak, Robert A. 1976. "Habit Formation and Long-Run Utility Functions." *Journal of Economic Theory* 13:272–97.

———. 1985. "A Transaction Cost Approach to Families and Households." *Journal of Economic Literature* 23:581–608.

Reskin, Barbara F., and Patricia Roos. 1990. *Job Queues, Gender Queues: Explaining Women's Inroads into Male Occupations*. Philadelphia: Temple University Press.

Schott, Robin May. 1988. *Cognition and Eros: A Critique of the Kantian Paradigm*. Boston: Beacon Press.

Sen, Amartya K. 1982. *Choice, Welfare and Measurement*. Cambridge, Mass.: MIT Press.

———. 1987. *On Ethics and Economics*. New York: Basil Blackwell.

Stigler, George, and Gary Becker. 1977. "De Gustabus Non Est Disputandum." *American Economic Review.* 67:76–90.

Varian, Hal. 1984. *Microeconomic Analysis.* 2d ed. New York: W. W. Norton.

Witte, Ann. 1980. "Estimating the Economic Model of Crime with Individual Data." *Quarterly Journal of Economics* 94:57–84.

3

Diana Strassmann

Not a Free Market: The Rhetoric of Disciplinary Authority in Economics

In recent years, mainstream American economics has increasingly been built around core ideas of self-interested individualism and contractual exchange. The central character of economic analysis is the autonomous agent who trades with other agents in order to maximize a utility or profit function. Both microeconomists and macroeconomists explain the economy in ways that are consistent with this microfoundations core. Modern mainstream economics therefore may be identified as an explanatory approach rather than as a domain of facts to be explained. An explanatory approach is unusual, however, for disciplines oriented toward explaining empirical phenomena. Most other empirical disciplines, such as the physical and biological sciences, define themselves in terms of the empirical domain to be explained (Shapere 1984).

How has the identification of economics as an approach rather than as an empirical domain become predominant? What voices have been included and represented in this construction of economics? How has this construction shaped economic research? My thesis is that the tendency of mainstream economics to be identified with an approach rather than with a set of empirical phenomena limits the kinds of explanations that the discipline can provide.[1]

This essay owes a great intellectual debt to Karey Harrison and develops some of the ideas expressed in our joint paper "Gender, Rhetoric, and Economic Theory" (1989). This essay has also benefited greatly from extensive conversations with Elizabeth Long, Julie Taylor, and Sharon Traweek, and from the very helpful comments and criticisms of Linda Lucas and those of the editors and other contributors to this volume. This essay also marked the beginning of my collaboration with Livia Polanyi, who gave detailed editorial help on numerous versions of the paper. In addition, she insisted upon the importance of including short summaries of each of the stories discussed here and suggested much of the language for these brief texts.

1. Although there is much diversity in economic thought in the United States, including institutionalist, Marxist, and other perspectives, the mainstream voice predominates at elite universities, in policy circles, and in the most widely read journals of the discipline. I do not claim that

By proscribing what can count as economics, this identification constrains the pattern of acceptable disagreement in a way that silences serious challenges to the primacy of self-interested individualism and contractual exchange. I shall argue that the resulting theories reflect a distinctly androcentric and Western perspective on selfhood and individual agency.

Core Ideas and the Shaping of Economic Research

A popular view among mainstream practitioners is that explanations based on self-interested individualism and contractual exchange merit their high status in economics because of their obvious logic or superior power. The conceptual structure of economics indeed appears natural and obvious to most practitioners in the discipline, and this is no accident. The selection and socialization process for becoming an economist ensures that those to whom this structure might be less obvious learn how to do proper economics or be screened out. Those who remain economists easily forget that the organization of the discipline, based on the core assumptions of self-interested individualism and contractual exchange, means that the construction of economic knowledge is partial.

Economists' typical description of a good model as focusing on the most "important" elements of some phenomenon displays an implicit recognition of the nature of models. Models, like maps, highlight certain aspects of a situation while suppressing others. Since a model can never completely capture the phenomenon in its entirety, questions of the "truth" or "falsity" of a model are less relevant to judgments about its quality than are questions of its appropriateness, aptness, and helpfulness in a given context. Our models can help us to understand those aspects of the world we choose to emphasize, but the principles or laws we derive from our models are "true" only in the model, not literally true in the world (Cartwright 1983).

Well-socialized economists, however, in practice tend to view their simplifications—especially those required by the core assumptions of self-interested individualism and contractual exchange—as relatively innocent. The prevalence of jokes about economists forgetting that assumptions are just assumptions is no accident.[2] The microfoundations of economic theory are seen as being approximately true rather than as only partially true. The notion of modeling as approximation, however, disguises the value judgments hidden

---

the mainstream speaks with one voice; indeed the mainstream is beset with fierce and substantive internal debates.

2. The can opener joke is the classic example of this genre. In brief, a physicist, a philosopher, and an economist are on a desert island with nothing to eat but a can of beans, but they have no can opener. The physicist and the philosopher have various unsuccessful solutions to the problem, but the economist knows how to solve the problem: "Assume a can opener!"

behind the decision to count some phenomena as more important than others. These judgments need to be understood in the context of the model-makers' own experience, and hence their partial views of the world.

Rather than encouraging a search for the most appropriate simplifications for a given context of application, the discipline requires that explanatory accounts be built on the foundational assumptions of self-interested individualism and contractual exchange, thereby insulating itself against accounts built on alternative assumptions. Four case studies of the partial nature of mainstream economics stories will illustrate the problems created, in theory and in policy, by the narrowness of the range of explanatory accounts in the discipline. I use the term "story" to highlight the nature of economic knowledge and the restrictions the discipline places on the acceptable structure of economic accounts.[3] Like any model, the story model is a partial description of accounts of the world.[4]

The Story of the Marketplace of Ideas

The story of the marketplace of ideas is a classical example of economic imperialism—the application of economic explanations to domains viewed as being outside the traditional purview of economics, in this case the philosophy of science and anthropology. In the marketplace of ideas the "best" ideas bubble to the top, rising in value according to merit. Ideas are exchanged as in a marketplace, their worth ascertained in a competitive process of bidding and exchange. This story implies that predominant economic theories are valued because of their worthiness, with no role for cultural values or institutional configurations. In Donald McCloskey's (1985) version of this story, the success of a theory depends on its inherent quality as well as on the quality of the rhetoric used to support it: the community of "honest" scholars is the judge. As McCloskey wrote, "The overlapping conversations provide the standards (for science). It is a market argument. There is no need for philosophical lawmaking or methodological regulation to keep the economy of intellect running just fine" (28).

But who are these judges in the "economy of intellect," those select and

3. I owe a great intellectual debt to the anthropologist Sharon Traweek for directing me to think about the nature of storytelling in economics. Her 1988 book, *Beamtimes and Lifetimes: The World of High Energy Physics,* and her 1992 essay, "Border Crossings: Narrative Strategies in Science Studies and among Physicists at Tsukuba Science City, Japan," which discusses reactions to her book, have been a major influence on my thinking. I recommend them most highly to anyone interested in the relationships among the construction of knowledge in the sciences, power relations, and cultural values. Also see McCloskey (1990) for a detailed discussion of narrative and storytelling in economics.

4. Stories and metaphors, for example, are two different kinds of explanations: one static, the other dynamic (McCloskey 1990). See Polanyi (1989) for a detailed discussion of different forms of explanatory accounts.

worthy scholars who have become economists? They have not been produced in a vacuum. The persuasiveness of any particular argument does not lie wholly in the argument itself; the success of an argument depends in part on the composition of the judging audience. The arguments that appeal to economists need to be understood in the context of the complex processes by which economists have been selected and socialized, and the processes by which other potential economists have been excluded.[5]

To the extent that the marketplace metaphor does indeed apply to the exchange of ideas, perfect competition does not predominate. The marketplace of academia lacks, for example, both free entry and perfect knowledge—essentials for perfect competition. So what happens if there is *imperfect* competition in the marketplace of ideas? Helen Longino (1990a) claims that objectivity within a discipline is enhanced when qualified practitioners share intellectual authority. Her arguments translate easily to the language of economics. The absence of free entry into the marketplace of economic ideas distorts the relative valuations of ideas in this arena, giving market power to dominant practitioners. The dominant practitioners may protect their intellectual stronghold with exclusionary practices. As any economist would agree, barriers to entry create price distortions. Exclusionary practices lead to a divergence between the social and private value of ideas. The private value is determined by the reward structure within the discipline and the subtle processes of selection, socialization, and exclusion.[6]

But even this story of imperfect competition in the marketplace of ideas obscures the influence of social and cultural values. When entry into the discipline is filtered by the requirement that members adhere to a core conceptual structure, dissenting voices are screened out. Dissenters' papers are relegated to marginal economics or interdisciplinary journals, or worse, to journals in other less reputable or less "rigorous" disciplines. Although women and minorities commonly experience dissonance with the standard models of economics, only those who adhere to foundational metaphors are allowed to participate in the conversations of the mainstream. The inability of economics to give much credence to issues of values, power, and social construction may be due to the way practitioners have been selected and socialized to discount the role of such factors, and to give excessive credence to stories based on core assumptions and models.

One example is the story of the benevolent patriarch.

5. Traweek (1988) describes these processes of socialization and exclusion in one subdiscipline of physics. In her study of the high energy physics communities in the United States and Japan, she finds that these complex processes differ markedly from stories physicists tell about talent rising to the top.

6. See Seiz (1992) for a parallel discussion of knowledge construction in the economics community.

The Story of the Benevolent Patriarch

The standard economic model of the family is a story of a benevolent patriarch.[7] In this story, the patriarch makes choices in the best interests of the family. A patriarch is necessarily male; as head of the prototypical family, he has a wife and one or more children dependent upon him for providing for their needs.[8] Although family members may have conflicting needs, the good provider dispassionately and rationally makes decisions that are in the best interests of the family. In particular, the patriarch participates in markets, making choices that link market values to his own assessment of family needs.

This story is useful for economic theory because it allows the family to be treated as an individual agent. The metaphor of the invisible hand and its modern expression in general equilibrium theory rest critically on this foundational story by linking decision-making with individual well-being. The link implicitly assumes that family decisions (made by the patriarch) give equal weight to the needs of all family members. By subsuming the needs of all family members into one utility function, the story of the benevolent patriarch provides an economic parallel to the historical invisibility of children and women in much of British and American law.

An individual patriarch may indeed take individual family members' preferences into account, perhaps far better than a distant bureaucrat would. However, the linking of decision-making with individual well-being need not necessarily hold for the dominant decision-makers in families, who are overwhelmingly male (Sen 1984). Widespread wife and child abuse as well as the substantial evidence for unequal food distribution within the family, which again harms women and children, clearly undermine the notion that family members necessarily behave altruistically (Sen 1984). Rather, the distribution of power among family members, often directly related to their individual resources, appears to play a major role in family decisions and the intrafamily distribution of resources.

---

7. See Folbre and Hartmann (1988) for a detailed discussion of the gender-related self-interest underlying the traditional acceptance of this model. The dichotomous assumptions of perfect selfishness in the marketplace and perfect altruism in the home were first made explicit by Adam Smith (1776). They remain the underpinnings for much current economic theory, including Becker's *A Treatise on the Family* (1981), which mathematically elaborates and extends the theory.

8. Families are, of course, more complex and diverse than this simple story indicates, but that is obscured when this background story is hidden from analysis. Recent game-theoretic accounts of family behavior challenge the story of the benevolent patriarch and explore a variety of issues related to decision-making in the family. See, for example, Manser and Brown (1980), McElroy and Horney (1981), Pollak (1985), and Lundberg and Pollak (1990). Although such accounts are mainstream in the sense of maintaining consistency with assumptions of individual optimization, they have been treated as relatively peripheral and have not been incorporated into economic theory more generally. See Cooper (1990) for an analysis of mainstream resistance to game-theoretic accounts of the family.

The story of the benevolent patriarch, like all stories, is partial. The problem is not the partiality of the story per se but its inappropriate use, which leads to numerous misguided policy judgments. In an early response to Milton Friedman's (1953) claim that the realism of assumptions does not matter, Robert Solow suggests that when theoretical results stem directly from a "crucial" assumption, that assumption should be reasonably realistic (1956, 65). I would like to call attention to the possibility that an assumption may be "crucial" for some application areas but not for others.

For example, the story of the benevolent patriarch serves as a background to theories of income distribution, taxation, welfare, and economic development. Although Amartya Sen's work shows that the linking of decision-making with individual well-being is a crucial assumption underlying many of these theories, such theories are not generally understood to be crucially dependent upon this linkage.[9] Children and women in particular get short-changed by some economic policies based on the story of the benevolent patriarch. Sen calls attention to "the grave tragedy of the disproportionate under-nourishment of children," "the sharper undernourishment of the female children in distress situations," and the "unusual morbidity of women" in India and in poverty more generally. Sen attributes these phenomena to the selfish behavior of family patriarchs and concludes that the failure of family decision-makers to behave altruistically calls into question the reliability of many of the economic analyses based upon this premise, including the traditional efficiency or optimality results related to the market mechanism (1984, 363, 364). For example, contrary to the story of the benevolent patriarch, there is evidence that children fare better in poor countries if transfers (government financial assistance) are given to mothers rather than fathers (Kumar 1979; Horton and Miller 1991). I suggest that the problem with the story of the benevolent patriarch is that economists fail to recognize the limited scope of application of models built on this story, a failure that has led to inadequate and inappropriate theories and policies in a wide variety of contexts.

The Story of the Woman of Leisure

Another old economic fable is that women do not work. The woman of leisure stays at home tending to the domestic needs of her family. Although she may perform many activities, these activities are limited to her family and have no value because they are not traded in the marketplace. Dependent on her husband, the benevolent patriarch, she relies on him and the money he earns from his productive and marketed activities to provide for her needs.

Unlike the story of the benevolent patriarch, however, the story that women

9. Samuels (1992) makes a related point in criticizing analyses that purport to reach "optimal" solutions on the basis of implicit normative premises.

do not work is slowly giving way to other stories, many of them told by the women who have become economists in recent decades.[10] Although labor economists have begun to recognize the concept of nonmarket production, the very term "household production" represents a borrowing from a category formed to describe male activity. While economists have given lip service to women's work in the home as one of those "unfortunate" exclusions from the national income accounts, gendered conceptualizations of what counts as work matter greatly for public policy. The exclusion of women's work from national income accounts, for example, has had particularly pernicious effects for women in developing nations (Waring 1988). That finding a way to measure and include nonmarket production has remained a low priority activity in the discipline attests to the small degree of concern over this exclusion.[11] The exclusion of nonmarketed women's work from the national income accounts is not an "accidental" oversight as is commonly believed. Nancy Folbre (1991) documents the origins of the "unproductive housewife" concept in economic theory and uncovers the gendered politics behind the development of economic theories that reduced nonmarketed "home production" to leisure.

The Story of Free Choice

Another partial story, related to the previous two, is the story of free choice. The agent in economic theory is a creature with wishes and desires as well as with various resources at his disposal. The agent can deploy his resources toward attaining these wants. Because his resources are always inadequate to attain all his wishes and desires, economic man must make choices. Faced with the available array of goods and services, each with an attached price, he dispassionately considers his various possibilities for satisfaction and carefully weighs their costs against their respective degrees of potential satisfaction. Eventually, he will conclude that he prefers one of these options, and that option becomes his choice. The agent in economic theory is a self-contained individual—an adult able to choose from an array of options, limited only by "constraints."

But by focusing on choice, the theory contains a number of ancillary, more hidden assumptions: (1) people are independent agents and unique selves, taking only their own needs and wishes into account; (2) people are able and responsible for taking care of their own needs.[12]

10. Differences in the stories people with different experiences tell illustrate how experiences may influence the way people construct accounts of the world. Brown (1989), for example, shows how economists' "discovery" of women workers coincides with the entry of the wives of these male economists into the marketplace.

11. The *American Economic Review* has not published a single article on this topic for at least the past ten years; details of such work elsewhere remain largely unknown to most economists.

12. Mansbridge's collection *Beyond-Self Interest* (1990) contains an excellent set of essays related to this topic.

Such assumptions are not actually intended by the theory (and indeed have been correctly analyzed and considered by a number of theorists), but are implicit in actual use. Economists do not universally deny that these assumptions are problematic, but, like the exclusion of women from national income accounts, these assumptions are viewed as fairly benign. Such assumptions indeed may be typical of the perceived experiences of adult, white, male, middle-class American economists, but they fail to capture economic reality for many others.[13] Economic theory's conception of selfhood and individual agency is located in Western cultural traditions as well as being distinctly androcentric.[14] Economic man is the Western romantic hero, a transcendent individual able to make choices and attain goals.

Are these assumptions really benign? Consider the case of infants and children, who do not make choices in a process of rational optimization. They are not calculating machines; their needs are met by others. The nursing relationship between mother and child, far more ancient than market relationships, is the natural mainstay of sustenance for infants. In this relationship, and in the other connective bonds between child and parent, one finds an interdependence that belies separative conceptions of the self. Infants do not choose what kind of diapers they wear nor what kind of care they receive. The choices that influence their welfare are made by adults. Most human capital investments are given to children by parents, yet economic theory focuses on the small amount of human capital that can be obtained by adults, able to choose. Because economic theory examines adult behavior, parents' gifts of time, love, and money to infants and children are reconceptualized as "natural endowments," and thus are hidden by a theory that focuses on how people get what they choose. These lost gifts, forgotten or ignored by economic theory, are yet another manifestation of the invisibility of women's work.[15]

Some economic theorists have attempted to explain gifts to children in the context of parents receiving some form of expected return. Such accounts reflect a general tautological tendency in economic theory, that is, defining any choices, including any form of giving, as being in an individual's self-interest—reconceptualizing any form of giving as self-interest. Virginia Held (1990) describes an alternative view of parent child relations. She defines a "mothering person" as someone, male or female, who is engaged in the prac-

13. Developments in a variety of disciplines have shown how the social construction of gender has created a tendency for men and women to differ in how they conceptualize their experiences, moral choices, and epistemological views as well as in their orientation toward separation and connection. See, for example, Chodorow (1978); England (1989); Gilligan (1982); Harding (1986); and Belenky et al. (1986).

14. See Kondo (1990) for a discussion of the relation between cultural traditions and conceptions of selfhood.

15. Although there is a growing literature on intergenerational transfers, much of this literature focuses on bequests and other pecuniary (male-identified) gifts rather than on gifts of time and attention.

tice of "mothering,"[16] and suggests that any element of a bargain between mothering person and child is very different from the bargain supposedly characteristic of the marketplace:

> If a parent thinks "I'll take care of you now so you'll take care of me when I'm old," it must be based, unlike the contracts of political and economic bargains, on enormous trust and on a virtual absence of enforcement. And few mothering persons have any such exchange in mind when they engage in the activities of mothering. At least the bargain would only be resorted to when the callousness or poverty of the society made the plight of the old person desperate. This is demonstrated in survey after survey; old persons certainly hope not to have to be a burden on their children. . . . So the intention and goal of mothering is to give of one's care without obtaining a return of a self-interested kind. The emotional satisfaction of a mothering person is a satisfaction in the well-being and happiness of another human being, and a satisfaction in the health of the relation between the two persons, not the gain that results from an egoistic bargain. (1990, 297–98)

A number of alternative conceptions of economic relations focus on giving and the satisfaction of human needs, concepts obscured by the standard economic metaphors tied to separative conceptions of selfhood. Genevieve Vaughan (1990) describes an alternative paradigm based on giving, which she calls the gift economy. Nancy Folbre and Heidi Hartmann quote Nancy Hartsock (1983, 41–42) in questioning why market exchange rather than the mother-infant relationship is taken to be the prototypical human interaction. They suggest that the economic individualism underlying neoclassical models of self-interested market behavior "would be better termed male individualism" (Folbre and Hartmann 1988, 186). Julie Nelson argues that an organizing metaphor of autonomous, individual market optimization deemphasizes and marginalizes phenomena characterized by connection, tradition, and domination, and is likely to create "a feeling of distortion, a feeling that that which is most important has been left out" (1990, 17). Dorinne Kondo (1990) shows how conceptions of the self are integrally connected to power and gender relations. That power matters in economic relations is obscured by standard models, which deemphasize such background circumstances as "constraints" or "differences in natural endowments."

When all important choices are made by others, as is the case for infants, constraints are all. The same is true for the elderly, the infirm, and the handicapped. Yet economic theory presents the ability to choose as the normal state of being. Economic theorists, it seems, have formed their conceptual repre-

16. She adds that "if men feel uncomfortable being referred to as, or even more so in being, 'mothering persons,' this may possibly mirror the discomfort many mothers feel adapting to the norms and practices, and language, of 'economic man' " (Held 1990, 290).

sentatives in their own image: autonomous individuals, privileged and free to choose. That the constraints faced by the young, by the old, by women, by political refugees (the list goes on) might be more significant than those of the average economist remains unnoticed. The lack of emphasis on constraints and interdependence stems from the way economic models focus on individual rational choice processes, a focus that deemphasizes (if not ignores) the fact that human beings begin (and often end) life in a state of helplessness and unchosen dependency. Although the dependency of infancy lessens, our lives are always a mix of connectedness and separation.

Economists *are* aware that constraints will theoretically influence outcomes. A theory that focuses on the choices people make assumes that individual outcomes are a consequence of those choices. Although choices are directly influenced by background circumstances and constraints, the emphasis on choice over constraints leads to the tendency to direct attention toward choice instead of toward the constraints that direct and underlie choices.[17] One may ask whether certain contemporary policy failures, particularly the undue suffering of infants and children, may be partially attributable to the current thinking, of economics, which coheres with the American story of resources going to those who work for and deserve them.[18]

Can Mainstream Theories Be Fixed?

Economists would like to believe that most difficulties and problems in standard theories can be resolved within the mainstream framework. They have worked hard to develop stories that reconcile the major "anomalies" with the standard economic approach.[19] For example, by fixing economic theory to provide better explanations of women's behavior, many such deficiencies in the theory have (in some sense) been resolved.[20] The likelihood of a mainstream "fix," however, depends upon the nature of the difficulty in

17. Pateman (1988) elaborates this point in her discussion of consent in family and sexual relationships.

18. Among the twenty leading industrialized nations, the United States is tied for last place in its high rate of infant mortality (Children's Defense Fund study, cited by David and David 1987). Moreover, 20 percent of all American children live in poverty. The percentages are even higher for African-American and Hispanic children: 45 and 39 percent, respectively (U.S. Department of Commerce 1990, 460).

19. Such modifications include some of the recent research on the family, symmetrical research programs on the theory of the firm, and research on the economic behavior of women and minorities.

20. However, theoretical changes regarding the treatment of women have often proceeded on a selective basis, resulting in ad hoc rather than theory-driven explanations for women's behavior. Brown describes how "explanations" of racial differences in women's labor force participation range from "matriarchal family structure" in black families to variations in the fear of losing husbands (1989, 9).

the standard story. Difficulties linked to core assumptions (such as self-interested individualism) will be extremely hard to change because of the identification of economics as an approach that uses those assumptions. Because any account of the world is constructed on the basis of a partial perspective, standard economic accounts do more than just leave out other voices. They create a conceptual framework for organizing an understanding of the world in which some features are prioritized over others. Therefore, problems less linked to core assumptions can be more easily changed within a mainstream framework. Consequently, women's activities in the home have been more easily reconceptualized as useful and productive (instead of as leisure) because nonmarketed exchanges are not inconsistent with foundational metaphors (although less prototypical than marketed exchanges).

Even where mainstream fixes are possible, however, such modifications often will remain peripheral to the theoretical core of the discipline. For example, the influence and centrality of game-theoretic reconceptualizations of the family, which extend self-interest into the family, are limited by the central role of the benevolent patriarch story with which they conflict. As long as adherence to central stories determines theoretical importance, modifications that do not adhere to these stories will be marginalized and known in detail almost exclusively by those who specialize in them. Furthermore, specialists are unlikely to be aware of the full extent to which the prototype fails over a broad range of economic contexts. Because few economists learn much about research on the "fringes," modifications to core theories cannot be easily coordinated to allow for the development of a unified conception of problems with core economic metaphors. Indeed, my discussion of impediments to alternative conceptualizations in economics conflicts with the popular story of the marketplace of ideas.

The conversation metaphor for knowledge construction used by Arjo Klamer (1984), Donald McCloskey (1985), and others has the potential to draw attention to questions obscured by the story of the marketplace of ideas (e.g., who gets to participate and who gets excluded? who listens and who gets listened to? who gets to decide which arguments are "good" and which are not?). McCloskey generally does not focus on these issues; he prefers to emphasize the protective aspects of the social character of science. He writes that "the social character of scientific knowledge does not make it arbitrary, touchie-feelie, mob-governed, or anything else likely to bring it into disrepute. It is still, for instance, 'objective,' if that is a worry" (1985, 152).[21]

But the social character of science protects it in a way that also "renders it vulnerable to social and political interests and values" (Longino 1990, 12). Helen Longino argues that reducing subjective preferences in science requires both that hypotheses and background assumptions be subjected to a variety of

---

21. Both McCloskey (1985, 152) and Longino (1990) give objectivity a social definition.

conceptual criticisms and that such criticisms can limit the acceptance of partial and idiosyncratic assumptions reflecting the views of a single same-minded group (1992, 21). Such a process cannot happen when "unreflective acceptance of assumptions" defines "what it is to be a member of such a community (thus making criticism impossible)" (1992, 17).

The entry of more women into the discipline may lead to theoretical changes that fit within the existing disciplinary framework of economics. But as long as dissent is labeled not economics and suppressed, critique of standard economic assumptions remains taboo.[22] Not surprisingly, neither anthropologists nor philosophers of science view the story of the marketplace of ideas as a fully credible or complete explanation of why some ideas or theories prevail over others. Their explanations include some features and questions that are left out of the story of the marketplace of ideas. A story that takes into account the incompleteness of models need not keep searching for the "best" model. Because models by their nature represent only a partial viewpoint, partiality or bias cannot be eliminated from theories. A greater openness to entertaining alternative perspectives is likely to lead to a multiplicity of perspectives that more adequately captures the complexity and diversity of economic activities.

References

Becker, Gary. 1981. *A Treatise on the Family.* Cambridge, Mass.: Harvard University Press.

Belenky, Mary, et al. 1986. *Women's Ways of Knowing.* New York: Basic Books.

Brown, Lisa Jo. 1989. "Gender and Economic Analysis: A Feminist Perspective." Paper presented at the American Economic Association annual meetings, December.

Cartwright, Nancy. 1983. *How the Laws of Physics Lie.* Oxford: Clarendon Press.

Chodorow, Nancy. 1978. *The Reproduction of Mothering: Psychoanalysis and the Sociology of Gender.* Berkeley: University of California Press.

Cooper, Brian. 1990. "Marital Problems: A Reconsideration of Neoclassical Bargaining Models of Household Decision-Making." Manuscript, Economics Department, Harvard University.

David, Lester, and Irene David. 1987. "How We Can Save Our Babies." *Health* (August), 29–31, 61–66.

England, Paula. 1989. "A Feminist Critique of Rational-Choice Theories: Implications for Sociology." *American Sociologist* 20(1): 14–28.

22. See Strassmann and Polanyi (1992) for further discussion of the status of critique in economic analysis and the relationship between critique and disciplinary membership.

Folbre, Nancy. 1991. "The Unproductive Housewife: Her Evolution in Nineteenth-Century Economic Thought." *Signs* 16(3): 463–84.

———, and Heidi Hartmann. 1988. "The Rhetoric of Self-Interest: Ideology and Gender in Economic Theory," in *The Consequences of Economic Rhetoric,* ed. Arjo Klamer, Donald N. McCloskey and Robert M. Solow, 184–203. New York: Cambridge University Press.

Friedman, Milton. 1953. "The Methodology of Positive Economics." In *Essays in Positive Economics,* 3–43. Chicago: University of Chicago Press.

Gilligan, Carol. 1982. *In a Different Voice: Psychological Theory and Women's Development.* Cambridge, Mass.: Harvard University Press.

Harding, Sandra. 1986. *The Science Question in Feminism.* Ithaca, N.Y.: Cornell University Press.

Hartsock, Nancy. 1983. *Money, Sex, and Power: Toward a Feminist Historical Materialism.* New York: Longman.

Held, Virginia. 1990. "Mothering versus Contract." In *Beyond Self-Interest,* ed. Jane Mansbridge, 287–304. Chicago: University of Chicago Press.

Horton, Susan, and Diane Miller. 1991. "The Effect of Gender of Household Head on Food Expenditure: Evidence from Low Income Households in Jamaica." Manuscript, Economics Department, University of Toronto.

Klamer, Arjo. 1984. *Conversations with Economists.* Totowa, N.J.: Rowman & Allanheld.

———, Donald N. McCloskey, and Robert M. Solow, eds. 1988. *The Consequences of Economic Rhetoric.* New York: Cambridge University Press.

Kondo, Dorinne. 1990. *Crafting Selves: Power, Gender, and Discourses of Identity in a Japanese Workplace.* Chicago: University of Chicago Press.

Kumar, S. 1979. *Impact of Subsidized Rice on Food Consumption and Nutrition in Kerala.* Washington D.C.: International Food Policy Research Institute.

Longino, Helen. 1990. *Science as Social Knowledge.* Princeton, N.J.: Princeton University Press.

———. 1992. "Essential Tensions—Phase Two: Feminist, Philosophical, and Social Studies of Science." In *Social Dimensions of Science,* ed. Ernan McMullin, 198–218. South Bend, Ind.: Notre Dame University Press.

Lundberg, Shelly, and Robert Pollak. 1990. "Gender Roles and Intrafamily Distribution." Manuscript, Economics Department, University of Washington.

Mansbridge, Jane, ed. 1990. *Beyond Self-Interest.* Chicago: University of Chicago Press.

Manser, Marilyn, and Murray Brown. 1980. "Marriage of Household Decisionmaking: A Bargaining Analysis," *International Economic Review* 21: 31–44.

McCloskey, Donald. 1985. *The Rhetoric of Economics*. Madison: University of Wisconsin Press.

———. 1988. "The Consequences of Rhetoric." In *The Consequences of Economic Rhetoric*, ed. Arjo Klamer, McCloskey, and Robert M. Solow, 280–93. New York: Cambridge University Press.

———. 1990. *If You're So Smart: The Narrative of Economic Expertise*. Chicago: University of Chicago Press.

McElroy, Marjorie B., and Mary Jean Horney. 1981. "Nash-Bargained Household Decisions: Toward a Generalization of the Theory of Demand." *International Economic Review* 22(2): 333–49.

Nelson, Julie. 1990. "Gender, Metaphor, and the Definition of Economics." Working Paper Series #350, University of California at Davis.

Pateman, Carole. 1988. *The Sexual Contract*. Stanford, Calif.: Stanford University Press.

Polanyi, Livia. 1989. *Telling the American Story: A Structural and Cultural Analysis of Conversational Storytelling*. Cambridge, Mass.: MIT Press.

Pollak, Robert A. 1985. "A Transaction Cost Approach to Families and Households." *Journal of Economic Literature* 23: 581–608.

Samuels, Warren. 1992. "Institutional Economics." In *Economics in Perspective*, ed. David Greenaway, Michael Bleaney, and Ian Stewart, London: Routledge.

Seiz, Janct. 1992. "Gender and Economic Research." In *Post-Popperian Methodology of Economics: Recovering Practice*, ed. Neil de Marchi, 273–319. Boston: Kluwer-Nijhoff.

Sen, Amartya. 1984. *Resources, Values and Development*. Cambridge, Mass.: Harvard University Press.

Shapere, Dudley. 1984. *Reason and the Search for Knowledge*. Dordrecht: D. Reidel.

Smith, Adam. 1937 [1776]. *An Inquiry into the Nature and Causes of the Wealth of Nations*. New York: Random House.

Solow, Robert. 1956. "A Contribution to the Theory of Economic Growth." *Quarterly Journal of Economics* (February), 65–94.

Strassmann, Diana, and Lyvia Polanyi. 1992. "Shifting the Paradigm: Value in Feminist Critiques of Economics." Paper presented at the First Annual Conference of the International Association for Feminist Economics, July 1992, Washington, D.C.

Traweek, Sharon. 1988. *Beamtimes and Lifetimes: The World of High Energy Physics*. Cambridge, Mass.: Harvard University Press.

———. 1992. "Border Crossings: Narrative Strategies in Science Studies among Physicists at Tsukuba Science City, Japan." In *Science as Practice and Culture*, ed. Andrew Pickering. Chicago: University of Chicago Press.

U.S. Department of Commerce. 1990. *Statistical Abstract of the U.S.* 110th ed., 460. Washington, D.C.: U.S. Government Printing Office.

Vaughan, Genevieve. 1990. "From Exchange to Gift Economy." Paper presented at The Other Economic Summit. July, Houston.

Waring, Marilyn. 1988. *If Women Counted: A New Feminist Economics.* San Francisco: Harper & Row.

4

Donald N. McCloskey

Some Consequences of a Conjective Economics

Let a man get up and say, "Behold, this is the truth," and instantly I perceive a sandy cat filching a piece of fish in the background. Look, you have forgotten the cat, I say.

Virginia Woolf, *The Waves* (1931)

Arjo Klamer (1990) has a way of describing what is peculiar about modern economics. He draws a square to stand for the rigid, axiomatic method that dominates most journals in the field. The square, he points out, is the ideal shape of modernist architecture and painting, of Mondrian and Mies van der Rohe. Squares are about facts and logic. Show me the theorem. Then he draws a circle some distance from the square. Circles are about metaphor and story. Circle reasoning is the other half. Tell me your story. Since the seventeenth century, and especially during the mid-twentieth century, the square and the circle have stood in nonoverlapping spheres, sneering at each other.

Klamer's diagrammatic parable, of course, has a feminist interpretation. Whether or not there is any truth to it, the myth of our culture says that men do the squares and women the circles. Regardless of what men and women actually do statistically speaking, the claims about what they do exist as cultural objects. It may or may not be correct that women in our culture have deeper friendships than men. But in any case the stereotype exists and can be used to criticize a foursquare economics that has no room for friendships, deep or otherwise. It may or may not be correct that women communicate

I thank the participants in the conference at the University of Iowa on Women's Bodies/Women's Voices: The Power of Difference, a seminar at Iowa's Project on Rhetoric of Inquiry, and the CSWEP session at the Southern Economic Association meetings in San Antonio for their comments. I have benefited from written comments by Barbara Bergmann, Kathleen Biddick, Eleanor Birch, Paula England, Susan Feiner, Tara Gray, Sarah Hanley, Katherine Hayles, Jane Humphries, Evelyn Fox Keller, Linda Kerber, Joanne McCloskey, Laura McCloskey, Marjorie McElroy, Julie Nelson, Elyce Rotella, Sibyl Schwarzbach, Diana Strassmann, and an anonymous referee for the University of Chicago Press. They do not agree with everything I say. Some of the themes in the paper are explored further in *If You're So Smart: The Narrative of Economic Expertise* (Chicago: University of Chicago Press, 1990) and in *Knowledge and Persuasion in Economics* (Cambridge: Cambridge University Press, 1993).

with stories of somebody's life, men with unnarrated facts such as astounding baseball trivia.[1] But in any case the stereotype can be used to criticize an economics that does not realize it depends on stories. The round, "feminine" arguments can be construed as "modes of argument suppressed by modern economics," which is square.

Klamer points out how crazy it is to insist that the only arguments that are really scientific are the square ones. Crazy, but common. His point can be put economically: argumentative styles, like countries, have different endowments and tastes; some trade between them would therefore be mutually advantageous.

That is, because men and women live somewhat differently they differ on average in their ways of approaching economics. The way certain women actually or might or should approach economics is good. Some of the limitations of economics can be traced to its square masculinity, understanding "masculinity" to be a cultural not a biological product. A feminine economics would in some ways be better. Above all, both modes of argument, round or square, should be available to economists, male or female, and both should be accorded scientific prestige.

That "feminine" qualities are not unique to women does not prevent an inquiry into a difference, as long as there is a notable difference on average. There is no need to take a stand on nature *versus* nurture to admit that for some reason men and women at present think rather differently, especially about society. The assertion is no more controversial than an assertion that Japanese and Americans at present think rather differently, especially about society. Yet women often think and act in ways that we stereotypically associate with men, and vice versa. Characteristics of women and men, Americans and Japanese, overlap, as in body weights and lengths of hair. We are mainly human beings, not women or Japanese. For most purposes a difference in gender or nationality is less important than what we have in common— human language, mathematics, history, social origin, passion, intelligence. For most scholarly purposes male and female economists have more in common with each other than with male and female classicists.

And yet the gender differences might be worth noting for describing the science. A "tetrad" in Greek is a set of four things. "Rhetoric" is the art of argument, good or bad, from Pythagoras to advertising. Sciences use four things to argue, the four of the "rhetorical tetrad": fact, logic, metaphor, and story. Half of the tetrad is the methodical dyad of fact and logic, that is, Klamer's square. The other half is the creative dyad of metaphor and story, Klamer's circle. But thinking requires both dyads, the whole tetrad: $2 + 2 = 4$ in a complete science. In truth, all four parts of the tetrad participate in me-

1. What major league pitcher retired every batter he faced for twelve innings yet lost the game? Answer: Harvey Haddix of the Pirates, May 26, 1959. He lost on an error, a walk, and a hit in the thirteenth inning. Wow!

thodicalness and in creativity. As it was put by the philosopher of science Mary Hesse, one of the early contributors to the new understanding of science, "rationality consists just in the continuous adaption of our language to our continually expanding world, and metaphor is one of the chief means by which this is accomplished" (1966, 176–77). Story, too. "We are storytelling animals," says Stephen Jay Gould, and shows the fact with the history of paleontology (1989, 70; 1980, ch. 3). All his works shows the storied character of evolution: "In the sterotyped image, scientists rely upon experiment and logic [—] a middle aged man in a white coat (most stereotypes are sexist). . . . But many sciences do not and cannot work this way. As a paleontologist and evolutionary biologist, my trade is the reconstruction of history" (1980, 27).

Pieces of the tetrad are not enough. The allegedly scientific and masculine half of the tetrad, the fact and logic, falls short of an adequate economic science, or even a science of stars or arthropods. The allegedly humanistic and feminine half falls short of an adequate art of economics, or even a criticism of form and color. Scientists, scholars, and artists had better be factual and logical. But they had also better be literary. The scientists had better devise good metaphors and tell good stories about the first three minutes of the universe or the last three months of the economy. A scientist with only half of the rhetorical tetrad is going to mess up her science.

It is easy to catch economists, as good scientists, in the act of using metaphors and stories for their science. Outsiders will find this easier to see than the economists will because the economists are trained to think of themselves as fact and logic users. They do not realize that they are also the poets and novelists of the ordinary business of life. To an outsider it is obvious that economists are using metaphors (analogies, similes, comparisons of one realm with another) when they speak of the demand "curve" for housing in New York City or the "human capital invested in a child, which is of course a durable good." It is obvious to the outsider that economists are using stories about a hog market once upon a time out of equilibrium or about the causes in the olden days of modern economic growth.

It is not an attack on economics to say that like other sciences it uses the whole of the tetrad. Let "God" be a metaphor of certitude beyond day-to-day persuasion (the God metaphor was lively and potent before the sea of faith receded, and nostalgia for its certitude remains). The truth is that not this "God" but we humans make the metaphors and tell the stories; not God but humans identify the facts and choose the logics (note the plurals). No part of the tetrad is wholly God-given and nonhuman, whether in physics or in economics. The models and histories in economics are not facts made by nature or logic immanent in the universe but words made by human art.

The art does not make them arbitrary; it merely makes them various. To admit that what we say in science is socially constructed is not to fall into

Valley-girl, touchy-feely relativism or to advocate anything goes. Niels Bohr, who was not a touchy-feely, said, "It is wrong to think that the task of physics is to find out how nature is. Physics concerns what we can say about nature. . . . We are suspended in language. . . . The word 'reality' is also a word, a word which we must learn to use correctly" (quoted in Moore 1966, 406).

In any event it is a crazy dualism to insist that *either* we merely read what God's Reality presents to us *or* we construct the world wholly without reference to the facts of the matter. The better model is fishing. The fish are there by God's command, and if they were not then no human ingenuity in making nets would bring them up. But likewise a sea full of fish does not feed humans without nets made by human hands. We need both to eat on Fridays.

A paleontologist, for example, is constrained by what in fact happened to life, and by what he thinks are relevant logics.[2] Nonetheless, with the same choice of fact and logic he can tell the story in varied ways—to use the words in paleontology, he can tell it as "gradualist" or "catastrophist." The movie can be run in dignified slow motion or in frantic lurches. The same sort of thing happens in economics. The workplace can be seen with a metaphor of conflict, as in Marxian economics, or with a metaphor of exit and entry to markets, as in neoclassical economics. How we judge the two depends on their fit with the facts, with the logic, with the story, and with the other metaphors we have found useful. The variety of metaphors and stories does not make all of them equally good or equally important for every purpose, any more than the variety of facts or logics makes all of them equally good or important for every purpose. No one is proposing, to repeat, that anything goes, merely that a life in science is more complicated than checking first-order predicate logic against uncontroversial facts. To criticize the varieties of facts, logics, metaphors, and stories you have to recognize that they are being constructed and postulated and imagined and told.

For about fifty years economists have believed themselves to be users only of fact and logic, the square rather than the circle, half of the rhetorical tetrad, the masculinist half. During the 1940s they shared belatedly in the temporary narrowing of Western culture called "positivism" or "modernism" (Booth 1974; Klamer 1990, 1987). Modernism has roots as deep as Descartes and Plato, but it became the whole of what we call thinking only in the early twentieth century. As Virginia Woolf said in 1924, "On or about December 1910, human character changed" (Woolf 1967 [1924], 320). Certain male philosophers in the West came suddenly to believe that their whole subject could be narrowed down to an artificial language; certain male architects narrowed

---

2. In the late twentieth century "logics," to repeat, are plural, like geometries. They are Aristotelian, first-order predicate, fuzzy, deontic, modal, relevant, multivalued, informal, epistemic, paraconsistent, and so on and so forth through the various ways that people can formalize what they are saying.

their whole subject to a cube; certain male painters narrowed their whole subject to a surface. Out of this narrowness was supposed to come insight and certitude.

Insight did come (not certitude, alas). After modernism in philosophy we know more about languages lacking human speakers. In architecture we know more about buildings lacking tops. In painting we know more about pictures lacking depth of field. When news of modernism got out to economics around 1940 it yielded some worthwhile insight, too. In economics after modernism, after the masculinist programs of Paul Samuelson and Tjalling Koopmans, we know more about economic models lacking contact with the world.

On the whole the narrowing did not work out very well. The failure of modernism in economics and elsewhere in the culture does not say it was a bad or stupid idea to try. And it certainly does not say that we should now abandon fact and logic, surface and cube, and surrender to the irrational. We are all very glad to keep whatever we have learned from the Bauhaus or the Vienna Circle or the running of rats. We in economics are all very thankful to Smith, Marx, and Marshall for inspiring those wonderfully theorems by Arrow, Robinson, and Samuelson. It says merely that we should turn back to the work at hand equipped now with the full tetrad of fact, logic, metaphor, and story.

The modernist experiment in getting along with fewer than all the resources of human reasoning puts one in mind of the Midwestern rural expression, "a few bricks short of a load." It means cracked, irrational. A masculinist economics, such as we have had in most refined form since the 1940s, is irrational. To admit now that metaphor and story also matter in human reasoning does not entail becoming less rational and less reasonable, dressing in saffron robes, or tuning into "New Directions." On the contrary it entails becoming more rational and more reasonable, because it puts more of what persuades serious people under the scrutiny of reason. Modernism was rigorous about a tiny part of reasoning and angrily (one might say hysterically) unreasonable about the rest. The typical article on international economics is arranged in the modernist form: scandalously vague motivation, rigorous middle, and vague, even reckless, "implications for policy."[3]

Modernism seized the word "science" for its purposes. In English the word for a long time has been a club with which to beat on arguments the modernists did not wish to hear. "Science" has been a verbal weapon within the intelligentsia. English speakers over the past century and a half have used it in a peculiar way, as in British academic usage, arts and sciences, the "arts" of literature and philosophy as against the "sciences" of chemistry and geology. A historical geologist in English is a scientist; a political historian is not. The

---

3. I have in mind some recent work by William Milberg (1991) and Hans Lind (1992), who have analyzed the rhetorical structure of typical articles in international economics.

usage in English would puzzle an Italian father boasting of his studious daughter, *mia scienziata,* my learned one. He does not mean that she is a nuclear physicist. Italian and other languages use the science word to mean simply "systematic inquiry," as do French, Spanish, German, Dutch, Icelandic, Norwegian, Swedish, Greek, Gaelic, Polish, Hindi, Bengali, Tamil, Hungarian, Turkish, Korean, and Hebrew. Only English, and only the English of the past century, has made physical and biological science (definition 5b in the old *Oxford English Dictionary* [Oxford, 1933]) into, as the *Supplement* (1982; compare *OED,* 2d ed., 1989) describes it, "the dominant sense in ordinary use." It would be a good idea to reclaim the word for reasonable and rigorous argument.

The English and modernist error, to put it another way, is thinking of science and literature as two cultures. The author of the phrase, the scientist-novelist C. P. Snow, can hardly be blamed, since he lived and wrote at the peak of an anxious masculinism in British and American science—evinced, for example, in the mistreatment of Rosalind Franklin in the uncovering of DNA. Literature since romanticism and most particularly since aestheticism was written off as airy-fairy. The very work of middle-class men was paper shuffling and feminine. Only tough science and Hemingwayesque literature could assuage their dread. As Barbara Laslett has argued persuasively in writing of William Fielding Ogburn (1886–1959), one of the founders of the Chicago school of sociology and in his uncertain youth an advocate of quantitative methods, "Science so defined simultaneously offered a cultural space to which men could aspire without threat to their masculinity and provided a gatekeeping mechanism that limited women's entry" (1990, 429).

The two-cultures talk is not written in the stars, though it is common enough and encouraged by the faculty and the deans. The dualism drips with sexist mythology, and the women co-opted by such dualism are not immune. A dean of research at a large state university gave a talk a couple of years ago in which she spoke of the humanities as what is left over after the (physical and biological) sciences, and then after them the social sciences, have expended their eloquence. The humanities in her mind are a residuum for the mystical and the ineffable, the stuff of circles, not squares. The dean, who was a social scientist, thought she was being good natured. The bad-natured remarks muttered from each side are worse: that if we mention metaphors we are committed to an arty irrationalism; that if we mention logic we are committed to a scientific autism.

One is tempted to shake them both and say, "Get serious." The sciences, such as economics, require supposedly humanistic and "feminine" methods in the middle of their sciences; likewise, the arts and humanities require fact and logic, right in the middle of their own systematic inquiries. It is not so much that metaphor is an alternative to fact (true though this sometimes is) as that the construction of facts requires metaphors—for example, the metaphor of light as quanta, as against waves, is essential for certain measurements in physics. Without the metaphor no one would have thought to do the measurements. So, too, in economics: without the metaphor of the nation as a business enterprise the measurement of the "national accounts" would not happen; without the story line of "development" the historical measurement of income would not happen. The items in the rhetorical tetrad work together, each necessary for the job of the other. Leonardo da Vinci used stories and logic; Newton used logic and metaphors; Darwin used facts and stories. Science is literary, requiring metaphors and stories in its daily work.

Speaking of a science such as economics in literary terms, of course, inverts a recent and anxiety-producing hierarchy. Science is masculine and high status; art is feminine and low status; therefore, for God's sake, let's demarcate science from art. But contrary to the century-long program to demarcate science from the rest of the culture—a strange program when you think of it—science is after all a matter of arguing. The ancient categories of argument still apply. Satisfying stories are recognized in a complete psychology (Gergen and Gergen 1986; Bruner 1986); beautiful metaphors in a complete physics (Weinberg 1983); so, too, in economics after modernism (Klamer, McCloskey, and Solow, eds. 1988).

The dualisms square/circle, fact/story, logic/metaphor, science/art, numbers/words, cognition/feeling, rigor/intuition, truth/opinion, fact/value, hard/soft, positive/normative, objective/subjective may be useful as tentative descriptions. Certainly they come up a lot in methodological disputes, usually as conversation stoppers. But they are crazy when they are imagined, as the modern byword has it, to cut the universe at its joints. Such dualisms, it need hardly be emphasized, reenact the Mother of All Dualisms, male/female, as Julie Nelson, Ann Jennings, and others point out in their essays in this volume. Men insist on square, fact, logic, science, numbers, cognition, rigor, truth, hardness, positiveness, and the objective with a comical, anxious rigidity of the sort the comedian John Cleese makes fun of. The anxiety resembles nothing more than a man worrying that he might be taken for a woman.

The distinction objective/subjective, for example, does not withstand much scrutiny. The modern usage (a reversal, incidentally, of the medieval usage) was popularized by Kant in the late eighteenth century and came into English with Coleridge in the early nineteenth century. For scientific purposes it is useless. We cannot know what is objective, if it means the Reality that is in the mind of God. In the twentieth century we humans are alone with the universe and have to make of it what we can with our human ways of seeing and talking. Two-and-a-half millennia of attempts since the Greeks to vault to a higher realm in which we will *know* the objective, will have *solved* the problem of epistemology, will *hear* what God is whispering to us, have failed.

Similarly, we cannot know what is subjective, if it means the wholly personal place from which each of us looks out. We cannot, after Freud, know it even in our own minds, and certainly never completely in someone else's.

What we can and do know, to coin a term, is the *conjective*. It is neither the square nor the circle, neither the objective nor the subjective. It is what we know together, by virtue of a common life and language. It is what economists know about the definition of the money supply or the prevalence of marginal cost pricing. It is what men and women know in their conversations, together or apart. As the mathematician Armand Borel noted, for practical purposes "something becomes objective . . . as soon as we are convinced that it exists in the minds of others in the same form that it does in ours, and that we can think about it and discuss it together" (1983, 13). Helen Longino, quoted in the introduction to this volume, gives the same social spin to "objectivity": it is "dependent upon the depth and scope of the transformative interrogation that occurs in any given scientific community." For practical purposes, in other words, we have only the "conjective."

The conjective is the milieu in which Klamer's square and circle sit. Imagine an amoebalike shape encompassing both the masculine square and the feminine circle, a fluid of words and symbols in which the two must float. That is where science actually goes on, never in the square or the circle alone but in the conversations that surround them. The conversations are subject to rigorous appraisal, more rigorous than the phony rigor of wholly square proofs or wholly round faiths. We do it daily in a science like economics, assessing a new paper on the basis of its fit in detail with our earlier conversations.

All right, so what? What is to be gained by such talk? This: a conjective economics, which admitted the "feminine" alongside the "masculine," would be better science because it would be more complete and persuasive. It would constitute a higher standard for a science, one of coherence in story as much as in axioms; of relevance in Bureau of Labor Statistics questionnaires administered as much as in its regressions.

The prefeminist economics I can speak of most convincingly is the neoclassical, a hard case in all senses. Compared with other schools of economics the neoclassicals are notably butch. They are a motorcycle gang among economists, strutting about the camp with clattering matrices and rigorously fixed points, sheathed in leather, repelling affection. They are not going to like being told that they should become more feminine.

Looking at the economy from a conjective point of view, putting the allegedly feminine and the allegedly masculine into conversation with each other, will, I say, enrich neoclassical economics. The project is enrichment, not impoverishment. I would *not* argue that economics is worthless in its square and masculine moods. But even the "conservative" and Chicago-school economics that I espouse, which seems to me admirably masculine, is open to feminine revision.

The purpose, in other words, is to encompass and extend what has been learned from men, not to dynamite it unthinkingly. As was noted recently by J. A. Boone, a feminist critic of literature, "the solution isn't simply to discard all 'offending' texts. . . . If we are to hang on to our Norman Mailers as well as our Margaret Atwoods, we need a more sophisticated means of evaluation than simply judging a book's contents in terms of its 'political correctness' " (1988, 2). He's right. We want to hang onto our Gary Beckers as well as our Joan Robinsons.

At a modest level one can beat masculine economics at its own game (pardon me) by a more conjective choice of postulates. Consider the economics of the family, explored by Becker and his associates (Becker 1981). In common with other Chicago economists working on law, history, politics, and economic development, Becker saw that economic reasoning could be applied to events beyond the usual, to families as much as to firms. Lucidity has come from this, and a welcome turn of economics to wide subjects.

For all its brilliance as a pioneering effort, though, Becker's program is constrained by its masculinity. For instance the family in Becker's world has one purpose, one utility function—guess whose?—unproblematically unified in the way that the neoclassical firm is supposed to be (see Folbre and Hartmann 1988, 188ff; and elsewhere in the present volume). Ironic commentary on the postulate of mastership within the family comes from a surprising direction. The late George Stigler, Becker's greatest fan and the very model of a modern Chicago economist, wrote: "It would of course be bizarre to look upon the typical family—that complex mixture of love, convenience, and frustration—as a business enterprise." Quite right. But then, with Stiglerian irony, he says truly that "therefore economists have devoted much skill and ingenuity to elaborating this approach" (1966, 21).

One neoclassical way to get beyond a masculine mastership has been illustrated by Marjorie B. McElroy and Mary Jean Horney in "Nash-Bargained Household Decisions: Towards a Generalization of the Theory of Demand" (1981). They view the household as a bargaining game among two players over the allocation of public and private goods. Consider it as double solitaire. To anyone in a family the setup has a familiar sound. The results of the McElroy-Horney model are detailed and plausible, yielding clean implications for labor force participation by women and by teenage children. It brings market solutions into the family (see, however, Brian Cooper's thorough and feminist commentary on such arguments [1990]).

A Darwinian route to the same result has been suggested by Howard Margolis in *Selfishness, Altruism, and Rationality: A Theory of Social Choice* (1982). He argues that for good evolutionary reasons a person is public spirited as well as narrowly selfish, having virtually two selves trading with each other. Margolis would probably agree that the argument applies literally to families: for some purposes (child-minding) the wife tends to be public spirited and the husband selfish; for others (protection) the man tends to be the public spirited one and the woman selfish.

Susan Feiner (1984), to give another example, takes a nonmarket view of the matter, making use of an analogy of families with serfdom. The analogy is again useful, though it would be more so if the Marxist economists would read more history. In the way that the serfdom of women threatens to break down under advanced capitalism, so, too, the serfdom of men in Western Europe broke down when it was pushed into contact with markets. (The push happened not in the sixteenth century, as a much-beloved piece of Marxist folklore says, but in the thirteenth.)

Another element in a conjective economics is taking difference seriously. From an Austrian perspective, for example, Karen Vaughn has questioned the neoclassical disdain for the committee, that ubiquitous and irritating institution, which so obviously does not achieve the efficient solution:

> The Austrian emphasis on the particularized and personalized qualities of knowledge are especially helpful to anyone who has ever worked closely with a group of people to get a job done, whether it be volunteer work in the neighborhood or church, organizing a project at work or running a family. People are all different, and women, I believe, are more tuned-in to that fact than most men. . . . Economists are predisposed to hate this kind of compromise since it probably isn't "the efficient solution." But the Austrian insight reminds us that for most problems where the welfare of many are concerned, there is no efficient solution. The committee is one way both to gather decentralized information and to get the affected parties to buy into the decision finally arrived at. (1988, 14–15)

I admit to harboring dark thoughts about committees myself, and have said frequently that the optimal size of an academic committee is one: all power to the deans. Dictatorship has been the man's model of society since Plato, or for that matter since the caves. Put a good man in charge. After all, says he, a football team has a quarterback who calls the plays and takes the blame. But the point made by Vaughn, presumably not the left guard of her high school football team, has merit as description and as democracy, in contrast to the military and sporting contexts in which men grow up.

Still further along the way to a conjective economics, and economics of what we know together, is taking solidarity seriously. After all, Adam Smith did: the book we economists all know is his book about greed; but his other great book, *The Theory of Moral Sentiments* (1759, 1790), is about love. I repeat that nothing biological is assumed in solidarity. In their essay on the sexist rhetoric of neoclassical and Marxist economics Nancy Folbre and Heidi

Hartmann quote with approval J. S. Mill's advanced views of 1869: "If women are better than men in anything it surely is in individual self-sacrifice for those of their own family. But I lay little stress on this, so long as they are universally taught that they are born and created for self-sacrifice" (1988, 194). Precisely. And I repeat that nothing especially virtuous about the stereotypical woman is being assumed either. Solidarity sounds like a swell idea until one reflects that Tojo, Hitler, and Mussolini raised empires by calling on it.

Anyway, neoclassical economics does not take solidarity seriously, except implicitly within the family and within the firm, and neither do any of the other schools. No wonder. *Vir economicus* sporting around the marketplace is stereotypically male: rule driven, simplemindedly selfish, uninterested in building relations for their own sake.[4] A cross between Rambo and an investment banker, our *vir economicus* has certain boyish charms, but a feminine solidarity is not one of them. When it suits his convenience he routinely defects from social arrangements, dumping externalities on the neighbors. *Femina economica,* by contrast, would more often walk down the beach to dispose of her McDonald's carton in a trash bin—not because she reasons in the manner of Kant (and again of men) that one must test one's behavior by hypothetical universalization ("Suppose *everyone* dumped their trash on their neighbors?") but because she feels solidarity with others. It is simply not done to dump trash on the beach; we do not treat our neighbors that way.

James Buchanan (another unexpected direction, this) has noted a consequence of taking *femina economica* and her solidarity seriously. If people

> do, in fact, behave in accordance with some version of the Kantian imperative [note that there is a conjective route to this], potential externalities, in the normal usage of this term, will tend to be internalized within the calculus of the actors. Individuals will tend to take into account the effects of their own actions on the situation of others than themselves. Hence [here is the remarkable turn], in such a world there can be no need for corrective collective or governmental intervention in the private decision process. It becomes impossible to observe "market failure" in the standard sense. (1979, 70ff)

A feminine economy would have less need of a paternalistic government. If everyone behaved like people do in Iowa, then socialism would have less to recommend it.

A related technical example in economics concerns the value of a human

4. By the way, Latin like many languages, but unlike modern English, had two words for man: *vir,* which means a "male adult" or "husband," like *Mann* in German or *anēr* in Greek, as distinct from *femina* or *mulier;* and *homo,* which means (and is cognate with the word) "human," like *Mensch* in German or *anthropos* in Greek. In patriarchal societies, of course, the distinction was a fine one. But *homo economicus* literally means "economic human," not "economic man."

life. The usual strategy is to infer the value from how individuals act when they buy insurance or choose risky but well-paying jobs. If a coal miner gets five dollars an hour more than a waiter/waitress of similar skill, and if enough people can move between the mine and the restaurant (a big if), then evidently the person just barely willing to switch to mining puts a value of five dollars on the dangers of the mine relative to work in the restaurant. The statistics of injury and death measure the danger she is actually facing. Therefore the implicit value she puts on her life, assuming she values it methodically and that there are no other amenities or disamenities of the two jobs, can be calculated. The same reasoning applies to more straightforward gambles with one's life, especially the gamble of life insurance. Alan Dillingham (1985) has summarized the estimates, arriving at a figure in the United States nowadays of one million dollars plus or minus half a million.

It has sometimes been noted, however, that individual self-valuation is only part of the value of a life (Usher 1985, 183). In a society with solidarity a life is technically speaking a public good, to be valued by summed values that the citizenry places on it. The whole value is the sum of all valuations of the life, by its owner and by others. Yet most economists have not noticed how it matters that the life is valued by him or her or thee. No human is an island; any human's death diminishes me because I am involved in humankind.

Remarkably, the only value of other lives recognized in the present literature is not the great misery of seeing others die but the cash *advantage* that accrues to the survivor through inheritance and the like. As an empirical matter these merely pecuniary advantages are probably dwarfed by the misery. Janet Guthrie may value her own life at $1,000,000, and enter formula-one auto racing with that figure in mind. But Jack Guthrie values her life, too, at $1,500,000, say, and Janet's mother values it at $2,000,000, her father at another $2,000,000, her best friend at another $1,000,000, and so on, down to the single dollar from that anonymous other part of humankind who never sends to know for whom the bell tolls.

The upshot is that the value of life calculated on the assumption of *vir economicus* is probably a small fraction of the correct, conjective measure, the result of our knowing value together, not as isolates. Janet is worth millions, not the one million at which she values herself. The consequences are grave. A value of human life, like it or not, must be used in designing roads and, when the courts allow more than earning power, in deciding personal injury cases. That's just economics. But a conjective economics would use a much higher figure than a masculine economics would, interfering more with the devil-may-care attitude of males, especially young ones, zooming about helmetless on their Kawasakis. Consequently, though a feminine economy would need spontaneously less interference, the interference that did take place would be more thorough—one might say, more motherly.

A conjective economics has other consequences, large and small. Hannah

Arendt once remarked that only a man would ignore a hurt to our grandchildren, which is to say that men might at present discount the future too much in pursuing present glory. Again, the omission of housework from the national income does not survive conjective scrutiny (see Folbre 1991; although even among male economists the omission has long seemed strange).[5] A conjective theory of labor relations, which would draw attention to the social meaning of employment and wages, might push farther down a road that men have tentatively explored, with their tortured and masculine notion of the "implicit contract" between worker and employer. A conjective view of immigration might find it harder to take the nationalist, I'm-all-right-Jack position that motivates present policy (Roback 1981). Economists better equipped than I am to see the economy with feminine eyes will think of twenty other ways in which an economics amended by women would differ from the male-centered version we now have.

Looking at the economy with feminine eyes, however, is made more difficult than it has to be by certain masculine rules of engagement. A conjective economics, valuing stereotypically feminine perspectives as much as stereotypically masculine perspectives, will be hobbled, corseted, awkwardly hoop-skirted at the start if it accedes without protest to the man-made rules of the game. The masculine rules need to be resisted.

For example, questionnaires are disdained on methodological grounds in a masculine economics. Robin Bartlett (1985) suggests quite plausibly that a conjective economics, using what we know together, would make more use of questionnaires than economics nowadays does; in her presidential address to the Eastern Economic Association Barbara Bergmann (1975) had made the same point. The small percentage of papers in the *American Economic Review* that depend on questionnaires would startle other social scientists.

The reason economists give is, "If you just *ask* someone what they are doing they will tell you lies." Male economists use the argument reflexively whenever someone proposes to ask businesspeople why they are hiring or to ask consumers why they are buying. But hostility to questionnaires among men, and their eagerness to reduce questionnaires to numbers before considering the very words, appears to reflect a masculine idea of the ends and means of conversation. To the masculine argument against questionnaires a woman might reply that the response of course needs to be probed, considered, interpreted; but that doesn't make it unscientific, or even, come to think

5. I once asked the great economist Margaret Reid, the actual implementer of household economics (invented by her Ph.D. supervisor Hazek Kirk), a friend and colleague of mine at Chicago, whether she thought the housewife's work should be included in national income. I was disappointed by her answer, which was the conventional one that it is difficult to estimate (which of course is also true of the value of owner-occupied houses, governmental services, and most capital goods, each included in national income).

of it, different from other evidence. The "nonquestionnaire" evidence, after all, comes from responses about one's state of employment spoken to the interviewer from the Department of Labor.

The responses are more than mute facts. As Karen Vaughn has pointed out, in the masculine and neoclassical view of the world the only information comes from bumping up against constraints. Nobody *tells* anyone anything. You can see the neoclassical assumption in the way the new experimental economists talk about their work: they could if they wished examine the rhetoric of markets but usually they prefer to keep their "market" participants in isolation booths. About a fellow economist who claimed that he never "preached" at his children, but merely presented them with the "correct incentive structure" (if you foul up, you get punished, and presumably learn), Vaughn remarks, "My reaction was, first of all, I didn't believe him. . . . Children do not only learn by doing, they also learn by exhortation, conversation, story-telling and example. The advantage of verbal learning over learning by doing is that it saves the child's time" (1988, 16–17). Vaughn is speaking as a mother; I agree as a father, though as a father I can see what her colleague had in mind. I do not know if learning by fouling up is an especially male way of behaving, but there can be little doubt that it is an especially male way of seeing behavior. Show me the budget constraint and then shut up. Where in economics have you heard that before?[6]

The reduction of empirical work in economics to statistical fitting of formal models is another saver of masculine labor. The male economist confronted with facts will immediately subordinate them to a model, then to a statistical mechanism, which, he will claim stoutly in the face of most scientific experience, "tests" the model (my own work in economic history has this character). Evelyn Fox Keller recalls the metaphor used by the men of the early seventeenth century, so skilled in torture: Nature is to be put on the rack and tortured until she confesses her formulas. (In the end Dame Nature almost always confesses to formulas surprisingly consistent with the male investigator's model, and so in the end did the witch confess to the male suggestion that she rode through the air on a broom.)

Consider by way of contrast the great biologist, Barbara McClintock, who approached Nature with the idea that, as Keller puts it in writing of Mc-Clintock,

> organisms have a life and an order of their own that scientists can only begin to fathom. . . . [McClintock said] "there's no such thing as a central dogma into which everything will fit." . . . The

6. Arjo Klamer and I have estimated that persuasion—managers persuading employees, entrepreneurs persuading bankers, retailers persuading customers, professors persuading students—amounts to about a quarter of national income (Klamer and McCloskey 1991). So the "feminine" matter of persuasion is not optional.

> need to "listen to the material" follows from her sense of the or-
> der of things. . . . The complexity of nature exceeds our own
> imaginative possibilities. . . . Her major criticism of contempo-
> rary research is based on what she sees as inadequate humil-
> ity. . . . [The dualisms of] subject-object, mind-matter, feeling-
> reason, disorder-law . . . are directed towards a cosmic unity
> typically excluding or devouring one of the pair. (1985, 162–63)

The style of empirical inquiry that spends six years on the aberrant pigmenta-
tion of a few kernels of corn is rare in economics, but no one is surprised to
find it disproportionately among female economists: Margaret Reid of Iowa
State and Chicago, for example, in her studies of the consumer spending and
death rates, or Mary Jean Bowman of Chicago in her studies of education, or
Dorothy Brady of Pennsylvania and of the Women's Bureau at the Department
of Labor in her studies of consumer spending in the distant past, or Anna
Jacobson Schwartz of the National Bureau of Economic Research and New
York University in her studies of money. "The thing was dear to you for a
period of time, you really had an affection for it," said McClintock (Keller
1985, 164). What is dear to male economists is not the thing itself but their
model of the thing. Disproportionately they scorn the rich and multiple stories
of the thing itself, the sandy cat in Woolf's perception filching a piece of fish.
The men want to impose their favorite metaphors on the world, not to remain
"content with multiplicity as an end in itself" (Keller 1985, 163). "I start with
the seedling," said McClintock, "and I don't want to leave it. I don't feel I
really know the story [note the word] if I don't watch the plant all the way
along" (Keller 1983, 198).

The point is that economics is at present dominated by a masculinist methodology, defended since Plato by a philosophical doctrine overstating its practical importance. To repeat, even male economists depend on analogy, storytelling, *verstehen*, appeals to authority, mucking about with the raw data, the
other half of the rhetorical tetrad; and they depend on them even in their most
logical and factual moods. The alternative is not to throw away proof and
curve fitting, which deserve a place of honor. The alternative is to make them
fruitful by recognizing that we economists already use massively another, parallel, more conjective and more feminine rhetoric.

The use of storytelling is a case in point. The literary critic Peter Brooks
says rightly that "our lives are ceaselessly intertwined with narrative, with the
stories that we dream or imagine or would like to tell, all of which are re-
worked in that story of our own lives that we narrate to ourselves. . . . We are
immersed in narrative" (1985, 1). Yet male economists sneer at the anecdote,
though it gives them most of their factual beliefs, and do not recognize that
they use storytelling conventions in their science daily (McCloskey 1990). An
eclectic Keynesian will tell the story that "oil prices caused inflation." To this
a monetarist will reply that "it is not an equilibrium," namely, that the curtain

has been lowered prematurely near the beginning of the second act: if aggregate demand is not changed by the oil prices, why would not other nominal prices fall? The Keynesian will reply in turn with his own drama criticism: "Well, you damned monetarists start the drama in the middle; where does all that money come from, before your play begins?"

In her recent book on biography, *Writing a Woman's Life,* Carolyn Heilbrun notes that "lives do not serve as models; only stories do that" (1988, 37). Her point is that "there will be narratives of female lives only when women no longer live their lives isolated in the houses and the stories of men" (47). An economics with its stories made explicit would be unable to carry on with merely masculine tales.

School librarians attest that girls disproportionately read stories, boys nonfiction. When the big boys reach economics they prefer metaphors of maximization to stories of entry and exit. Notice that there is no epistemological ranking between the two, a metaphor being just as humanistic, if that's how you want to put it, as a story. If a seventeenth-century Darwin had published *The Origin of Species* in 1687 and some Newton had waited until 1859 to publish *Philosophae naturalis principia mathematica* we would now perhaps think of stories as hard science and metaphors as soft. A conjective rhetoric of economics would exploit the Darwinian niche provided by the neglect of explicit storytelling in economics. Joan Robinson, who admittedly is a hard case, converted around 1940 from modeling maximization, at which she excelled, to the telling of evolutionary and Marxist stories, at which she also excelled. The exemplar of a "feminine" economics would be biology, not physics, and McClintock's biology at that, not a biochemistry revolutionized by guilty but still model-building physicists after the Second World War (as Keller has argued elsewhere).

Discussions of economic methodology involve few women participants. Men more than women tend to be fascinated by the rules of the game (Klant 1985). Women economists often appear to find the discussion vacuous, though most seem to have been persuaded to obey its conclusions. The literary critics Annis V. Pratt and Mary Daly attack "methodolatry" (Pratt's word): "the insistence on a single method is not only dysfunctional but an attribute of the patriarchy" (quoted in Ruthven 1984, 25). "Methodocide" (Daly's word) is a good option. But if we insist on continuing the conventional conversation of methodology, at least the conversation should be opened.

In an illuminating study, "Sex Differences in Games Children Play," Janet Lever noted that "boys were seen quarreling all the time, but not once was a game terminated because of a quarrel. . . . The P.E. teacher in one school noted that the boys seemed to enjoy the legal debates every bit as much as the game itself. Even players who were marginal because of lesser skills or size took equal part in these recurring squabbles" (1976, 482). The boys' game went on, and on, and on, through recess, through every quarrel. By contrast, "most girls interviewed claimed that when a quarrel begins [among them], the game breaks up. . . . And some complained that their [girl] friends could not resolve the basic issues of choosing up sides, deciding who is to be captain, which team will start, and sometimes not even what game to play" (483).

Methodological disputes in economics and elsewhere run parallel to disputes about kickball and Monopoly. The Swiss psychologist Jean Piaget noted in 1932 a contrast between the "polymorphism and tolerance" of girls' games and "the splendid codification and complicated jurisprudence of the [boys'] game of marbles" (76, 70). Men and boys decide rules of the game and decide to discuss the rules endlessly because they think rules are important, the only important thing. As Carol Gilligan (1982) noted in her discussion of this literature of games, girls and women could not care less. My daughter's girl friends gather in social clusters on the soccer field while the boys quarrel passionately about the rules or bury themselves in lonely fantasies of sporting greatness. Girls and women in our culture, it seems, stress community, conversation, solidarity, and other nonrule values, of the sort that Richard Rorty has embraced as the values of the "new fuzzies" (1987, 41; see Laura McCloskey 1987 on the conversation of girls and boys). When the game no longer serves these values they abandon it. They therefore are defined as incompetent in a game not of their choosing.

The point is to imagine a conversation among economists ruled in this cooperative, antiauthoritarian, anarchopacifist, conjective way, what we know together. Susan Feiner, Barbara Morgan, and Bruce Roberts, in a paper taking a Marxist look at race and gender in introductory economics texts (1988), quote Richard Rorty on the matter a good deal. Certainly Richard Rorty has it right. But I recommend, too, Amelie Oksenberg Rorty. In writing on Descartes' strange and masculine rhetoric of science she argued that what is crucial in distinguishing genuine intellectual life from system-building lunacy is "our ability to engage in continuous conversation, testing one another, discovering our hidden presuppositions, changing our minds because we have listened to the voices of our fellows. Lunatics also change their minds, but their minds change with the tides of the moon and not because they have listened, really listened, to their friends' questions and objections" (1983, 562). A conversation in which economists listened, really listened, to their friends' questions and objections would not sound much like a conversation of men.

Masculine rhetoric in economics has long possessed certain conversation stoppers, notably mathematical proof. The alleged superiority of mathematical proof favors men, who more commonly believe it and believe it deeply. It is notable, by the way, that physicists do not believe it. Contrary to what mathematical economists tell their students, physicists are irritated and embarrassed by the mathematical attitudes of the mathematics department. Math-department mathematics is qualitative, not quantitative. It does not depend on actual measurements, merely existence (see McCloskey 1993, ch. 9).

By contrast, in economics one encounters repeatedly the rhetorical turn of a "disproof" of marginal productivity theory (e.g., Feiner, Morgan, and Roberts 1988, 15–19) or a "proof" of the existence and stability of competitive equilibrium (e.g., Hahn 1986). One finds, that is, a man with chalk dust on his jacket trying to persuade you that *set theory shows* that people do not earn their worth under capitalism or that *game theory shows* that capitalism is after all a workable social arrangement.

The notion that one can prove or disprove a great social truth by standing at a blackboard is a peculiarly masculine delusion. The women can do the math, of course. But they are less inclined to accept it as all there is. It is something of which women students of economics are disproportionately skeptical, I think, though usually silent in their skepticism. Men, especially young men, are typically able to believe any crazy abstraction about society, and stand ready to impose it by force of arms because they do not know what a "society" is. Many more women know, even when young, and are appalled by the shallow summaries of society displayed in the words and graphs and mathematics of economics. Perhaps this contributes to their lack of enthusiasm for economics as presently taught.

I am not suggesting that there is some error in the proofs that competitive equilibrium can be derived from axioms of choice or, to name another male obsession since Hobbes, that there is some error in the proofs that civil society can be derived from axioms of selfishness. They are "right" when they are right. But they are right in such a narrow sense, so removed from the concerns of a community that already has approximate equilibrium and already has a semblance of civility, that someone not half in love with easeful narrowness would wonder what the fuss is all about.

The mathematical economist Frank Hahn, for instance, a man's man in this line of work, wrote that Arrow and Debreu "*demonstrated* . . . the logical possibility of the truth of [Adam] Smith's claims." Many male economists, like Hahn, take this Arrow-Debreu theorem to be the essence of modern economics: "these were remarkable achievements not only for what had been *demonstrated* but for the *conclusive manner* in which it was done. . . . The theory . . . is *all we have of honest and powerful thinking* on the subject [of how economies might behave]" (Hahn 1986, 833; my emphasis). What in fact was done was to show in a couple of pages that certain mathematical objects called "economies" can be looked at mathematically in two ways at least. Using a style of proof fashionable circa 1910, a certain mathematical expression was shown to be equivalent to another.

Worthwhile as the equivalence is—the point here is not to abandon mathematics, considering as I have noted that identical points can be made about wholly nonmathematical work in the tradition of Hobbes—it is limited as science. No historical evidence was adduced; no common experience was reinterpreted; no new way of viewing society was revealed; no deep insight into human behavior was put forward. Without the substance of economics the proof is just not very useful. Only a man, and a man in love with black-boards, would be likely to be caught saying that such writing was "all we [economists] have of honest and powerful thinking."

Looking at the formalisms of economics in a conjective way can help. For instance, the vocabulary of the neoclassical "production function," as a self-consciously conjective style of reasoning would recognize, is intrinsically analogical: we imagine that production is a function of capital and labor. I am arguing that self-consciousness about analogizing and storytelling are femi-nine in our culture; literalism, a belief in the Reality of this or that analogy or story, is masculine. As Roslyn Willett notes:

> For reasons that are not entirely clear, men seem to fantasize more than women. . . . Men tend to impose abstract structures on reality, and then to perceive reality in terms of their abstrac-tions. . . . Economic theory [for example] is elaborated but quite often fails to be predictive, although that is its ostensible pur-pose. . . . The whole male-dominated world shows symptoms of a progressive removal from the real world with its stubborn ad-hoc-ness and variability. (1972, 526, 528; compare McClintock's words above)

"Aggregate capital" involves an analogy of "capital" (itself analogical) with something—sand, bricks, shmoos—that can be "added" in a meaningful way; so does "aggregate labor," with the additional peculiarity that the thing added is not a thing but hours of conscientious attentiveness. The very idea of a "production function" involves the astonishing analogy of the subject, the fabrication of things, about which it is appropriate to think in terms of inge-nuity, discipline, and planning, with the modifier, a mathematical function, about which it is appropriate to think in terms of height, shape, and single valuedness. The metaphorical content of these ideas was alive to their inven-tors in the nineteenth century. It is largely dead to twentieth-century male economists. The men do not notice that they are perceiving reality in terms of their metaphorical fantasies.

During the 1960s the dead metaphor of the production function got out of its coffin Bela Lugosi style for the debate of the two Cambridges. The Marxist economists of Cambridge, England, who did not believe in production func-tions, battled with the neoclassical economists of Cambridge, Massachusetts, who did. (The British group was led of course by that same Joan Robinson.) All sides agree that after a few quarters of play Cambridge, England was ahead on points, although penalized frequently for eye-gouging and groin-kicking. But suddenly, on account of injuries and the lack of a crowd, to the dismay of the Cambridge, England group, the game was abandoned.

The game itself was testimony to the importance of metaphorical questions in economics. Its very violence suggests that boys' rules were in force, and that something beyond simple fact or elementary logic was at stake. The combatants hurled logic at each other. The important and unanswered questions, however, were those one would ask of a metaphor, which could be asked only with a conjective self-consciousness about such matters—is the metaphor of a production function illuminating, is it satisfying, is it apt? How do you know? How does it compare with other economic poetry? After some tactical retreats by Cambridge, Massachusetts on matters of ultimate metaphysics irrelevant to these important questions, mutual boredom and exhaustion set in, without decision.

The reason there was no decision was that the important questions were literary, not logical. No one noticed this, and the game therefore breaks out in back alleys from time to time under the old rules. The Cambridge Marxists are properly irritated about the lack of outcome, because after all they won the game fair and square on a logical field laid out by their opponents. Yet they lost the larger argument. The continued vitality of the idea of an aggregate production function in the face of logical proofs of its impossibility can only be explained this way: that logical proof, the masculine weapon, is not a perfect winner of arguments.

Nor should it be, on the frequent occasions when the main issue is not a matter of properly translating one expression deductively into another. The "proofs" of the possibility or impossibility of an aggregate production function are equivalent to telling Shakespeare that he must abandon a metaphor because, you know, it is logically "impossible." "You are being illogical, my dear William, to compare your beloved to a summer's day: a human being is surely flesh and blood—a fact indeed that I have proven experimentally. It is not rough winds and darling buds. Break off this madness, dearest Will, and return to the sure path of literal experiment and conclusive proof." Francis Bacon and Descartes, eloquent against rhetoric, could almost have argued so.

The question between neoclassicals and Marxists in the Cambridge Controversy, in short, was a question of metaphor. Can you write down a blueprint for a factory (one of Samuelson's self-conscious metaphors for a production function) and expect to get it built? No, not if the carpenters and electricians and secretaries on the job do not possess "kinds of skills [that] could not even in principle be written down" (Vaughn 1988, 10). The visualization of the metaphor in action is a more persuasive criticism of it than the logic. Nothing was settled forever and ever by hauling in the logic and declaring the matter resolved.

In discussing another "one of the most perfect examples in the history of economic thought of a total failure of a conversation to take place," the Hayek/ Lange debate about the feasibility of socialism, Vaughn notes that Oskar Lange "thought the whole debate concerned and could be settled by mathematical reasoning" (1988, 8). He was that kind of guy. The figure of speech "you-are-inconsistent-and-that's-all-I-need-to-show" dominates the rhetoric of masculine argument, as many wives have had occasion to note. Consistency is not the hobgoblin only of little minds; it is more particularly the hobgoblin of little masculine minds. The demonstration that this or that neoclassical idea is incoherent mathematically by a narrow definition of "coherence" settles something worth settling. But it is after all not much. It is sometimes interesting and occasionally important. Hardly ever is it decisive.

Likewise the usual demonstrations that Marxist economics leaves something to be desired "empirically," by which the man using the word will mean "according to some 3×5-card definition of consulting The Facts," is not decisive. Nor should it be. There are many reasons for adopting one or the other view, and all are subject to conversation. The actual conversation of science and scholarship leads to conclusions more definite than those achieved by the narrow and official and nonconjective methods—this contrary to the main virtue alleged for the official methods, that they are supposed to yield conclusions. Name the conclusion produced by highbrow mathematical or econometric means since the Second World War. Go ahead: no fair merely citing the literature; tell me the substantive gain to economic thinking that has come by the highbrow route. The test is embarrassing to the overblown promise of formalism in economics. The plan to reduce all science to authoritarian pronouncements of true theorems and nonfalsified predictions reflects a masculine notion of life's simplicity. It overvalues "that mass of small intellectual tricks, that complex of petty knowledge, that collection of cerebral rubber stamps, which constitute the chief mental equipment of the average male" (Mencken 1963 [1922], 8). It is a 3×5-card philosophy of inquiry.

The usual criticisms in economics of other people's research programs are notably simpleminded, and notably masculine. Men tend to think it satisfactory to find one loose end and pull hard. The young Karl Popper advocated just such a procedure, a thought-saver beloved ever since by young men. It makes scholarship into a game of marbles, scoring points under the rules of falsification and quitting promptly when time is called. It rejects the notion of an agreement arrived at through long and serious discussion. If you can falsify Marxist economics by "proving" that "Marx's predictions were wrong" or falsify Chicago economics by "proving" that "a full set of contingent markets are necessary for efficiency," then you can quit early and go have a beer. There is no need—a conjective need, creative of scholarly community—to synthesize, to compromise, to hear the other person's opinion, to spend time listening, really listening, to one's colleagues' questions and objections.

A conjective economics might humanize economics and enlarge it, and it might make economists better scholars. Economics through feminine eyes would not lack seriousness or rigor, unless the women economists allow the feminine to be defined as marginal, pushing Virginia Woolf, Joan Robinson, Emily Dickinson, and Margaret Reid off to one side in favor of Serious Work.

Men and women already must use a wide and conjective rhetoric in doing economics, but are not aware of it. If they became aware of it they would do their economics better and would keep their tempers better. They could speak then in their own voice but with a tolerant confidence, without shouting or sneering. And perhaps they could speak better in the voice of the other, too.

References

Bartlett, Robin L. 1985. "Integrating the New Scholarship on Women into an Introductory Economics Course." Paper presented at session on Gender and Race in the Economics Curriculum, meetings of the American Economic Association, December, New York.

Becker, Gary. 1981. *A Treatise on the Family.* Cambridge, Mass.: Harvard University Press.

Bergmann, Barbara. 1975. "Have Economists Failed?" *Eastern Economic Journal* 2 (July): 16–24.

Boone, Joseph A. 1988. "Feminist Criticism and the Study of Literature: What Difference Does Difference Make?" *Harvard Graduate Society Newsletter* (Spring): 1–3.

Booth, Wayne C. 1974. *Modern Dogma and the Rhetoric of Assent.* Chicago: University of Chicago Press.

Borel, Armand. 1983. "Mathematics: Art and Science." *Mathematical Intelligencer* 5 (4): 9–17.

Brooks, Peter. 1985. *Reading for the Plot: Design and Intention in Narrative.* New York: Vintage.

Bruner, Jerome. 1986. *Actual Minds, Possible Worlds.* Cambridge, Mass.: Harvard University Press.

Buchanan, James M. 1979. "Professor Alchian on Economic Method." In *What Should Economists Do?*, 65–79. Indianapolis: Liberty Press.

Cooper, Brian. 1990. "Marital Problems: A Reconsideration of Neoclassical Models of Household Decision-Making." Manuscript, Department of Economics, Harvard University.

Dillingham, Alan E. 1985. "The Influence of Risk Variable Definition in Value-of-Life Estimates." *Economic Inquiry* 24 (April): 277–94.

Feiner, Susan F. 1984. "The Household Class Process and Imperialism: An Alternative View of the Family Wage." Manuscript, Department of Economics, Virginia Commonwealth University.

———, Barbara A. Morgan, and Bruce B. Roberts. 1988. "Hidden by the Invisible Hand: Race and Gender in Introductory Economics Texts." Paper for session on Gender and Race in the Economics Curriculum, American Economic Association meetings, and for the CSWEP session, Southern Economic Association; November, San Antonio.

Folbre, Nancy. 1991. "The Unproductive Housewife: Her Evolution in Nineteenth-Century Economic Thought." *Signs* 16 (3): 463–84.

———, and Heidi Hartmann. 1988. "The Rhetoric of Self-Interest: Ideology and Gender in Economic Theory." In *The Consequences of Economic Rhetoric,* ed. Arjo Klamer, Donald N. McCloskey, and Robert M. Solow, 184– 203. New York: Cambridge University Press.

Gergen, Kenneth J., and Mary M. Gergen. 1986. "Narrative Form and the Construction of Psychological Science." In *Narrative Psychology: The Storied Nature of Human Conduct,* ed. T. R. Sarbin, 22–44. New York: Praeger.

Gilligan, Carol. 1982. *In a Different Voice: Psychological Theory and Women's Development.* Cambridge, Mass.: Harvard University Press.

Gould, Stephen Jay. 1980. *The Panda's Thumb.* New York: W. W. Norton.

———. 1989. *Wonderful Life: The Burgess Shale and the Nature of History.* New York: W. W. Norton.

Hahn, Frank. 1986. "Living with Uncertainty in Economics: A Review of Kenneth Arrow's Collected Papers." *Times Literary Supplement.* 1 August, 833–34.

Heilbrun, Carolyn G. 1988. *Writing a Woman's Life.* New York: Ballantine Books.

Hesse, Mary. 1966. *Models and Analogies in Science.* South Bend, Ind.: University of Notre Dame Press.

Keller, Evelyn Fox. 1983. *A Feeling for the Organism: The Life and Work of Barbara McClintock.* New York: Freeman.

Keller, Evelyn Fox. 1985. *Reflections on Gender and Science.* New Haven, Conn.: Yale University Press.

Klamer, Arjo. 1987. "The Advent of Modernism in Economics." Manuscript, Department of Economics, George Washington University.

———. 1990. "Towards the Native's Point of View: The Difficulty of Changing the Conversation." In *Economics and Hermeneutics,* ed. Don Lavoie, 19–33. London and New York: Routledge.

———, Donald N. McCloskey, Robert M. Solow, eds. 1988. *The Consequences of Economic Rhetoric.* New York: Cambridge University Press.

——— and D. N. McCloskey. 1991. "The Economy as a Conversation." Manuscript, Department of Economics, University of Iowa.

Klant, J. J. 1985. *The Rules of the Game.* Cambridge: Cambridge University Press.

Laslett, Barbara. 1990. "Unfeeling Knowledge: Emotion and Objectivity in the History of Sociology." *Sociological Forum* 5 (3): 413–33.

Lever, Janet. 1976. "Sex Differences in Games Children Play." *Social Problems* 23:478–87.

Margolis, Howard. 1982. *Selfishness, Altruism, and Rationality: A Theory of Social Choice.* Chicago: University of Chicago Press.

McCloskey, Donald N. 1990. *If You're So Smart: The Narrative of Economic Expertise.* Chicago: University of Chicago Press.

———. 1993. *Knowledge and Persuasion in Economics.* Cambridge: Cambridge University Press.

McCloskey, Laura A. 1987. "Gender and Conversation: Mixing and Matching Styles." In *Current Conceptions of Sex Roles and Sex Typing: Theory and Research,* ed. D. B. Carter, 139–53. New York: Praeger.

McElroy, Marjorie B., and Mary Jean Horney. 1981. "Nash-Bargained Household Decisions: Towards a Generalization of the Theory of Demand." *International Economic Review* 22 (2): 333–49.

Mencken, H. L. 1963 [1922]. *In Defense of Women.* New York: Time Inc.

Moore, Ruth. 1985 [1966]. *Niels Bohr: The Man, His Science, and the World They Changed.* Cambridge, Mass.: MIT Press.

Oxford. 1933. *The Oxford English Dictionary,* vol. 9, S–Soldo. Oxford: Clarendon Press.

Oxford. 1982. *A Supplement to the Oxford English Dictionary,* vol. 3, O–Scz. Oxford: Clarendon Press.

Oxford. 1989. *The Oxford English Dictionary.* 2d ed. Vol. 14, Rob–Sequyle. Oxford: Clarendon Press.

Piaget, Jean. 1932. *The Moral Judgment of the Child.* Trans. Marjorie Gabain. London: Routledge and Kegan Paul.

Roback, Jennifer. 1981. "Immigration Policy: A New Approach." Policy analysis paper, Cato Institute.

Rorty, Amelie Oksenberg. 1983. "Experiments in Philosophical Genre: Descartes' *Meditations.*" *Critical Inquiry* 9 (March): 545–65.

Rorty, Richard. 1987. "Science as Solidarity." In *The Rhetoric of the Human Sciences: Language and Argument in Scholarship and Public Affairs,* ed. J. S. Nelson, A. Megill, and D. N. McCloskey, 38–52. Madison: University of Wisconsin Press.

Ruthven, K. K. 1984. *Feminist Literary Studies: An Introduction.* Cambridge: Cambridge University Press.

Stigler, George. 1966. *The Theory of Price.* 3d ed. New York: Macmillan.

Usher, Dan. 1985. "The Value of Life for Decision Making in the Public Sector." In *Ethics and Economics,* ed. Ellen Frankel Paul, F. D. Miller, Jr., and J. Paul, 168–91. London: Basil Blackwell, for the Social Philosophy and Policy Center, Bowling Green State University.

Vaughn, Karen I. 1988. "Austrian Economics/Feminine Economics." Paper presented to the CSWEP session, Southern Economic Association, November, San Antonio.

Weinberg, Steven. 1983. "Beautiful Theories." Revision of the Second Annual Gordon Mills Lecture on Science and the Humanities, University of Texas, 5 April. Typescript.

Willett, Roslyn S. 1972. "Working in 'A Man's World': The Woman Executive." In *Woman in Sexist Society,* ed. Vivian Gornick and Barbara K. Moran, 511–32. New York: Mentor.

Woolf, Virginia. 1931. *The Waves.* New York: Harcourt, Brace.

———. 1967 [1924]. *Collected Essays.* Vol. 1. New York: Harcourt, Brace, and World.

5 Nancy Folbre

Socialism, Feminist and Scientific

In 1878, Friedrich Engels distinguished the impractical demands of the early nineteenth-century socialists from the theoretical contributions to which he and Karl Marx laid claim. In his words, socialism could be either "utopian" or "scientific."[1] He argued that the former was idealist, naively confident of the ultimate victory of reason and goodwill, while the latter was materialist, based on scientific principles. Engels was wrong, in more ways than one.

Marx and Engels were no more and no less "scientific" in methodology than their Irish precursor, William Thompson. What distinguished them most clearly from earlier socialist theorists was their focus on the exploitation of the industrial proletariat and their related conviction that gender inequality was of distinctly lesser importance. Yet most historians of economic thought have implicitly accepted Engels's dichotomy, according Marxian theory at least cursory examination but omitting any serious consideration of early socialist feminist theorists.

This omission is one example of economists' general lack of interest in feminist theory, which may be explained partly by a positivist tendency to define the scientific canon in androcentric terms.[2] Omissions have a way of reproducing themselves—the common misperception that women's rights were seldom debated by economists before the 1960s has only recently been

I gratefully acknowledge the comments and criticisms of the editors and other contributors to this volume. Thanks also to Robert Dworak, Ann Ferguson, and Robin Hahnel.

1. Originally published in 1878 as part of a book entitled *The Anti-Duhring*, "Socialism: Utopian and Scientific" later was distributed separately in pamphlet form.

2. This point is addressed by the other essays in this volume as well as by McCloskey (1985) and Nelson (1992). I merely wish to point out its relevance to the history of economic thought. See, for instance, Mark Blaug's emphasis on "maximizing facts and minimizing values" (1980, 156).

contravened.[3] Economists prone to label these as political and social rather than economic concerns might note that the married women's property acts passed in 1870 and 1882 represented one of the greatest redistributions of wealth in English history (Holcombe 1983, 217).

This essay explores the rhetoric of women's rights within the socialist tradition, broadly defined. It both defends the scientific insights of early socialist feminist theory and criticizes the meaning Marx and Engels attached to "scientific" socialism. The first section critically reviews the writings of the well-known Robert Owen, making a case for the greater theoretical contributions of William Thompson and his occasional collaborator, Anna Wheeler. The second section suggests that Karl Marx and Friedrich Engels downplayed feminist concerns partly to strengthen their claims to a "scientific" approach. The socialist feminist legacy was better advanced by August Bebel, the prominent German Social Democrat later vilified by Leninists as a revisionist. The final section emphasizes that Owen, Thompson, Wheeler, and Bebel anticipated many later feminist criticisms of economic orthodoxy. They questioned conventional assumptions that juxtaposed perfect selfishness in the market with perfect altruism in the home. They emphasized the productivity of household labor and explored means of making it more efficient. Finally, they challenged Malthus's assertion that contraception was immoral, insisting that reason could and should be applied to reproduction.

The Early Socialist Feminists

The word "socialism," based on the Latin word for friendliness, came into common English parlance around 1830, largely in connection with the name of Robert Owen. Those who welcomed the label were a motley group, encompassing Owen himself, adherents of the Ricardian labor theory of value like Robert Bray, and outspoken feminists such as William Thompson and Anna Wheeler. Virtually all, however, rejected the arguments and assumptions of "political economy"—particularly its confidence in untrammeled pursuit of individual self-interest. As an alternative, they offered an approach and a term of their own—"social science" (Harrison 1969).

Their distinctly rationalist stance manifested itself in their dissent from traditional religious views and sympathy for women's political and economic rights. Their views on the family, however, were by no means unanimous. Robert Owen was a paternalist who described socialism as an easy generalization of family life. William Thompson and Anna Wheeler, on the other hand, criticized the patriarchal character of traditional families and demanded individual rights for women and children.

3. See Pujol (1989, 1992), Folbre and Hartmann (1988), Rendall (1987), Boralevi (1987).

Robert Owen

Robert Owen is the only early socialist widely represented in histories of economic thought.[4] His life history is certainly the most remarkable. A successful industrialist and advocate of child labor laws, he sacrificed respectability when he began to criticize religion and promote communal experiments after 1813. Most of his biographers celebrate his early contributions to social reform and apologize for his later eccentricities, which included calls for revision of marriage laws and support for contraception.[5] Yet Owen and his followers had a significant impact on English politics between 1820 and 1845, contesting Chartists and trade unionists who occasionally called for the exclusion of married women from paid work (Taylor 1983; Thompson 1984).

Owen was clearly an idealist, a man who wanted to bring utopias to life. One of his most important ideals, however, was commitment to reason and social science. He built on the philosophical foundations for social reform laid by other representatives of the Enlightenment tradition, such as Thomas Paine, William Godwin, Mary Wolstonecraft and Jeremy Bentham. Like them, he was a vehement critic of accepted religious doctrine.

Owen's ideas, not his idealism, undermined his effectiveness. As Marx, Engels, and other "scientific" socialists rightly complained, Owen addressed his manifestos to a ruling class whose cultivated intelligence he always praised, whose motives he never questioned. In 1833 he published "An Appeal to the Rich." In "Revolution by Reason" he proclaimed, "This great change . . . must and will be accomplished by the rich and powerful." On his last trip to America, he appealed "To the Capitalists" (Morton 1963, 125, 149).

His trust in the "rich and powerful," one aspect of his confidence in the scientific reason of his arguments, might be explained partly by his own experience as a successful industrialist. But it was also rooted in a larger view of society as a family in which employers were fathers and workers were children. Always paternalistic in attitude and demeanor, Owen was sometimes referred to by his followers as "The Social Father" (Harrison 1969, 157).[6]

4. See, for instance, Robert Heilbroner's immensely popular *The Worldly Philosophers,* which warns, "There is no use trying to read the Utopians" (1972, 330). Mark Blaug ignores the early socialists altogether, attributing "the first appearance of the subject of socialism in a major treatise of economics" to John Stuart Mill's *Principles of Political Economy* (1987, 191). E. K. Hunt (1979), a rare exception to the rule, gives William Thompson careful consideration.

5. Cole writes, "His enemies, and the foes of Socialism, naturally fastened on this book, and denounced Owen and the Owenites as not only infidels and blasphemers, but also open advocates of sexual immorality" (1965, 297). See also Podmore (1907, 211). Owen's later views regarding women and the family have received relatively little attention from either his biographers or historians of economic thought. Claey's recent book (1987), for instance, ignores these issues altogether. Taylor's account (1983) is a notable exception.

6. Harrison also notes Owen's "unresolved ambivalence" between paternalism and equalitarianism (1969, 76).

Virtually everything he wrote was infused with paternal imagery. *A New View of Society,* addressed to His Royal Highness the Prince Regent, explained the necessity not merely of educating but of reforming the character of the poor and working classes (1817, 15). The great error of all previous theories, by Owen's account, was the notion that men formed their own character; in reality, their predecessors and educators bore responsibility for their conduct (1817, 91, 107). *The Book of the New Moral World,* prefaced by a letter to His Majesty William IV, reiterated the vision of a rising generation "educated from birth to become superior, in character and conduct, to all past generations" (1836, xii).

Both he and his sympathizers played on the metaphor of society as a family writ large. John Bray prescribed a new society organized as a vast insurance company for the bearing of all losses from fire, shipwreck, old age, and widowhood (Lowenthal 1911, 98). Socialism would be "as if one family had multiplied as to fill the earth" and was then "by the stipulations of kindred . . . pledged to co-operation in the full extent" (Taylor 1983, 49).

In his first *Essay on the Principle of Population,* published in 1798, Malthus had argued vociferously that such brotherly love would lead to unlimited population growth and economic disaster. Owen disparaged this argument in *A New View of Society,* first published in 1813. In the fifth edition of his *Essay* (1817), Malthus returned the compliment, adding a formal rejoinder to Owen to his general critique of all egalitarian systems. In addition to ignoring the need for a "stimulus of inequality," Malthus wrote, Owen had failed to suggest any means of limiting population growth that was not "unnatural, immoral, or cruel in high degree" (1817, 285). He was referring here to Owen's implied advocacy of contraception. After 1823, Owen became actively involved in the birth control movement (Himes 1928). In this respect, certainly, he assumed a more "scientific" posture than his adversary, who endorsed the traditional religious view that efforts to prevent conception in sexual intercourse were immoral.[7]

Malthus, like Adam Smith before him, drew a strict boundary between the market economy, in which individuals should pursue their individual self-interest, and family life, in which individuals should observe "the moral sentiments" and exercise benevolence (Folbre and Hartmann 1988). Owen wanted to eliminate this boundary because he felt that family allegiances took a basically self-interested form. In his *Lectures on the Marriages of the Priesthood of the Old Immoral World,* he wrote:

> The children within these dens of selfishness and hypocrisy are taught to consider their own individual family their own world, and that it is the duty and interest of all within this little orb to do

7. For a more detailed discussion of Malthus's attitudes toward contraception, as well as those of Bentham, Mill, and Francis Place, see Folbre (1992).

whatever they can to promote the advantages of all the legitimate members of it. With these persons it is my house, my estate, my children, or my husband. . . . No arrangement could be better calculated to produce division and disunion in society.(1840, 30)

If the superstitions of religion could be transcended and the binding constraints of marriage released, a broader form of cooperation would emerge. In this respect, Owen was less the Enlightenment scientist than the passionate romantic. He saw no need for a social contract that would stipulate individuals' responsibilities to each other or to children. Natural sentiment would suffice. His critics were quick to warn of the dire consequences, for women and children, of such "free love" (Taylor 1983, 187).

Ironically, it was Owen's very confidence in paternal benevolence and familial altruism—which he shared with Smith and Malthus—that undermined his larger vision. While the ideals of family life offered a model for social cooperation, real family life was hardly democratic or egalitarian. Rather, it was governed by strict legal rules, economic practices, and cultural norms that gave men authority over their wives and children and defined their responsibilities to them.

The family proved a powerful but problematic metaphor for socialism, one that worked only if the most powerful family members naturally subordinated themselves to the needs of the family as a whole. Were individual fathers any more likely than individual kings to exercise perfect benevolence? The feminists among Owen's adherents answered this question decisively: No.

William Thompson and Anna Wheeler

William Thompson was an Irish landlord whose interest in political economy and social reform was informed by his friendship with Jeremy Bentham as well as Robert Owen. Between 1824 and 1830 he wrote three books that placed him in the intellectual leadership of the socialist movement. His ideas regarding surplus value anticipated Marx and Engels; he also had a discernible influence on John Stuart Mill (Pankhurst 1954). But while Alfred Marshall and Thorstein Veblen respectfully cited his work, few twentieth-century economists have ever heard of him.[8]

Thompson espoused a political labor theory of value, claiming not only that workers should have control over the products of their labor but that control had been wrested from them by organized force and violence. His *Inquiry into the Principles of the Distribution of Wealth,* published in 1824, employed utilitarian reasoning, pointing out that inherited property was inconsistent

8. See Marshall's *Principles of Economics* (1890, 619–20) and Veblen's *The Place of Science in Modern Civilization* (1932, 412–13, 491), cited in Pankhurst (1954).

with meritocratic ideals. The unequal distribution of wealth, he argued, inevitably resulted in unequal exchange in the marketplace.[9]

Like Owen, Thompson advocated social solidarity rather than individual competition. He criticized competition based on individual pursuit of self-interest specifically on the grounds that it was disadvantageous to women. Men would always prevail in individual competition due to their greater physical strength and "exertion uninterrupted by gestation" (1824, 372, 373). He also dwelt on the inefficiencies of a system of domestic labor in which women were condemned to seclusion and drudgery in the home.

Thompson acknowledged that rapid population growth could have ill effects, but he contended that prosperity would lead to a decline in fertility (1824, 544–45). He was even more forthright than Owen in advocating contraception: "A mental effort on the side of refinement, not of grossness, is all the price necessary to be paid, and by only one party, for early marriages and mutual endearments, where the circumstances of society permit no increase of population" (1824, 549).

Thompson did far more than simply concern himself with issues of special import to women. He developed a critique of patriarchal authority that became central to his larger vision of socialism. James Mill, the eminent Utilitarian, provided the impetus in 1825, with an article published in *Encyclopaedia Britannica* reiterating the traditional principle of paternal benevolence. Women did not need political rights, he explained, because their interests were represented by their fathers and husbands.

Thompson immediately wrote a spirited but systematic rejoinder in collaboration with the socialist journalist Anna Wheeler (he credited her contributions in a lengthy preface). This second book was entitled *Appeal of One Half the Human Race, Women, Against the Pretensions of the Other Half, Men, to Retain Them in Political, and Thence in Civil and Domestic Slavery* (1825).[10] Far more than a mere proclamation of support for women's right to vote, the *Appeal* systematically explored the contradictions of a theory of political economy that held men to be wholly self-interested in their dealings with each other but wholly altruistic in their dealings with women and children.

The argument was put most concisely in the outline of topics covered in part I, which addressed Mill's claim:

> 1. The general argument of the "Article" for Human Rights, is founded on the universal love of power of all human beings over

9. Thompson's approach clearly foreshadows John Roemer (1988), who rejects Marx's labor theory of value as a theory of relative prices but models the impact of unequal property allocations on the exploitation of labor.

10. For more discussion of the authorship of the *Appeal*, see Taylor (1983, 22–23). For more information regarding Anna Wheeler, see Pankhurst (1954).

all their fellow-creatures for selfish purposes. This is stated to be the grand governing law of human nature. . . .

2. But, if in the disposition of one half the human race, men, an exception from this grand governing law exists towards the other half, women, what becomes of the law itself and the arguments founded on it? (1825, B)

The following sections argued both for an extension of liberal democratic rights and for a transition toward a more cooperative, less "self-interested" economy. In dialogue format, Thompson presented and rebutted every possible rationale for denying women the same political and civil rights as men. Contesting the claim that marriage was an agreement between free and equal individuals, he detailed the married woman's lack of rights under English common law, which constrained her to become "an involuntary breeding machine and household slave" (1825, 63). In a related article, published in *The Co-Operative Magazine,* Thompson rejected Owen's assumption of paternal altruism and argued that patriarchal rather than capitalist authority had distorted the natural instincts of cooperation: "Every family is a centre of absolute despotism, where of course, intelligence and persuasion are quite superfluous to him who has only to command to be obeyed: from these centres, in the midst of which all mankind are now trained, spreads the contagion of selfishness and the love of domination through all human transactions" (cited in Taylor 1983, 38).

Reiterating the arguments advanced in his earlier *Inquiry,* Thompson insisted that women would never gain true equality in a system based on individual competition. Then, he converged with Owen, calling for the establishment of communities of cooperation. Detailed plans for efficient collectivization of domestic labor were proffered in his *Practical Directions for the Speedy and Economical Establishment of Communities on the Principles of Mutual Co-operation, United Possessions and Equality of Exertions and of the Means of Enjoyments* (1830). Owen later offered similar specifics in his *Book of the New Moral World* (1836), which suggested replacing the sexual division of labor with an age-based system (housework to be performed by children of eleven years or younger).

While few of the communal experiments lasted more than a few years, their principles greatly influenced the development of the cooperative and trade union movements (Thompson 1984; Taylor 1983). Whatever one may conclude about the political efficacy of Thompson's socialist concepts, his feminist arguments proved prophetic. Many of the political reforms he and Anna Wheeler called for were later realized, with important economic consequences for women. Their *Appeal* represented far more than a statement of political or moral values. It contributed to the development of a science of political economy in at least two ways: by exposing the inconsistencies of the theory of paternal benevolence and by explaining the tension between competitive individualism in the market and altruism in the home.

The Marxian Tradition

Serious consideration of the early socialist feminists casts a rather unflattering light on the self-designated "scientific socialists," who have occasionally been pardoned for their lack of concern with gender inequality on the grounds that they had little previous scholarship to draw from (Vogel 1983, 59). Marx and Engels condemned the oppression of women under capitalism, but insisted that their emancipation would follow inevitably from the successful resolution of the class struggle. Engels's celebrated *Origin of the Family, Private Property and the State* was written only after August Bebel had gained a wide audience with the more assertively feminist tract, *Women and Socialism.*

Marx and Engels

Unlike his socialist precursors, Karl Marx developed a critique of capitalism informed by the precepts of classical political economy that guaranteed him an important place in the history of economic thought (Blaug 1987, 286). His revision of the Ricardian labor theory of value provided a theoretical underpinning for the claim that wage earners were exploited by capitalists despite the fact that they were actually paid the value of their labor power. Marx redirected socialist attention from relations of distribution, which he believed could be judged only in moral terms, to relations of capitalist production, which he believed could be scientifically shown vulnerable to crisis.

Marx and Engels did not dismiss their feminist predecessors entirely. Both agreed that woman's position was a measure of the general level of social development, her wretched condition under capitalism one more indicator of the need to supersede that system. But they were the first to apply the "utopian" label to Owen and others, in *The Communist Manifesto* first published in 1848. In the later *Anti-Duhring* (1878) Engels credited Owen for his materialist analysis of education but ridiculed his naïveté. He never alluded to issues of women's rights or mentioned Thompson or Wheeler.[11] Apparently these were not within the purview of scientific socialism.

Marx and Engels often used the adjective "patriarchal" to modify the word

11. It is interesting to note that Thompson used the phrase "surplus value" before Marx. Anton Menger argued in 1899 that Marx's analysis was derivative of Thompson's; Sidney and Beatrice Webb described Marx as the "illustrious disciple" of Thompson and Thomas Hodgskin. See the discussion in Pankhurst (1954, 216).

"family" in their early writings. Yet they tended to locate patriarchy in the past, describing it as an outmoded, almost anachronistic set of authority relations. Where it did exist under capitalism, it lacked significant economic implications—the working class family unit was unified by mutual benevolence. Influenced, perhaps, by Hegel's vision of the family as a wholly ethical realm (Landes 1982), Marx wrote that "individual labour powers, by their very nature, act only as instruments of the joint labour power of the family" (1977, 171).[12]

Engels was more interested in the internal dynamics of family life. *The Condition of the Working Class in England,* a detailed descriptive study he published in 1845, dwelt at length on the perverse reversal of traditional gender roles in areas where high male unemployment made husbands dependent on their wives' earnings. "The wife is the breadwinner while her husband stays at home to look after the children and to do the cooking and cleaning. . . . In Manchester alone there are many hundreds of men who are condemned to perform household duties. One may well imagine the righteous indignation of the workers at being virtually turned into eunuchs" (1958, 162).

To his credit, Engels realized he was in danger of some inconsistency, adding "if the rule of the wife over her husband—a natural consequence of the factory system—is unnatural, then the former rule of the husband over the wife must also have been unnatural" (1958, 164). But the weight of his argument supported the popular trade unionist demand that married women's participation in wage labor should be restricted, that men and women should be segregated in the workplace, and that men but not women should earn a "family wage."

Scientific socialism defined class interests largely in terms of the interests of working-class men. This theory "incorporated basic elements of the outlook of the organized, mainly skilled working men of the 1840s, including the male worker's conception of himself as the sole, rightful breadwinner for the working class family" (Benenson 1984, 1; Seccombe 1986). Neither Marx nor Engels disagreed that women were oppressed, but they linked this oppression to the consequences of private property and the interests of capital rather than to men's interests or men's power. As a result, they believed that resolution of "the woman issue" could be achieved only by resolution of "the class issue." Efforts to reverse, or even to equalize, these priorities were considered counterproductive.

In the late 1860s, for instance, two factions of the International Workingmen's Association emerged in the United States. One, dominated primarily by native-born radicals, included a large number of militant women, including the indomitable feminist Victoria Woodhull. The other faction, comprised

---

12. Joint labor power, in this context, is directly analogous to the neoclassical economic concept of joint utility. For further discussion, see Folbre and Hartmann (1988).

primarily of immigrant Germans, clung to traditional notions of family life. As the two factions began sparring, Marx himself recommended the expulsion of the faction that gave "precedence to the woman's question over the question of labor" (Buhle 1981, xiv). In a letter to a friend in the late 1860s, Marx spoke derisively of women's suffrage, explaining that "German women should have begun by driving their men to self-emancipation" rather than "seeking emancipation for themselves directly" (Buhle 1981, 11).[13]

These political priorities were reinforced by the assumption that family labor could not be analyzed in the scientific terminology of "value." Marx treated labor itself as a nonproduced commodity—childbearing and childrearing were considered not only unproductive of surplus value but also irrelevant to its realization. Domestic tasks were never described as aspects of a creative labor process; they were relegated to the noneconomic world of nature and instinct, analogous to a spider weaving a web or a bee building a honeycomb (O'Brien 1981; Clark and Lange 1979).[14]

In the 1880s, both the "woman question" and the "population question" were hotly debated by the German Social Democrats. August Bebel's *Women and Socialism* (1879) was widely acclaimed in Germany but greeted unenthusiastically by Marx and Engels. Shortly after Marx died, Engels took time off from the task of editing the final volumes of *Capital* to write a response to Bebel, a manuscript based on the findings of the American anthropologist Lewis Morgan and Marx's notes on the subject. *The Origin of the Family, Private Property and the State* applied the theory of historical materialism to explain the coevolution of class relations and family types. Engels described the overthrow of an original matriarchy, based on "mother right," as the result of the emergence of forms of property that men wanted to control and pass on to their heirs in the male line. Men's desire to ensure paternity led them to establish control over women's sexuality in the form of strict female monog-

13. His views may have changed over time. In 1871, with his encouragement, the International Workingmen's Association recommended the establishment of female branches, without precluding mixed-gender branches (Vogel 1983, 71).

14. Sometimes it seems as though Marx was aware of these factors but considered them beyond the scope of his analysis. For instance, in volume 1 of *Capital* he wrote:

There are, besides, two other facts that enter into the determination of the value of labour-power. One is the cost of developing that power, which varies with the mode of production. The other is the natural diversity of labour-power, the difference between the labour-power of men and women, children and adults. The utilization of these different sorts of labour-power, which is in turn conditioned by the mode of production, makes for great variations in the cost of reproducing the worker's family, and in the value of the labour-power of the adult male. Both these factors, however, are excluded in the following investigation.(1977, 655)

In the 1970s, Marxist theorists debated these issues at length in the so-called "domestic labour debates"; see, for instance, Seccombe (1973). Folbre (1982) presents a more detailed critique of Marx's failure to recognize the importance of production and distribution in the household.

amy; their monopoly over economic activities outside the home enhanced their power over the emergent state.

This book made a genuine effort to explain gender inequality in terms of the science of historical materialism. Whatever the inaccuracies in the ethnographic account (and there were many) *The Origin* argued persuasively that gender inequality was rooted in the process of social evolution, not in biological differences between men and women. Yet Engels carefully absolved the proletarian family of any potential for internal conflict. There both husband and wife were propertyless, both likely to engage in wage labor. The transition to socialism, and a concomitant increase in women's participation in "social labor," would be sufficient to guarantee their complete liberation because domestic labor and child-rearing could easily be "industrialized." Whatever tasks remained, women would naturally, and lovingly, assume.

Despite these limitations, or perhaps because of them, *The Origin* became known as the classic Marxian account of women's oppression. This designation contributed to the consolidation of a Marxian tradition that was unsympathetic, though not overtly hostile, to feminist concerns. However historically significant, gender inequality was deemed irrelevant to the scientific "laws of motion" of capitalism. Only a few Marxists dissented from this view.

August Bebel

First published in 1879, Bebel's *Women and Socialism* was banned by German antisocialist laws until 1890, but it nonetheless became one of the best-selling books of its day. By 1910 it had gone through fifty editions and had been widely translated. (It sometimes appeared in English under the title *Women under Socialism.*) The greatly expanded ninth edition of 1891, which incorporated many of Engels's arguments in its historical section, became the best-known and most widely cited version (Vogel 1983, 97–98). Yet Bebel's analysis remained quite distinct from Engels's in its appreciation and support for feminist struggles.

As a prominent member of the German Second International Workingmen's Association, Bebel advocated the electorally based reformism that many later Marxists (academics as well as activists) condemned as apostasy. Within the International, left-wing militants such as Clara Zetkin and Vladimir Lenin argued that issues such as sexuality, marriage, and divorce were diversionary because they were not class based.[15] Still, Bebel's views were quite influential and probably shaped some of the family policies originally implemented by the Bolshevik regime.

The first sentence of his first chapter boldly asserts the parallels between class and gender: "Woman and the workingman have, since old, had this in common—oppression" (1971, 9). Bebel went on to argue that all social de-

15. For an articulate modern version of this argument, see Vogel (1983).

pendence and oppression was rooted in economic dependence, or lack of independent property rights. His sweeping history of the emergence of patriarchal and capitalist hierarchy dwelt on the role of force and violence, establishment of arbitrary laws, and cultural and religious norms.

Women and Socialism provided an encyclopedic account of legal injustices, ranging from generalities regarding married women's lack of control over earnings to specificities such as the Prussian law giving the husband the right to dictate how long his wife should suckle a child (1971, 216). Along the way, Bebel entertained various arguments regarding the age of sexual ripeness and the merits of vegetarianism. He also recited a catechism of arguments in defense of women's capacities, rebutting misogyny from Plato to Schopenhauer.

The book was daring and innovative in its attention to issues typically ignored by political economists. The increased costs of raising children, Bebel argued, were driving many women to resort to abortions that threatened their health (1971, 109). He documented new laws in France and Germany that made it difficult for unwed mothers to gain any support from the fathers of their children. He deplored the increasing use of contraception, not because it was immoral but because under a socialist regime all children would be considered economic assets. At the same time, he suggested that improvements in women's position would result in fertility decline:

> Leaving exceptions aside, intelligent and energetic women are not as a rule inclined to give life to a large number of children as "the gift of God" and to spend the best years of their own lives in pregnancy, or with a child at their breasts. This disinclination for numerous children, which even now is entertained by most women, may—all the solicitude notwithstanding that a Socialist society will bestow on pregnant women and mothers—be rather strengthened than weakened. In our opinion, there lies in this the great probability that the increase of population will proceed slower than in bourgeois society. (1971, 370)

Still, like Engels, Bebel saw children as essentially women's responsibility, cheerfully predicting that under socialism "nurses, teachers, female friends, and the rising female generation" would be on hand to help individual mothers (1971, 347). Also like Engels, he believed that housework would soon be obsolete. His evidence on this count included a glowing description of the centralized modern kitchen exhibited at the Columbian Exposition of 1893 and an extremely funny description of a recently invented shoe-polishing machine (1971, 338–41).

Most distinctively, (and, from the point of view of orthodox Marxists, most culpably) Bebel refused to blame women's oppression simply on the interests of the ruling class. He welcomed Engels's contribution to the history of gender inequality and reiterated his colleague's point that its forms were various.

Yet he singled out one major point of resistance to women's demands for greater independence and better jobs:

> The favorite objection raised against them is that they are not fit for such pursuits, not being intended therefor by Nature. The question of engaging in the higher professional occupations concerns at present only a small number of women in modern society; it is, however, important in point of principle. The large majority of men believe in all seriousness that, mentally as well, woman must ever remain subordinate to them, and, hence, has no right to equality. They are, accordingly, the most determined opponents of woman's aspirations. (1971, 187)

In sum, Bebel advanced the socialist feminist tradition inaugurated by William Thompson and Anna Wheeler. He might have been more successful had the Social Democrats prevailed. In the aftermath of World War I, however, the Bolshevik party enforced more orthodox interpretations of scientific socialism.

Reprise

The nineteenth-century socialist feminists did more than express surprisingly "modern" attitudes about women's rights. Their concern for such rights led them to explore at least three issues that classical political economy ignored: the juxtaposition of individual self-interest with paternal benevolence, the organization of household production, and the potential for birth control. Their insights anticipated contemporary economic arguments that could have been (and still could be) strengthened by greater appreciation of their efforts.

When Owen, Thompson, Wheeler, and Bebel railed against competitive individualism and called for greater social cooperation, they invoked moral categories of right and wrong, fair and unfair. But their arguments were systematically presented and reasonably argued, certainly no less "scientific" than Malthusian warnings against assistance to the poor or Marxist predictions of capitalist crisis. Thompson and Wheeler explicitly criticized the assumption that men were self-interested in their dealings with other men but altruistic in their dealings with women and children. In this, they foreshadowed Amartya Sen's critique of the rationality of pure self-interest (1977) and recent efforts to apply bargaining models to the family (Pollak 1985).

Political economists from Adam Smith to Alfred Marshall not only ignored household labor; they explicitly argued that it was "unproductive" (Folbre 1991). The early socialist feminists, on the other hand, addressed issues of productivity and equity in domestic labor later explored by economists at the University of Chicago (Reid 1934). Socialist efforts to develop "communities of cooperation" with central kitchens and "industrialized" domestic labor were not particularly successful (Hayden 1981). But discussion and debate over such issues surely encouraged housewives and their families to demand municipal facilities such as plumbing, gas, and electricity, and services such as nurseries and schools, which, after all, "socialized" many aspects of housework.

Finally, the socialist feminists departed from traditional orthodoxy in their advocacy of contraception. Their confidence in rational, scientific efforts to limit fertility contributed to the emergence of the birth control movement in England and the United States. Their prediction that economic growth and improvements in women's rights would foster fertility decline proved basically correct (Caldwell 1982).

Engels asserted that socialists could be either utopian or scientific and assigned feminists to the former category. Most historians of economic thought followed suit. This paper has praised the contributions of socialist theorists who were both feminist and scientific. Their commitment to women's rights did not diminish their theoretical insights. Rather, it provided them with a useful vantage point for a critique of the assumptions of classical political economy.

References

Bebel, August. 1971. *Women and Socialism*. Trans. Daniel De Leon. New York: Schocken Books.

Benenson, Harold. 1984. "Victorian Sexual Ideology and Marx's Theory of the Working Class." *International Labor and Working Class History* 25 (Spring): 1–23.

Blaug, Mark. 1980. *The Methodology of Economics, or How Economists Explain*. Cambridge: Cambridge University Press.

———. 1987. *Economic Theory in Retrospect*. 4th ed. Cambridge: Cambridge University Press.

Boralevi, Lea Campos. 1987. "Utilitarianism and Feminism." In *Women in Western Political Philosophy*, ed. Ellen Kennedy and Susan Mendus, 159–78. New York: St. Martin's Press.

Buhle, Mary Jo. 1981. *Women and American Socialism, 1870–1920*. Urbana: University of Illinois Press.

Caldwell, John. 1982. *The Theory of Fertility Decline*. New York: Academic Press.

Claeys, Gregory. 1987. *Machinery, Money and the Millennium: From Moral Economy to Socialism, 1815–60*. Cambridge: Polity.

Clark, Lorenne M. G., and Lynda Lange. 1979. *The Sexism of Social and Political Theory: Women and Reproduction from Plato to Nietzsche*. Toronto: University of Toronto Press.

Cole, G. D. H. 1965. *The Life of Robert Owen*. London: Frank Cass and Company.

Engels, Friedrich. 1935. *Socialism Utopian and Scientific*. Trans. Edward Aveling. New York: International Publishers.

———. 1948. *The Origin of the Family, Private Property and the State*. Moscow: Progress Publishers.

———. 1958. *The Condition of the Working Class in England*. Trans. and ed. W. O. Henderson and W. H. Chaloner. Stanford, Calif.: Stanford University Press.

Folbre, Nancy. 1982. "Exploitation Comes Home: A Critique of the Marxian Theory of Family Labour." *Cambridge Journal of Economics* 6:317–29.

———. 1991. "The Unproductive Housewife: Her Evolution in Nineteenth-Century Economic Thought." *Signs* 16 (3): 463–84.

———. 1992. "The Improper Arts: Sex in Classical Political Economy." Forthcoming in *Population and Development Review* 18(1).

———, and Heidi Hartmann. 1988. "The Rhetoric of Self-Interest and the Ideology of Gender." In *The Consequences of Economic Rhetoric*, ed. Arjo Klamer, Donald N. McCloskey, and Robert M. Solow, 184–206. Cambridge: Cambridge University Press.

Harrison, John F. C. 1969. *Quest for the New Moral World. Robert Owen and the Owenites in Britain and America*. New York: Charles Scribner's Sons.

Hayden, Dolores. 1981. *The Grand Domestic Revolution: A History of Feminist Designs for American Homes, Neighborhoods, and Cities*. Cambridge, Mass.: MIT Press.

Heilbroner, Robert. 1972. *The Worldly Philosophers. The Lives, Times and Ideas of the Great Economic Thinkers*. 4th ed. New York: Simon and Schuster.

Himes, Normal E. 1928. "The Place of John Stuart Mill and of Robert Owen in the History of English Neo-Malthusianism," *Quarterly Journal of Economics* 42:627–40.

Holcombe, Lee. 1983. *Wives and Property: Reform of the Married Women's Property Law in Nineteenth-Century England*. Toronto: University of Toronto Press.

Hunt, E. K. 1979. *History of Economic Thought: A Critical Perspective*. Belmont, Calif.: Wadsworth Publishing Company.

Landes, Joan. 1982. "Hegel's Conception of the Family." In *The Family in Political Thought*, ed. Jean Bethke Elshtain, 125–44. Amherst: University of Massachusetts Press.

Lowenthal, Esther. 1911. *The Ricardian Socialists*. Columbia University Studies in History, Economics, and Public Law, vol. 46, no. 1. New York: Longmans, Green and Co.

Malthus, T. R. 1817. *An Essay on the Principle of Population*. 5th ed. London: John Murray, Albemarle Street.

Marx, Karl. 1977. *Capital*. Vol. 1. Trans. Ben Fowkes. New York: Vintage Books.

———, and Friedrich Engels. 1972. "Manifesto of the Communist Party." In *The Marx-Engels Reader,* ed. Robert Tucker, 331–62. New York: W. W. Norton.

McCloskey, Donald N. 1985. *The Rhetoric of Economics*. Madison: University of Wisconsin Press.

Morton, A. L. 1963. *The Life and Ideas of Robert Owen*. New York: Monthly Review Press.

Nelson, Julie. 1992. "Gender, Metaphor, and the Definition of Economics," *Economics and Philosophy* 8(1): 103–25.

O'Brien, Mary. 1981. *The Politics of Reproduction*. Boston: Routledge and Kegan Paul.

Owen, Robert. 1817. *A New View of Society: or, Essays on the Formation of the Human Character, Preparatory to the Development of a Plan for Gradually Ameliorating the Condition of Mankind*. 3d ed. London: R. and A. Taylor.

———. 1836. *The Book of the New Moral World, Containing the Rational System of Society*. London: Effingham Wilson, Royal Exchange.

———. 1840 [1835]. *Lectures on the Marriages of the Priesthood of the Old Immoral World . . . with an Appendix containing the Marriage System of the New Moral World*. Leeds: J. Hobson.

Paine, Thomas. 1961. *Rights of Man*. New York: Heritage Press.

Pankhurst, Richard K. P. 1954a. "Anna Wheeler: A Pioneer Socialist and Feminist." *Political Quarterly* 25 (2): 132–43.

———. 1954b. *William Thompson: Britain's Pioneer Socialist, Feminist and Cooperator*. London: Watts and Co.

Podmore, Frank. 1907. *Robert Owen: A Biography*. New York: D. Appleton and Company.

Pollak, Robert A. 1985. "A Transaction Cost Approach to Families and Households." *Journal of Economic Literature* 203 (2): 581–608.

Pujol, Michèle. 1989. "Economic Efficiency or Economic Chivalry? Women's Status and Women's Work in Early Neo-Classical Economics." Ph.D. diss., Simon Fraser University.

———. 1992. *Feminism and Antifeminism in Early Economic Thought*. New York: Gower Press.

Reid, Margaret. 1934. *The Economics of Household Production*. New York: John Wiley and Sons.

Rendall, Jane. 1987. "Virtue and Commerce: Women in the Making of Adam Smith's Political Economy." In *Women in Western Political Philosophy,* ed. Ellen Kennedy and Susan Mendus, 44–57. New York: St. Martin's Press.

Roemer, John. 1988. *Free to Lose: An Introduction to Marxist Economic Philosophy*. Cambridge, Mass.: Harvard University Press.

Seccombe, Wally. 1973. "The Housewife and Her Labour Under Capitalism." *New Left Review* 83 (Jan.–Feb.): 3–24.

―――. 1986. "Patriarchy Stabilized: The Construction of the Male Breadwinner Wage Norm in Nineteenth-Century Britain," *Social History* 2 (1): 53–76.

Sen, Amartya. 1977. "Rational Fools: A Critique of the Behavioral Foundations of Economic Theory." *Philosophy and Public Affairs* 6(4): 317–44.

Taylor, Barbara. 1983. *Eve and the New Jerusalem: Socialism and Feminism in the Nineteenth Century.* New York: Pantheon Books.

Thompson, Noel. 1984. *The People's Science: The Popular Political Economy of Exploitation and Crisis, 1816–1834.* New York: Cambridge University Press.

Thompson, William. 1825. *Appeal of One Half the Human Race, Women, Against the Pretensions of the Other Half, Men, to Retain Them in Political, and Thence in Civil and Domestic Slavery.* London: Printed for Longman, Hurst, Rees, Orme, Brown, and Green, Paternoster Row; and Wheatley and Adlard, 108 Strand.

―――. 1830. *Practical Directions for the Speedy and Economical Establishment of Communities on the Principles of Mutual Co-operation, United Possessions and Equality of Exertions and of the Means of Enjoyments.* London: Printed for Longman, Hurst, Rees, Orme, Brown, and Green, Paternoster Row; and Wheatley and Adlard, 108 Strand.

―――. 1963 [1824]. *Inquiry into the Principles of the Distribution of Wealth Most Conducive to Human Happiness.* Reprints of Economic Classics. New York: August M. Kelley, Bookseller, 1963.

Vogel, Lise. 1983. *Marxism and the Oppression of Women.* New Brunswick, N.J.: Rutgers University Press.

6

Ann L. Jennings

Public or Private? Institutional Economics and Feminism

As the title of this book suggests, scholars, particularly feminist scholars, are taking new directions, asking new questions, and challenging old answers. They take issue with the notion of "man" as a universal category of human beings and with "economic man" as a metaphor for all economic behavior. Some also ask whether these categories, as generally used, even refer to all men; working-class, nonwhite, and non-Western men often appear to be excluded as well. These issues have been raised in many quarters, both within and outside economics.

This chapter explores economic relationships from a feminist perspective within institutional economics. A comparison of the foundations of institutional economics and feminist theory reveals important similarities. Both approaches (in at least some of their manifestations) view the acquisition of knowledge as a cultural enterprise, challenge dualistic understandings of knowledge and social life, and have a high regard for historical context. Institutionalism, therefore, affords unusual opportunities for feminist theorizing in economics. Feminist theory, in turn, offers institutionalism a way of broadening its analysis.

Varieties of Institutional Economics

There are at least three basic schools of institutional economics. The first combines the American tradition of Thorstein Veblen with the European tradition of Karl Polanyi and Gunnar Myrdal. After briefly discussing institutional labor economics and the "new institutional economics" (NIE), I will explore this American-European version of institutionalism.

Institutional labor economics, currently most closely associated with Michael Piore, emerged mainly from the pre-1960s "old labor economics" of Clark Kerr, John Dunlop, and Lloyd Reynolds (Cain 1976), although it sometimes draws from the American institutionalist John R. Commons as well as from Karl Polanyi and Thorstein Veblen (Brown 1988). Economists of this school tend to emphasize the social context of labor markets as well as house-hold/labor market relationships. Some, like Clair Brown and Myra Strober, have also contributed significantly to feminist discussions of the evolution of women's labor market and family roles.[1] Although many institutional labor economists reject the individualism of orthodox human capital theory (Piore 1983), this is not uniformly true (Amsden 1980). Others have continued to use neoclassical tools, neglected discussions of cultural foundations, or fo-cused rather narrowly on processes affecting labor markets. These factors make the institutional labor economics approach difficult to link directly with the feminist theories discussed in this chapter.

The NIE tradition of Oliver Williamson and others (Williamson et al. 1975) is much closer to a neoclassical perspective and retains its individualistic foundations. It employs some concepts developed by Commons, such as "working rules," as a foundation of "bounded rationality" principles operating when transactions cost are high (Pollak 1985), but it has no developed concept of culture. It is largely incompatible with the feminist theories discussed in this chapter and with American-European institutionalist cultural interpreta-tions (Dugger 1983).

Early Institutionalist Feminism

Feminist arguments have always been found in institutional eco-nomics. The founder of American institutionalism, Thorstein Veblen, placed socially constructed distinctions between men and women at the center of his first major work, *The Theory of the Leisure Class* (1899). There he argued that, historically, women had been viewed first as objects of seizure, then as producers of consumption goods for their masters, and, finally, as idle objects for the display of men's wealth. In modern society, status, which rests on ownership and the ability to consume without personal effort, was now most effectively demonstrated by men through women. Men's social reputations now depended upon their wives refraining from openly productive effort. Women's increasingly restrictive dress became an outward sign of wealth suf-ficient to relieve them of the need for useful effort, and even men who had to work for income could salvage their reputations by maintaining the illusion that their wives enjoyed leisure. Consequently, women were trained to be homemakers and consumers, ornaments for men; only disreputable women worked for money.

Veblen detested these social norms and favored women's rights, not just because he opposed invidious distinctions based on wealth but also because

1. See, for instance, Brown (1982, 1988) and Strober and Arnold (1987).

he abhorred the waste they honored.[2] Veblen also argued that men's market activities are often equally wasteful. He rejected conventional associations of the market with useful economic activity and understood the real economy as a social provisioning process, largely excluding "pecuniary exploit" and financial manipulation (Veblen 1961 [1901]).[3] He included many of women's domestic activities in provisioning, yet he noted that only their enforced wastefulness was socially reputable. Even today, the social image of women as frivolous and extravagant consumers has been only partially eclipsed by the fact that most women work openly for money; the economic importance of their domestic efforts remains understated. Thus, although Veblen's arguments need updating, they are generally consistent with many current feminist views.

Institutional economics, which initially expressed concern with the status of women, has only recently begun to reclaim this interest. Veblen's views of the "barbarian status of women" were linked to a larger opposition to social hierarchy rooted in invidious distinctions. Subsequent institutionalists retained the broader concern but for decades added few new feminist insights (Greenwood 1984), despite evolving social relationships and theoretical interpretations. Recently, however, some varieties of feminism have given increased emphasis to the cultural construction of social distinctions and have become increasingly reliant on philosophical approaches similar to those of institutionalism. This has yielded a foundational alignment that is highly favorable to the renewal of feminist institutionalism.

Foundations of the American-European Perspective

The American-European institutionalist perspective is the variety of institutionalism most compatible with the feminist theories I will discuss later. At its base is the concept of culture, borrowed from anthropology. Culture may be defined as a system of symbolic interpretation that unites human thought and action. It provides the basis for common social understandings and for community-based knowledge. Such common meanings order human existence and make coherent systems of thought and action possible. As Marshall Sahlins says, the concept of culture "leaves behind such antique dualisms as mind and matter, idealism and materialism, . . . [and the] worldless subject confronting the thoughtless object." Dualism is replaced by "a *tertium*

2. The origins of Veblen's feminism are unclear but appear to derive from anthropological rather than feminist sources. Charlotte Perkins Gilman's *Women and Economics* (1898) predated *The Theory of the Leisure Class* by one year, but Veblen's views were developing as early as 1894, as seen in his earliest articles on women reprinted in *Essays in Our Changing Order* (1934).

3. The recent spate of hostile takeovers, raiding, and insider trading are current reminders of Veblen's views on the wastefulness of masculine financial exploit.

quid, culture, not merely mediating the human relationship to the world by a social logic of significance, but constituting by that scheme the relative subjective and objective terms of the relationship" (1976, ix–x).

Culture has several connotations for institutionalists. First, culture implies an essential continuity of all human social activity as necessary to viable and coherent social arrangements. Institutionalists view theories that posit the separateness of any sphere of endeavor as cultural defenses of existing social distinctions, interpretations that rank various social groups and behaviors by first establishing their dissimilarities. Instead, institutionalists understand all behavior as multidimensional and complex, having various economic, political, and reproductive aspects that cannot be separated. This does not mean that activities cannot conflict; indeed, conflict routinely results from and cumulatively causes social evolution (Jennings and Waller 1992).

The concept of culture further implies that social processes are not governed by universal laws and do not have universal meanings; rather, processes and meanings are mutually and historically determined. Cultural analysis also eschews notions of functional necessity in the ways that human needs are met, except in the very narrow sense that existing social values may create cultural blindness to alternative arrangements and interpretations. Finally, the institutionalist view prescribes a mode of social inquiry that places cultural and historical context in the foreground and that freely crosses disciplinary boundaries. It also recognizes that social beliefs often perpetuate rather than illuminate cultural blindness, so that knowledge tends to incorporate cultural biases and frequently contains inaccurate accounts of social behavior and arrangements.

Both Veblen and Polanyi emphasized the possibility of substantive inaccuracy in social theory. Veblen regarded neoclassical economics as a reflection of market values and reverence for wealth in modern "pecuniary culture," and found in economics a perverse tendency to devalue processes that actually meet human needs. He saw the belief that "captains of industry" contribute to production through their financial manipulations as a myth dating from an earlier era of small-scale enterprise (Veblen 1961 [1901]). According to his theory of institutional lag, cultural habits of thought impede awareness of change and limit receptiveness to new ideas. Novel possibilities do result from the advance of "matter-of-fact knowledge," but Veblen was deeply skeptical of our will to break free from old habits. He emphasized the grasp of "imbecile institutions" that tend to preserve existing systems of status and privilege.[4]

---

4. Institutionalists often refer to Veblen's discussion of dynamic and static elements in cultural processes as the "Veblenian dichotomy." Several more or less parallel versions exist, including Veblen's institutional/technological form and his distinction between pecuniary and industrial employments. The form of this dichotomy most commonly used by institutionalists today is Ayres's (1961) ceremonial/instrumental distinction.

Polanyi (1944) also opposed "formalist" economic theory because it abstracts from cultural circumstances and misinterprets the nature of social arrangements. He challenged the view that market behavior characterized most economic relationships before the nineteenth century and doubted whether economic relationships could be easily distinguished from other social relationships in earlier periods. He suggested further that greed and self-interest were not naturally the preeminent motives of human beings, since before the nineteenth century these impulses were subordinated to other cultural values. Polanyi saw both individualism and laissez-faire as cultural reflections of a new faith in the self-regulating power of markets, which he mistrusted.[5]

Clarence Ayres (1961) added explicit linkages between cultural perspectives and pragmatist philosophy to institutionalism. He updated Veblen's anthropology and connected cultural myths to master/servant hierarchies and dualistic modes of thought in Western society. Ayres, who drew heavily on the work of John Dewey (Tilman 1990), also replaced Veblen's skepticism about social progress with Dewey's optimism.

Dewey's work has been influential in institutionalism because he rejected dualistic beliefs as both inadequate and socially invidious (Dewey 1929). His belief in the fundamental unity of reality and human experience paralleled Veblen's emphasis on cultural continuity; both used it as an argument for social change and greater social equality.[6] Dewey also understood truth to be an open-ended social process of inquiry and a guide to human problem solving rather than a conclusion of inquiry. These views remain important in institutionalism, although Dewey's optimistic belief in social progress has been tempered in more recent accounts.[7]

Foundations of Feminist Perspectives

Feminism, like institutionalism, is a label that has been applied to significantly different perspectives. Most feminists share the basic insight that women have been assigned second-class status in Western and most other societies, but the ways they explain women's disadvantages vary, as do their

5. While Polanyi was by no means a feminist, his concern with state/economy relationships may be seen as an additional aspect of the private/public distinctions that have engaged feminists.

6. Veblen, interestingly, was also briefly a student of another pragmatist philosopher, C. S. Peirce, and later a colleague of Dewey. The parallels his work shows to pragmatism are not coincidental.

7. Dewey (1929) took modern science as his open-ended model of progressive truth. While he saw science as offering only provisional truth and denied most claims to "objective truth," some institutionalists have argued more recently that science can be "captured" by elites and used for their own purposes. Called "ceremonial encapsulation" (Junker 1983; Bush 1986), this view restores Veblen's emphasis on social evolution as a process of change but not necessarily of progress and is consistent with feminist critiques of science (Harding 1986; Waller and Jennings 1990).

views of how gender inequality is related to other social inequalities, such as race and class (Jaggar 1983). An important strain in feminist philosophy emphasizes the cultural origins of knowledge and the need to overcome dualistic thinking. The works of three feminists discussed below link dualistic thinking to invidious gender distinctions in society and offer new interpretations of historical developments.

In *The Science Question in Feminism* (1986), Sandra Harding recognizes that knowledge is culturally constructed and analyzes the significance of this challenge to traditional views of scientific knowledge. The practice of science, she argues, has taken on a quasi-religious, authoritarian character because science claims to have unique methods of knowledge production, insulated from cultural biases, that yield "objective truths." Such practice also denies that scientists' cultural identities influence their scientific beliefs, as long as they rigorously pursue prescribed methods. Harding challenges each of these claims, identifies their foundations in dualistic, subjective/objective views of knowledge, and suggests that the claim of exclusive status is crucial to the use of science as a tool and transmitter of social hierarchy.

Harding argues further that science incorporates the dominant gender metaphors of modern society. These metaphors link cultural gender roles and individual gender identities to gendered thought processes that commonly exclude women, women's questions, and feminine values from privileged social spheres, including science. Such metaphors are asymmetrical in the sense that the masculine/feminine dualisms are hierarchical. Masculine persons (men), masculine activities (science), and masculine values (rational objectivity) are universalized while feminine persons (women), feminine activities (service and nurturance), and feminine values (emotional subjectivity) are personalized and particularized;[8] reason triumphs over emotion, science triumphs over particularized nature, and men subordinate women.

Harding's view of gender asymmetry implies that women cannot simply be "added" to science to correct its masculine bias. What is "only particular" can have little effect on what is already "universal." Nor can the debunking of fact/value dualisms alone transform science. Masculinity and femininity, like science, are not mere intellectual constructions; they are lived cultural processes and norms that cannot be changed by simple philosophical or personal insight (Harding 1987). Science must be "destabilized" through social struggle to transform cultural experience and awareness.[9] Since Harding rejects any

8. Harding (1987) also notes the dangers of universalizing the category "woman." Her views are consistent with those of black feminists who have criticized tendencies of feminists to adopt a white, European, middle-class perspective. Feminists on the left have recognized this problem but have not yet achieved a satisfactory theoretical articulation of race, gender and ethnicity/culture. These issues are discussed more extensively in Jennings and Waller (1990b) and Jennings (1992a).

9. Helen Longino (1992) frames this problem somewhat differently, arguing that divergent views of and within science are a source of useful tension, provided that dominant views are not permitted to override alternative perspectives. Relativism (the acceptance of pluralism without

claim that science possesses a "special practice," her arguments also clearly apply to economics, where gender asymmetries are also likely to be found.

Susan Bordo's *The Flight to Objectivity* (1987) contains a second account of culture and false dualisms. Bordo shows the rise of modern dualisms in the mind/body distinctions of Descartes. His work both reflects and contributed to a cultural "flight from the feminine" world of emotional connections to a masculine world of rational separateness.

Bordo describes Cartesian dualism as an alienated response to the social instability of the seventeenth century, an effort to compensate for the loss of social unity through egocentric claims to mastery over the physical world of nature. The adequacy of Descartes's method was challenged even during his own time (Bordo 1987), but gained acceptance nonetheless. Since that time, the conceptions of the masculine mind as the seat of pure reason and of the feminine body as an unreliable source of sensation and emotion remained dominant in Western philosophy until the twentieth century ushered in a new period of doubt. It was common for scientific accounts to speak of the need to penetrate and subjugate feminine nature; her mysterious secrets were to be wrested from her.

The masculine principles of Cartesian dualism also appear in individualistic philosophies of self-determination and self-interest, which also refer to the traditional prerogatives of men. In *Gender and History* (1986), Linda Nicholson traces the development of individualism in Anglo-American society since the seventeenth century. She associates the rise of modern individualism with the emergence of public/private distinctions and with liberal theories of the state, finding that these distinctions between social spheres have also constructed cultural masculinity and femininity.

Nicholson argues that distinct spheres of social life did not exist before the seventeenth century; economic, political, and kinship relationships largely overlapped, and no distinct sphere of "private" life was identifiable. She identifies the seventeenth-century emergence of such distinctions in the political theories of John Locke. Locke, who located the social basis of the (public) state in the free association of isolated heads of (private) landed households, challenged earlier social understandings that had grounded political legitimacy in patriarchal and interhousehold kinship connections.[10] In Locke's work, individualism became a structuring principle reflecting privileges of personal ownership and access to the public sphere. Women, as well as men who were not heads of propertied households, were denied social visibility and status as individuals. While Locke considered both women's labor and

recognition of the need for engaged debate), however, is to be rejected for promoting the dominance of established views.

10. Nicholson (1986) also suggests that Locke obscured the way political relations evolved historically out of kinship relations by creating a fictitious account of the origins of the state; his "natural order" perspective contributed to the universalization of public/private distinctions.

maternal roles important, the economic and reproductive aspects of household activities were not socially distinguished; neither formed the basis of public standing. Only legal ownership of property—a public political relationship—conferred social status (Jennings and Waller 1990b).

Locke's seventeenth-century "political split" of public and private spheres evolved into an "economic split" as nineteenth-century industrialization removed much production from the control of private households. The social importance of markets increased and the "cult of domesticity," which assigned women exclusive familial roles outside the market, emerged. Although Nicholson does not discuss it, the prerogatives of individualism were also extended to all (white) men, based on their now public economic roles and wage contracts, but women remained excluded, since the cult of domesticity denied their economic function.[11]

Nicholson relies on Polanyi in portions of her account, and both Nicholson and Polanyi focus on the historical novelty of the nineteenth-century separation of the economy from other social spheres. But, as Nicholson notes,

> Polanyi claims that the defining condition of the market economy is a separation of the economic and political. Not noted by him, but also essential, is the separation of the economic from the domestic and political. Indeed when we think of what is pivotal about industrialization it is that the production of goods ceases to be organized by kinship relationships and to be an activity of the household. (1986, 190)

Nicholson argues that it was mainly households, not the state, that ceded control over production and the disposition of men's labor. Households retained control over women's labor, but that labor was no longer recognized as productive.

Nicholson's view of shifting public/private distinctions implies that the nineteenth-century split left a smaller private domestic domain. The public sphere of individualism grew, and has continued to grow as women have fought for political and economic rights, for claims to public status as individuals. An alternative formulation, suggesting that two forms of dualistic individualism and two sets of public/private distinctions emerged in the nineteenth century, will be offered here.

When Institutionalism and Feminism Meet

It is clear from the above examples that institutionalist and feminist writers have in some cases reached quite similar conclusions about the

11. This indicates a change in the relation of the individual and property. The Chartist position was that all men have property in the form of their own labor (Jennings and Waller 1990b). An-

continuity of culture, the problems and hierarchies created by dualistic constructions, and the importance of historical accounts. This is not to say, however, that all institutionalists are necessarily feminist (some are quite notably not) or that all feminists think in terms compatible with institutionalist analysis.

Consistent with the primacy assigned to economic causality in conventional economic analysis, some feminists argue that women's relative lack of economic power explains their social disadvantages. Institutionalists, on the other hand, question this view. They accept neither the priority of "the economic" as universal nor the market as the sole provisioning domain. Further, they see the cultural prioritizing of markets as reinforcing existing status hierarchies and are critical of measurements of social worth in market prices. Veblen maintained that many market activities—such as saving, speculation, and corporate finance—make little contribution to provisioning and that ownership mainly sets the legal "limits of permissible fraud." While ownership legitimates flows of economic resources to the wealthy, it does not augment economic provisioning and has less economic significance than women's domestic labor.

Following this lead, feminist institutionalists are not content with most discussions that stress women's lack of economic power or roles. They challenge the very definition of "economic pursuits," question cultural interpretations that prioritize "the economic," explore the historical origins of modern cultural beliefs and practices, and describe the gender dimensions of existing distinctions between "economic" and "noneconomic" pursuits. Such issues are rarely considered in mainstream feminist discussions of economics.

Public or Private? A Feminist Institutionalist Approach

Feminist institutionalism, which relies on a concept of culture that unifies social habits of thought and behavior and rejects dualism, is concerned with the cultural manifestations of dualisms in social compartmentalizations and social rankings. The history of these social constructions may be traced partly through patterns of public/private distinctions. Two sets of associated distinctions have been identified as influential in Anglo-American society since the nineteenth century. Both serve to distinguish and prioritize the "the economy" or "the market" over other spheres in conventional understandings, and to rank social groups according to their presumed relationships to the privileges and spheres defined.

Nicholson never specifically describes public/private distinctions as dualistic, but Michelle Rosaldo has done so:

---

other view is that the right to own property, not actual ownership, was the new basis for individual standing. Women, of course, lacked both for most of the nineteenth century.

> Victorian theory cast the sexes in dichotomous and contrastive
> terms, describing home and woman not primarily as they were,
> but as they *had to be,* given an ideology that opposed natural,
> moral, and essentially unchanging private realms to the vagaries
> of a progressive masculine society. (1980, 404)

She continues:

> The most serious deficiency of a model based on two opposed
> spheres appears, in short, in its alliance with the dualisms of the
> past, dichotomies which teach that women must be understood
> not in terms of relationship—with other women and with men—
> but of difference and apartness. (409)

Cultural dualisms, like philosophical dualisms, are almost inevitably hier-archical, legitimizing master/servant relationships. In the seventeenth century, when public/private distinctions took the form of state/household separation, culturally recognized rankings were based mainly on political distinctions be-cause the state was the public realm of privilege. While property grounded class distinctions, such distinctions largely involved political rights, access, and prerogatives. In the nineteenth century, however, the political sphere lost ground to the economic sphere and distinctions of rank came to be based mainly on economic prerogatives. These shifts in cultural interpretation, as-sociated with industrialization, the creation of separate spheres for men and women, and the rise of economic individualism, also yielded a realignment of state/economy relationships expressed in the laissez-faire doctrines of classi-cal economics.

The writers and public figures active in early nineteenth-century economic discussions took little notice of women, the family, or even consumption.[12] Nor did the new economy/family split Nicholson discusses cause any social controversy (Jennings and Waller 1990b). Gary Langer's *The Coming of Age of Political Economy* (1987) shows instead that the main target of the new "political economists" was state control over economic affairs. Polanyi also described the challenges launched in Britain to mercantilism, the poor laws, and the corn laws as part of an effort to separate the economy from the state.[13] The state was to be limited to pursuits that private, self-interested entrepre-neurs could not undertake themselves. "State" and "economy" did not share the "public" sphere, but were demarcated according to an altered form of the public/private distinction that assigned preeminence to the market economy.

---

12. The main exceptions were Malthus, who discussed population growth, and J. S. Mill, who was concerned with women's rights.

13. Hirschman (1977), among others, shows that the relationship of the state and economic self-interest was frequently discussed before the nineteenth century. Interestingly, however, the primary concern in earlier treatments was with the possible influence of economic interests on the state rather than with the detrimental effects of the state on economic interests.

An interesting ambiguity in conventional understandings of public and private resulted. While markets became "public" with respect to the "private" family in the nineteenth century, they retained their "private" status vis-à-vis the "public" state. In both cases, public/private distinctions privileged the market but, because the market had become both public and private, the social ranking of public and private varied accordingly.

These insights permit us to reinterpret Veblen's view of "pecuniary culture," a culture characterized by the social dominance of the "captains of industry" and monetary standards of social worth. Once "market" and "economy" were set apart from other social pursuits, coterminously defined, and the social primacy of markets accepted, those who could manipulate the market standard of value for their own benefit were assured of privileged status as benefactors to society.[14] In the nineteenth century the state, which was not considered part of the economy, became the handmaiden of wealthy elites while the family, also not seen as part of the economy, became the sphere in which wealth was to be demonstrated through conspicuous consumption and the display of women's idleness. Veblen, of course, attacked these social habits as wasteful, based on myth, and oppressive, and dismissed individualistic social interpretations as a defense of the status quo.

Recent feminist work on both dualistic constructions and cultural compartmentalization is useful in restoring and updating Veblen's understandings and feminist discussion. From a feminist institutionalist standpoint, pecuniary culture is clearly dualistic and gendered. A simple and revealing exercise lays out the interconnected web of dualistic meanings in the public/private distinctions that emerged in the nineteenth century. On the economy/family side of the "double dualism" (Jennings 1992b), a partial list of social distinctions might read:

public / private
(market) economy / family
man / woman
rational / emotional
mind / body
historical / natural
objective / subjective
science / humanities
economics / sociology
competitive / nurturant
independent / dependent
individual / ?

14. The classical belief that the "money veil" merely reflects underlying real values and processes assisted in this deception. Veblen's full-length analysis of the destabilizing nature of financial manipulation, in his *Theory of Business Enterprise* (1904), foreshadowed Keynes's and many Post-Keynesian arguments.

No word is paired with "individual" since there is no good term for "non-public" persons, perhaps because such persons are "represented" by their public counterparts.

These oppositional pairings augment one another and are not independent constructions. Moreover, the meaning of the terms on one side of the division overlap, creating ambiguity in our conventional associations. This ambiguity is seldom critically examined; rather, it is generally exploited so that the terms become metaphors for one another.

While meanings on the same side are associated, the terms within each pair are opposed in an asymmetrical and hierarchical fashion (Harding 1987). Woman is defined as different from man: woman is "not man," just as the family is "not the economy." Man, however, is not defined as "not woman" but as a universal category, parallel to and informed by the economy. It is also noteworthy that this schematic set of public/private distinctions encompasses key portions of Harding's view of "scientific method," Bordo's account of Cartesian dualism, Nicholson's discussion of individualism, as well as institutionalist critiques of mainstream economic theories portraying the market as rational and universal.

These patterns of metaphorical linkage and dualistic exclusion explain the historical origin of "economic man." "Economic" and "man" have been linked in social understandings that also have imbued the competitive struggles of economic man with historical rationality. Both "woman" and "the familial" have been excluded from this social Darwinist teleology. When the familial or woman is considered explicitly, each is found to differ from, and to be deficient with respect to, the culturally prioritized category. Although they may have their own virtues, these categories are viewed as being insufficiently rational and insufficiently competitive; history leaves them behind. The prominence of the term "economic man" is an artifact originating in nineteenth-century cultural interpretations, which conflated man with dynamic market activity and woman with unchanging familial roles.[15]

The conflation of women with the family, expressed in the nineteenth-century cult of domesticity, remains deeply embedded in our culture. This may explain why so many feminists, determined to challenge women's disadvantaged status, still uncritically accept the notion that gender is rooted in the family. However, it is the association of women with the family and of

15. It is interesting that the dislocations caused by economic change are often regarded as necessary to discipline the lazy and weed out the uncompetitive, while changes in family structure are greeted with dire warnings. Fears about the decline of the American family—usually referring to the incidence of women having sole responsibility for the economic well-being of the household—were expressed as early as the nineteenth century. They are often used today to advocate the reinforcement of traditional familial norms rather than to champion the improvement of market prospects for women.

men with the market economy, and their dualistic separation, that has been the main foundation of gender distinction since the nineteenth century.

The social concept of economic man also has an anchor on the economy/state side of the double dualism. A second list of opposing concepts can be presented, although it is somewhat shorter because it does not carry the main burden of gender distinctions. Such a list might read:

private / public

(market) economy / state

individual / social

amoral / moral

freedom / regulation

enterprise / constraint

efficiency / inefficiency

objective / subjective

science / politics

In these constructions private outranks public, as in the ideology of laissez-faire and homage to free private enterprise, displacing the seventeenth-century prioritization of public political activity. Vestiges of the state/household split continued into the nineteenth century, however, in that the economic and the familial aspects of the earlier household remained distinguished from the state. Economic man is not viewed as a political animal, and market economy and the state do not share "the public sphere." The state likewise continued to be opposed to the considerably narrowed family, although individuals' terms of access to the political sphere were no longer as important as their terms of access to the market.

The declining importance of the political relative to the economic sphere may also explain why nineteenth-century feminists were far more successful in acquiring political rights than economic rights for women. The new definition of women as noneconomic beings was crucial to the interpretation of their roles in pecuniary society whereas their former definition as nonpolitical beings was no longer essential to that interpretation (Jennings 1992b).

The two halves of the double dualism reveal interesting relationships when combined. First, individualism in a market society involves the prescriptive freedom of economic enterprise from political interference on the one hand, and prescriptive gender distinctions between women's and men's status as economic individuals on the other hand. Second, the two sets of dualisms define the market as being more objective and rational than either political processes or familial principles; they define economics as scientific in contrast to politics, the humanities, and sociology.[16]

16. This second point offers an interesting perspective on recent comparable worth debates. Neoclassical economists tend to argue against comparable worth on the grounds that political

This approach not only offers a novel interpretation of the relationship between dualistic constructions and social hierarchy; it also reinterprets the individualistic premises of mainstream economic theory as exclusionary and constitutes a critique of the "animating myths" of our culture (Jones 1983). As Ayres (1961) noted, such myths are used to preserve rank and privilege. They serve to universalize existing conditions, justify cultural distinctions, and inform us of the catastrophic consequences of violating sacred taboos.

"Economism," the social prioritizing of market processes as the desiderata of social well-being and a basic principle of mainstream economic theory, is a cultural myth with quasi-religious status that perpetuates itself by exclusion and invidious distinction. It is also a Procrustean bed that accommodates the historical record only by dismissing its own origins, along with other inconvenient information. In part because our compartmentalized notions are falsely universalized, we are blinded to alternative interpretations; we see distinctions between social spheres as functionally necessary and fail to note how dualistic interpretations are central to our traditional views of knowledge itself. The recognition that knowledge is culturally determined leads to an understanding of cultural continuity that challenges dualistic constructions and compartmentalizations, and prompts the suspicion that our myths do not describe the historical record very well.

Human activities regularly have transgressed the nineteenth-century boundaries between spheres. Ironically, those transgressions often have been pursued in the name of laissez-faire or separate gender spheres. For example, both the creation of "social homemaking" professions for woman and the suffrage movement often relied on an idea of women's special moral and maternal nature to gain access for women to public spheres (Matthaei 1982; Degler 1980). These struggles exploited the ambiguity of social meanings that results from the basic multidimensionality of human thought and activities. Such multidimensionality, which challenges the facile compartmentalization of activities and roles, must be denied by conservative interests seeking to sustain existing categorizations and distinctions.

The historical record does not show that women were economically inactive during the nineteenth century but rather reveals cultural prescriptions of economic inactivity. Actual activity was often disguised to conform to cultural norms (Goldin 1990). The record also reveals that gender and class distinctions were closely related. The dominant norms of gender were associated with the middle class while the working class, for the most part, could only aspire to those norms. The ability of a household to achieve "proper" gender

---

evaluation of the skill content of jobs is subjective, whereas "impersonal" market forces are seen as objective (Raisian et al. 1988). Feminist institutionalism finds such distinctions both fictional and invidious.

roles was an important component of social standing. Such issues form the context for understanding struggles over the "family wage" (Jennings and Waller 1990b). In the United States gender norms have informed and sustained racial distinctions as well. African-Americans have long been chastised for not sustaining proper gender roles, and their families have been described as pathological (Moynihan 1965).[17]

The boundary between the state and the economy is much more ambiguous than the boundary between the family and the economy. Under laissez-faire the state is to provide only those goods and services that the market cannot provide. Such a "rule" is compatible with most political interventions short of price controls. Yet it still leaves the principle of nonintervention comfortably intact for elites to assert when they choose. U.S. federal government actions in markets were modest prior to the New Deal, but interventions by state and local governments, as well as by the judiciary, were far more frequent and more substantial (Horwitz 1977; Katznelson 1985; Skocpol and Ikenberry 1983). Thus, laissez-faire is largely mythical and misleading, despite its importance as a taboo on public policy that might upset the status quo of privilege and rank.

The bifurcations, fictions, and blindness associated with dualistic beliefs tend to close off the range of possibilities for the future. Under the double dualism political processes are interpreted as socially ineffectual and are usually denied the resources they need to promote social change. Remedying women's noneconomic status or rectifying market inequities will rarely be attempted if "politics" are successfully portrayed as being less rational than the "apolitical" market, and if women's socially assigned roles are seen as natural, unchanging, and distinct from more worthy "economic" roles. Yet cultural interpretations do change in response to both evolving circumstances and social struggles to reinterpret reality. These struggles are not over. The task of feminist economics is to assist in creating possibilities for a better future by illuminating the blindness of both past and present social interpretations.

Concluding Remarks

The lesson of feminist institutionalism is that cultural reality must be reinterpreted according to the principles of continuity, antidualism, and historical substance. "Economistic" beliefs must be challenged as hierarchical and invidious, and economic principles must be reconnected to the full range of human activities, most of which have provisioning significance (though

17. Gender norms are clearly not the only constituent of race distinctions in the United States, and no reductionism is intended here. Elsewhere I have advocated the black feminist position that race, gender, and class distinctions are "simultaneous" and mutually informing (Jennings 1992a).

sometimes negative), as well as to the political and reproductive aspects of those activities. Feminist and institutionalist theories are often in substantial agreement; both point to the need for nonexclusionary theory, policy, and everyday behavior. In this essay I have emphasized theory. But policies flow from cultural interpretations, and in the modern age of professionalization, theory is a potent expression of cultural belief and practice.

One final point about the exclusionary nature of conventional economics must be made. Neoclassical economists recently have applied their tools in the "new home economics" and in the "new political economy," thus extending the definition of the economy to include the family and the political arena. This does not, however, overcome compartmentalization; rather, it reflects the continuing dominance of individualism and market economy, still rooted in dualistic separations. The new home economics effectively strengthens women's association with domestic roles and justifies their low wages by linking them to economic self-interest (Becker 1981; Jennings and Waller 1990a). The effect of the new political economy, meanwhile, is to deny any real possibility of political action that is not self-interested; it largely erases "the social" from theoretical vocabularies in favor of "the individual" (Buchanan and Tollison 1984). Hence these new theories retain economic individualism, its social premises, and its support for existing social distinctions.

From the perspective of feminist institutionalism, the solution to "economism" is a cultural reconnection of home, workplace, and polity that recognizes the reproductive, productive, and political aspects of most human activities in all institutional settings and in all social milieux. Only when this happens can established beliefs in the essential dissimilarity of spheres, pursuits, and social groups—the precondition for devaluation—be transformed. What is separate is rarely, if ever, equal.

References

Amsden, Alice. 1980. *The Economics of Women and Work.* New York: St. Martin's Press.

Ayres, Clarence. 1961. *Toward a Reasonable Society.* Austin: University of Texas Press.

Becker, Gary S. 1981. *A Treatise on the Family.* Cambridge, Mass.: Harvard University Press.

Bordo, Susan. 1987. *The Flight to Objectivity.* Albany: SUNY Press.

Brown, Clair. 1982. "Home Production for Use in a Market Economy." In *Rethinking the Family,* ed. Barrie Thorne and Marilyn Yalom, 151–67. New York: Longman.

———. 1988. "Income Distribution in an Institutional World." In *Three*

Worlds of Labor Economics, ed. Garth Mangum and Peter Philips, 51–63. Armonk, N.Y.: M. E. Sharpe.

Buchanan, James, and Robert Tollison. 1984. *The Theory of Public Choice.* Ann Arbor: University of Michigan Press.

Bush, Paul D. 1986. "On the Concept of Ceremonial Encapsulation." *Review of Institutionalist Thought* 3:25–45.

Cain, Glen. 1976. "The Challenge of Segmented Labor Market Theory to Orthodox Theory: A Survey." *Journal of Economic Literature* 14:1215–57.

Degler, Carl. 1980. *At Odds: Women and the Family in America from the Revolution to the Present.* New York: Oxford University Press.

Dewey, John. 1929. *The Quest for Certainty.* New York: Capricorn Books.

Dugger, William. 1983. "The Transaction Cost Approach of Oliver E. Williamson." *Journal of Economic Issues* 17:95–114.

Gilman, Charlotte Perkins. 1966 [1898]. *Women and Economics.* New York: Harper & Row.

Goldin, Claudia. 1990. *Understanding the Gender Gap: An Economic History of American Women.* New York: Oxford University Press.

Greenwood, Daphne. 1984. "The Economic Significance of 'Women's Place' in Society: A New-Institutionalist View." *Journal of Economic Issues* 18:663–80.

Harding, Sandra. 1986. *The Science Question in Feminism.* Ithaca, N.Y.: Cornell University Press.

———. 1987. "The Instability of the Analytical Categories of Feminist Theory." In *Sex and Scientific Inquiry,* ed. Harding and Jean O'Barr, 283–302. Chicago: University of Chicago Press.

Hirschman, Albert. 1977. *The Passions and the Interests.* Princeton, N.J.: Princeton University Press.

Horwitz, Morton. 1977. *The Transformation of American Law.* Cambridge, Mass.: Harvard University Press.

Jaggar, Alison. 1983. *Feminist Politics and Human Nature.* Totowa, N.J.: Rowman and Allenheld.

Jennings, Ann. 1992a. "The Cultural Contours of Race, Gender, and Class Distinctions." Rev. ed. of paper presented at the Institutionalist Conference on Gender, Flagstaff, Ariz., 1991.

———. 1992b. "Not the Economy." In *The Stratified State,* ed. William Dugger and William Waller. Armonk, N.Y.: M. E. Sharpe.

———, and William Waller. 1990a. "Constructions of Social Hierarchy." *Journal of Economic Issues* 24:623–32.

———, and William Waller. 1990b. "Rethinking Class and Social Stratification." Paper presented at the annual meeting of the Southern Economics Association, New Orleans.

———, and William Waller. 1992. "Evolutionary Economics and Cultural

Hermeneutics: Beyond Blind Drift?" Paper presented at the annual meeting of the Association for Evolutionary Economics, New Orleans.

Jones, Gareth Stedman. 1983. *Languages of Class.* Cambridge: Cambridge University Press.

Junker, Louis. 1983. "The Conflict between the Scientific-Technological Process and Malignant Ceremonialism." *American Journal of Economics and Sociology* 42:341–51.

Katznelson, Ira. 1985. "Working Class Formation and the State." In *Bringing the State Back In,* ed. Peter Evans, Dietrich Rueschemeyer, and Theda Skocpol, 257–84. New York: Cambridge University Press.

Langer, Gary. 1987. *The Coming of Age of Political Economy, 1815–1825.* New York: Greenwood.

Longino, Helen. 1992. "Essential Tensions—Phase Two: Feminist, Philosophical, and Social Studies of Science." In *The Social Dimensions of Science,* ed. Ernan McMullin, 198–216. South Bend, Ind.: Notre Dame University Press.

Matthaei, Julie. 1982. *An Economic History of Women in America.* New York: Schocken.

Moynihan, Daniel P., for the U.S. Department of Labor, Office of Policy Planning. *The Negro Family: The Case for National Action.* Washington, D.C.: U.S. Government Printing Office.

Nicholson, Linda. 1986. *Gender and History.* New York: Columbia University Press.

Piore, Michael. 1983. "Labor Market Segmentation: To What Paradigm Does It Belong?" *American Economic Review* 73:249–53.

Polanyi, Karl. 1944. *The Great Transformation.* Boston: Beacon Books.

Pollak, Robert. 1985. "A Transactions Cost Approach to Families and Households." *Journal of Economic Literature* 23:581–608.

Raisian, John, et al. 1988. "Implementing Comparable Worth." In *Three Worlds of Labor Economics,* ed. Garth Mangum and Peter Philips, 183–200. Armonk, N.Y.: M. E. Sharpe.

Rosaldo, Michelle. 1980. "The Use and Abuse of Anthropology." *Signs* 5:391–417.

Sahlins, Marshall. 1976. *Culture and Practical Reason.* Chicago: University of Chicago Press.

Skocpol, Theda, and John Ikenberry. 1983. "The Political Formation of the American Welfare State." In *Comparative Social Research,* vol. 6, ed. Richard Tomasson, 98–119. Greenwich, Conn.: JAI Press.

Strober, Myra, and Carolyn Arnold. 1987. "The Dynamics of Occupational Segregation by Gender: Bank Tellers (1950–1980)." In *Gender in the Workplace,* ed. Clair Brown and Joseph Pechman. Washington, D.C.: Brookings Institution.

Tilman, Rick. 1990. "Dewey, Ayres, and the Development of Evolutionary Economics." *Journal of Economic Issues* 24:963–79.

Veblen, Thorstein. 1899. *The Theory of the Leisure Class*. New York: Mentor.

———. 1904. *The Theory of Business Enterprise*. New York: Mentor.

———. 1934. *Essays in Our Changing Order*. New York: Augustus M. Kelley.

———. 1961 [1901]. "Industrial and Pecuniary Employments." In *The Place of Science in Modern Civilization*, 279–323. New York: Russell and Russell.

Waller, William, and Ann Jennings. 1990. "On the Possibility of a Feminist Economics: The Convergence of Institutional and Feminist Methodology." *Journal of Economic Issues* 24:613–22.

Williamson, Oliver, et al. 1975. "Understanding the Employment Relationship: The Analysis of Idiosyncratic Exchange." *Bell Journal of Economics* (Spring): 250–78.

7

Rebecca M. Blank
Rhonda M. Williams
Robert M. Solow
Helen E. Longino

Discussion and Challenges

Rebecca M. Blank

What Should Mainstream Economists Learn from Feminist Theory?

I come to my role as a discussant for this volume with some hesitation. These chapters attempt to define a new approach to economics, informed by feminist theory. As an empirical labor economist who works predominantly in the mainstream tradition of economics, probably the best I can say to justify my role as a discussant is that I've read more feminist literature than most economists. But as anyone who knows the economics profession will realize, this is faint justification indeed. Such a claim can probably be made by any person who once glanced at a book in the women's studies section of the bookstore. I have read with interest, however, feminist scholarship in other branches of the social sciences, and I am deeply interested in the emergence of feminist scholarship within economics. My comments on this volume will give particular attention to the arguments in the chapters by Julie Nelson, Ann Jennings, Nancy Folbre, and Donald McCloskey.

In the time-honored tradition of placing one's biases up front, I should note that I come to this volume with a great deal of sympathy for what it is trying to do. I freely admit to dissatisfaction with some of the assumptions and applications of mainstream economics, dissatisfaction that is closely related to many of the issues discussed in this book. I came to economics out of an interest in social science and human behavior. Too often, during a seminar or a conversation with a colleague, I've suddenly realized with surprise, "He really *believes* all this stuff about individuals constantly making fully informed and rational choices accounting for all expected lifetime costs and benefits." It never occurred to me, even in graduate school, that this model was meant to be more than a partial picture of reality. It is perhaps a stereotypical female reaction to say that by the time I was old enough to be in graduate school the rational economic choice model just felt wrong for certain situations and problems. (Although I knew from late-night conversations with fellow graduate students that this reaction was surely not limited to women.) The analytical cleanliness and mathematical manipulability of the economic model, while enormously attractive intellectually, was never convincing enough to overcome my intuitive reaction: "This model should never be confused with reality." Thus, I continue to be somewhat amused and somewhat appalled when I meet those true-believer economists who think that they

Thanks are due to Jane Mansbridge, James Montgomery, Robert Pollak, and the editors of this volume for useful comments on earlier drafts of this chapter.

really understand human behavior because they understand the economic model of human behavior.

Unlike some of the authors in this book, however, I continue to find the economic model of choice-based behavior an extremely powerful and useful analytical tool. I place myself firmly in that group of female economists described by Marianne Ferber and Julie Nelson—"feminist empiricists" who believe that much of the problem in economics lies not with the model itself but with its interpretation and use. In other words, I have little difficulty using the economic model as an analytical tool in my own work, much of which is concerned with labor market behavior and the interaction between public policy and the labor market. I will discuss what I consider to be the real analytical attractions of the economic model of choice below. Yet I am critical of the way others use this model at times. Because economists are not trained to understand the limitations of their models, the choice model is too often used to draw sweeping conclusions from uncomfortably narrow evidence.

A Critical View of the Current Economics Profession

The authors in this book use feminist perspectives to criticize the economics profession in two ways. First, they detail the unique and important ways in which gender interacts with the economic structure of society. They argue that the economic decisions and constraints faced by women—the economic reality of their world—differ consistently and substantially from the economic reality faced by men. The authors claim that past and current economic analysis has, at worst, actively denied this fact, or, at best, ignored it or only partially attempted to understand it. This criticism applies not only to mainstream economics. Nancy Folbre shows how Marx and Engels devalued the role of gender in their analysis. Ann Jennings attempts to integrate a fuller understanding of gender into institutional economics.

The call to include the specific concerns of women and to be aware of the effects of gender in the economy runs through all of the chapters in this book. Other than noting that I am in strong agreement, I will say little more about this argument in these comments. In far too many cases, economists generalize about household and individual behavior from studies based on male behavior. There is substantial evidence that in many situations women face different constraints than men. In the standard economic model, this means that they will make different choices and face different outcomes. It is crucial that we understand the differences in the constraints that affect women's behavior if we want to claim to understand economic behavior in general.

The second (and much more important and fundamental) argument of the book, however, is the claim that economics needs to be redefined and reformed. The inadequacy of the economic treatment of gender issues is used to introduce a broader criticism of economics. As Donald McCloskey would say, in these chapters the treatment of gender in economics functions as a metaphor for a larger set of problems within the discipline. The authors call for reevaluation and revision of widely held assumptions about how economics is defined and about what good economic research should require. Hence, these chapters reflect the widely held view among feminist scholars that feminist theory is concerned with far more than gender issues and that it provides an alternative perspective on all aspects of social analysis. Writing from a feminist perspective, these authors argue for remaking the entire discipline of economics.

There is actually substantial agreement among the authors in this volume on the general nature of the changes that should be considered. I would broadly characterize these arguments by saying that the authors want to make economics a more *inclusive* discipline. They propose three particular ways of doing this.

First, several authors explicitly call for greater inclusiveness in the definition of economics. Julie Nelson and Ann Jennings both trace the historical development of the science of economics, indicating how the definition of the study of economics narrowed over time. They argue that economics has come to be defined as "the market." In fact, Nelson argues that the discipline has even, at times, come to define itself not by its subject matter but by its model of behavior: economics is "choice theory." Both authors argue that economic science should be broadened to include a wider range of issues. Nelson wants economics to be known as "the study of the basis of human material welfare," focusing on the "provisioning" of human life. Jennings calls for a redefinition of "economic" pursuits. McCloskey's discussion of the need to include women's home production in the measurement of gross national product echoes this same concern.

These authors are trying to develop a humanistic definition of economics as well. Nelson's attempt to define economics as concerned with human welfare encourages a communal perspective on the sharing of economic resources. The emphasis is shifted from efficiency to well-being and equity. This is in the philosophical tradition of Rawls, who argues that a society must consider the well-being of its worst-off member. It is in the public policy tradition which argues that the defining question for public policy should be "what does it do for the poor?"

Redefining economics, however, is only part of the challenge. These authors also favor greater inclusiveness in the methodologies economics uses to explore the world. Nelson argues that economic truth can emerge both from "rigorous" mathematical and logical analysis and from more intuitive ways of knowing. She refers to this latter form of reasoning as "reasoning beyond logic" or as "imaginative rationality." This is the primary point of McCloskey's chapter as well. He proposes a new term for what he seeks economics to be, a *conjective* science, which uses fact and logic as well as metaphor and story to develop its arguments.

Both of these authors emphasize this is not an either-or choice: fact and logic are informed by story and metaphor, and vice versa. They do not argue that economics should leave its mathematical equations behind but that it should include forms of proof that are not mathematical as well as those that are. From a feminist perspective, Nelson describes this as recognizing that there are both good and bad elements in hard "masculine" logic, and good and bad elements in "feminine" intuitive reasoning. Both are strengthened when they are used together to test and check one another.

The third way in which these scholars propose to change the structure of the discipline of economics is by moving away from individualistic models toward more inclusive models of human behavior. All of the papers in this volume criticize the focus of most of modern economics on individuals as separative selves who make autonomous decisions. Jennings wants to eliminate dualistic thinking that separates economic decisions from familial or public decisions. She wants to emphasize the shared cultural determinants of human behavior. Folbre questions the focus on public/private boundaries coming out of traditional Marxist analysis. McCloskey suggests that economists should recognize the fact that the world would be better if we all behaved as if we were from Iowa, i.e., as if we all had a sense of shared responsibility.

Criticism of the assumption of autonomous individuals within standard economic models is not unique to feminism. Other disciplines have long criticized economics for assuming preferences are fixed and separate across individuals. Models of human development in psychology often emphasize the dependence of individual decisions on the opinions of peers or older role models. Models of cultural determinism in sociology emphasize the role of group norms or ethnic ties on individual behavior. It would be interesting to see how a feminist model of personal interconnectedness differs from these other theoretical approaches, and also how it differs from the growing economics literature on altruism or linked preferences.

It probably does not need to be said that these proposed changes are fundamental and radical to modern economics. As Jennings notes, this is not just a call to "add women" to economic models; this is a call to change the whole structure of how economists think and how they conduct their research.

What's Missing?

These chapters provide some indications of how a restructured "feminist economics" might differ from the existing mainstream approaches. But a reader who hopes to glean a clear model of feminist economics from this book will come away disappointed. It is surely setting far too strong a standard to ask for a fully developed model at this stage of analysis. New paradigms are developed over time; they gain structure and complexity as more people become interested in them. Because scholars have just begun to apply feminist theory to economics, it seems somewhat churlish to complain that the full model isn't clear yet. But there are some crucial gaps in these chapters.

The feminist economics literature is too caught up in criticizing what it does not like in the existing work of the economics profession and has not yet adequately focused on clearly defining an alternative. Any new theoretical approach grows out of accumulated dissatisfaction with existing work. And it is perhaps a truism that it is always easier to criticize what you do not like than to construct it in a different way. But at some point, if a perspective is to gain long-term legitimacy, it must shift from criticism to construction.

I admit to some impatience, in particular, with extensive analysis of how the development of science went wrong in the seventeenth century with Descartes. There is an extensive and growing literature by feminist social scientists that analyzes the evolution of science across the past several centuries and points out how the individualistic, math-bound "masculine" approach to science has come to dominate and devalue the intuitive and inclusive "feminine" approach. Almost all of the papers in this volume reference and reiterate this literature. Let me be clear that I am not expressing impatience with critical historical analysis per se; in order to understand where we are now we must understand how we got here. But this sort of historical research is not going to produce a persuasive and usable model of feminist economics for the next generation of scholars.

Feminist scholars need to be explicit about what they would include in a broader definition of the "economic realm." They need to be explicit in modeling individual interconnectedness within families and within communities, to show how these models produce new insights for both macroeconomic and microeconomic behavior. They need to provide concrete examples of research that utilizes broader methodologies to produce more informative and more convincing empirical results than traditional economic approaches do. To gain wider interest and respect within the profession, feminist economists must move from historical analysis and general theoretical statements of principle to clearly constructed models of human behavior, whose implications and structure can be compared to existing models.

I was disappointed at how few attempts were made in this volume to provide actual examples of how a feminist focus on economic behavior would lead to new insights. If we redefine economics in the more inclusive way Nelson suggests, which issues would we look at differently? Are there examples where certain individuals are already pursuing such work? If we include more historical/cultural specificity in economic models as Jennings urges us to do, how would this change our view of economic behavior? How well do current attempts to link cultural and economic issues accomplish what Jennings wants to see done?

The only author who attempts to provide an explicit sense of how existing economic models would be changed with more feminist analysis is Mc-Closkey. He cites several examples of how specific economic approaches (Becker's theory of the family, the valuation of life, the understanding of self-interested behavior) might change with more inclusive and feminist thinking. I found this among the most useful reading in the volume.

I was struck by the lack of examples in most of these chapters partly because I have a sense that a number of economic researchers are already trying to do what these authors are calling for. Let me give two examples. First, within the literature on poverty there has been a vast explosion of interest among both economists and sociologists in "neighborhood effects"—the effect of the attitudes and behaviors of one's neighbors on an individual's propensity to work, drop out of school, become pregnant, or use welfare. Such an attempt to study the links between economic and family behavior and social networks strikes me as very close to Jennings's call to link cultural and economic factors.[1] Second, there is a growing body of work on immigration that focuses explicitly on ethnic differences between different immigrant groups. This literature explores the overlap between ethnic background and economic opportunities, and the manner in which different immigrant groups enter and make their way through the U.S. labor market.[2] Such work surely reflects an effort to use a more inclusive definition of "economic influences."

I do not believe any of the researchers working on these topics would define themselves as "feminist economists," yet their approaches seem at least consistent with the desire expressed in this volume for more inclusive models of economic behavior. I would like to see those who want to pursue feminist models evaluate this existing literature and indicate how they would alter or add to it, or present their own examples of good feminist economic research.

The Strengths of the Mainstream Economic Model of Human Behavior

Despite ongoing challenges from many fronts, the mainstream model of rational choice behavior has proved to be remarkably durable. If

1. For instance, see the theoretical work by James Montgomery,"Is Underclass Behavior Contagious? A Rational-Choice Analysis," Center for Urban Affairs Working Paper WP-90-9, Northwestern University, 1990, or see the empirical work by Anne Case and Lawrence Katz, "The Company You Keep: The Effects of Family and Neighborhood in Disadvantaged Youths," National Bureau of Economic Research Working Paper No. 3705, May 1991.

2. For instance, see the recent book by George Borjas, *Friends or Strangers* (New York: Basic Books, 1990), or the research by Cordelia Reimers, such as "Cultural Differences in Labor Force Participation among Married Women," *American Economic Review* 75 (May 1985): 251–55.

feminist economists hope to make inroads against this model and implement the reforms they call for, they must confront directly the perceived strengths of the choice-based model of economic behavior.

I want to say a few words of support for individual choice models, perhaps a foolish task in this volume, but one I nonetheless think is useful. What is it that the rational choice model does well, which feminist models will have to deal with? Or, stated more personally, with all the problems I have with certain widely used assumptions within mainstream economics, why do I continue to utilize such models?

First, the mainstream economic model provides a null hypothesis: people's choices are based on informed, autonomous decisions made under the conditions of a competitive market. You might believe this extremely simple null hypothesis is wrong 98 percent of the time in the real world. I'd be sympathetic. But as an analytical device, a standardized and widely accepted null hypothesis is a wonderful thing to have. It is relatively easy to be clear in speaking to my colleagues about my assumptions in any particular piece of research: I am going to assume a lack of accurate information, the presence of uncertainty, the existence of monopoly, or the presence of discontinuous institutional constraints in the labor market. Even economists who believe that the assumptions of the simple model of economic behavior are unlikely to be true nonetheless find it a useful "defining device" they can evoke as a "base case," from which they then can develop more realistic variations.

Second, the mainstream model has powerful predictive ability in a number of situations that are common in industrialized societies. I do not have to believe that economic incentives fully determine behavior in order to believe that economic incentives matter at the margin for behavior. Even in situations where choices are extremely bounded, it can still be useful to analyze the situation as one where the participants choose the best option. It becomes an empirical question whether these choice effects are large or small.

I am particularly convinced of the usefulness of the standard economic model in which choice-based behavior responds to economic incentives for analyzing public policy questions. For a whole host of reasons, most industrialized societies have only a limited set of preferred public policy levers and these tend to be incentive-oriented rather than mandated. It is expensive to enforce behavior, and strong government mandates often go against the grain of democratic principles; thus most governments would like to run programs that will produce compliance without extensive monitoring. In addition, most industrialized societies are filled with individuals and families who have become "market-oriented" and who do see themselves as having choices over at least some range of issues. Thus, for many relevant policy questions, economic models are useful. What happens if the government cuts college subsidies to the middle class? What happens if Mississippi raises its welfare payments? What happens if legislation is passed to regulate automotive emissions?

I do not know of a better model than the standard economic model as a first-pass, simple, and reasonably reliable way to answer such questions in a consistent manner. Of course, the magnitude of response will vary among different cultures, different ethnic groups, different family settings, and different age groups. But that just says we should not assume the economic model gives us a complete answer, merely that it gives us a way to think coherently about some of the important responses with which we are concerned. The wise researcher will always be concerned about the interactions of his or her model with a broader range of variables, including race, age, gender, and ethnic background.

Third, with some hesitation, I will note as an advantage the ease with which the standard economic model can be directly translated into tractable mathematical forms. I say this with hesitation because I have real sympathy for McCloskey's description of the problems that such a link between economics and mathematics has generated. It has limited too many economic researchers to only those questions that can be tractably dealt with in elegant mathematics, so "interesting economics" becomes limited by mathematical rigor. But the fact that mathematical elegance has drawbacks does not refute the fact that it also has advantages. Cumulation of knowledge in the social sciences requires theoretical precision. Mathematical formalism is one way (though not the only way) to produce theoretical precision. As such, the high degree of mathematical rigor in economics creates a clear sense of what we know and what we don't know, at least within certain limits: We know which problems have been "solved" and which have not. This helps us to understand the current boundaries of the discipline and to evaluate the contribution of new research. The real sophistication we have gained over the last decade about the effect of imperfect information or future risk and uncertainty on the behavior of individuals and firms has been possible only because of the insights gained through abstract and formalized mathematical models.

In short, even as I agree with many of the limitations and problems that economics faces because of its insistence on a relatively simple underlying model of maximizing choice in competitive equilibrium, I also think it is important to recognize some of the real benefits that have emerged from that model.

Is "Feminist Economics" the Best Label for a New Economic Paradigm?

As noted above, the treatment of gender in standard economic analysis is used as a metaphor in this volume for a broader set of problems in economic theory. The authors argue that a new "feminist economics" could provide a better explanation of human behavior over a broader range of economic situations. I am somewhat more hesitant about the use of gender as the organizing principle around which the economic model can best be criticized. While I largely agree that economics has dealt rather inadequately with many gender-related issues, I am not persuaded that the most convincing criticism of economic models emerges from a feminist or gender-based lens.

Rather, the assumption that I find most problematic in the standard economic model is that in all cases *choice* is taken as the most useful characterization of how individuals respond to their social and economic environment. Our prototypical story about economic behavior describes an *empowered* individual. This is a person (male or female) who has a sense of choice in his or her life, who consciously seeks information on a broad range of subjects, and who engages in conscious and rational planning with the expectation that it will produce better results. In short, this is a person with a sense of control over his or her life, who perceives choices and acts on them. There is not a glimmer in this basic model that any individual might ever feel dominated, oppressed, passive, stuck, ill, unsure about his or her abilities, or unaware of alternatives. There is no recognition that many people in many situations will not perceive that any choices are available to them.

There is truth in the standard economic model, but it is only a partial truth. As a representation of white, middle-income persons in a democratic, industrialized, and Westernized society, it is probably a very good approximation of reality. It is really quite effective at predicting how people in these societies go about acquiring education, finding jobs, or responding to government policies. But the farther one moves away from empowered, in-control Westernized individuals, the less attractive this model becomes as a paradigm for individual behavior. People who study street-corner society in extremely poor urban ghettos will tell you that this is not how their subjects think about life; social workers who deal with abused women and children will tell you this does not describe their clients' behavioral patterns. This does not say the model is useless; it merely says that the choice-based behavior such a model posits may be more dominant in certain situations than in others.

At no point in the last two paragraphs have I made any explicit reference to feminist theory. Although these arguments could be developed out of a feminist perspective, they could be developed out of other psychological, sociological, or institutional perspectives as well. The inadequacy of economics in dealing with gender-related issues is only one aspect of the overall "partial truth" nature of the economic model of behavior. Just as this model has not always adequately described the full range of forces that motivate the behavior of many women, so it has inadequately described the full range of experiences of many low-income men, many nonwhite men and women, and many nonassimilated immigrants.

Thus, if we are to work on developing alternatives to the standard economic model—a task I strongly applaud—it strikes me as not necessarily useful to identify this alternative as "feminist." While recognizing that feminism involves far more than gender, the name still raises the presumption that gender issues are the predominant concern. I would prefer language that is open to a wider range of persons, who might share many of the feminist concerns with the current state of economics but who arrive at this point through a variety of nongender-related issues. In this way, I like McCloskey's attempt to coin a new word, conjective economics, to describe what is being done. I admit, however, that I don't like the term "conjective" itself. It isn't as resonant a term as I'd like and it conveys no sense of its meaning to the uninformed reader, but it does have the advantage of sounding quite "scientific," thereby soothing all those "masculine" scientific types who will be suspicious of this enterprise.

The Problems Faced by a Discipline with Only One Widely Used Model

The heavy reliance on a single model of individual behavior in economics has some real disciplinary advantages. It provides a strong sense of cohesion among economists, for we are all trained to speak the same language. It makes it easy to define the core economics curriculum for graduate study. It makes it possible to readily translate work across fields, applying developments in one area of economics to other areas. It may decrease some of the internecine feuding that goes on within any discipline. But there are also real costs associated with such heavy reliance on a single model. Even if I were entirely satisfied with the broad applicability of the standard economic model to a wider range of human behaviors, I still could see the advantages of some degree of theoretical diversity within the discipline.

Some will argue that the remarkable perseverance of the economic model as a tool used by economists is proof of its accuracy and reliability. But when one particular approach becomes predominant, its use can become self-fulfilling. If the "standard economic model" is what you must believe in order to do good (or at least disciplinarily acceptable) economics, then anyone interested in pursuing other approaches is by definition "not an economist" and is discouraged from entering the profession.

In introductory undergraduate microeconomics courses I have the sense that the following scenario is frequent: out of a class of one hundred students, ninety-nine will listen to the lectures and think to themselves, "Although interesting, this is sort of crazy; nobody really thinks this way." Those students do what they must to pass the course and forget it soon afterwards. But the one remaining person in that class lights up. This is almost always a male. He realizes this model describes the way that he thinks and acts. To that person, the economic model *is* intuitively obvious. It is that one person who is most likely to become an economist. Small wonder then that fifteen years later, sitting around the lunch table with a group of other similar selectively chosen economists, everyone believes that the standard economic model indeed describes how most people think about the world. It's certainly the way most people who choose to study economics think about the world.

I've recently started teaching an intermediate microeconomics class to a group of noneconomics social science Ph.D. students. These are not undergraduates coming to class without any patterned beliefs about human behavior. The class is a mix of people trained to think in terms of specific theories common in psychology, human development, and sociology. They find the economic model extremely interesting, but none of them find it very plausible. It turns on no light bulbs in their heads—they do not think this way nor do they believe others think this way. They can recognize the usefulness of the model, and I can get most of the class to "think like an economist" about the effects and implications of policy changes. But they are really baffled when confronted with a reading from one of the economic "true believers," someone who thinks this model accurately describes the core aspects of a wide range of human behavior. They come to discussion section with a list of alternative theories of human behavior and ask, "How can economics ignore these other perspectives?"

The danger of having a discipline centered around only one model of behavior is that there is little incentive for anyone within that discipline to explore beyond that model. There is no encouragement to read theories of adult development and aging or to be familiar with ethnographic descriptions of particular communities. The discipline limits the wisdom it allows itself to use by providing no reward to those who seek additional sources of knowledge. There is little to be lost and potentially much to be gained if the economics discipline were to accept a wider range of theoretical and methodological approaches as valid forms of economic inquiry.

This volume presents some beginning attempts to move economics toward a more diverse set of models. Through feminist theory, the authors argue for making economics more inclusive, both in its theory and in its methodology. These authors argue that there are many paths to truth, and that economics would be better off if it recognized and encouraged more of those paths. While I do not think that "feminist economics" is yet at the point where it provides a usable alternative model of economic decision-making, I strongly support the effort of this book to push the discipline into broader ways of thinking and doing economics.

Rhonda M. Williams

Race, Deconstruction, and the Emergent Agenda of Feminist Economic Theory

Feminists in dialogue with post-structuralist theory continue to critique the incompleteness of analytic and political projects that employ "women" as an already constituted and undifferentiated group, and "gender" as a stable social and symbolic category. By expanding discussions developed in the introduction, this essay explores the extent to which the chapters in this volume universalize gender categories and the specific theoretical consequences of that tendency. I begin by developing at greater length the "curious coincidence" to which Ferber and Nelson allude in their introductory chapter, i.e., Sandra Harding's analysis of the similarities between some feminist and Africanist worldviews.[1] By way of making concrete my argument for a feminist economic theory that explicitly deconstructs[2] the differences masked in our binary oppositions, I argue the importance of racializing our theorizing of gender.

As several authors in this volume observe, many (although not exclusively) feminist theorists have noted that post-Enlightenment Western philosophy is rooted in a deeply gendered web of conceptual dualisms: objectivity vs. subjectivity, reason vs. emotion, culture vs. nature, positive vs. normative, mind vs. body, public vs. private, quantitative vs. qualitative, etc. Modern science identifies masculinity with the first term of each pair, femininity with the second. The presumption of fixed opposition conceals the hierarchical interdependence of these terms and the extent to which they depend on one another for their meanings.

These Cartesian-inspired dualisms mark the methods and self-understanding of many contemporary economic theorists. Thus Nelson explains how the professional hegemony of choice-theoretic economics both obscures and devalues other ways of knowing, and Jennings's analysis of the gendered dualism of pecuniary culture unveils the genealogy of "economic man." England convincingly demonstrates the Cartesian roots of the separative, choosing masculine self who stalks the pages of standard economic theory; Strassmann chastises those practitioners who use choice theory as an occasion to trivialize constraints that either inform or preclude substantive

---

1. Sandra Harding, *The Science Question in Feminism* (Ithaca, N.Y.: Cornell University Press, 1986).

2. Deconstruction is the process of analyzing the conventions used to create meaning. Deconstruction reveals the ideological nature of text, i.e., how a particular discourse poses as universal, general, and objective.

choice; and McCloskey challenges economic theorists who believe that their adherence to particular methodologies somehow liberates them from the taint of womanish metaphor. He and Nelson argue that insofar as metaphor and analogy already mediate rationality, those who assert the contrary contribute to the propagation of a masculine science that is insufficiently self-critical and thwart the humanization of economic theory. Each author's deconstruction reveals the masculinist subtext of neoclassical theorizing. As the brainchild of Western man's philosophical traditions, *homo economicus* bears the markings of his fathers' profoundly gendered social and cultural lives.

At the same time, forefathers of neoclassical economic theory were also the children of an imperialist world, one in which enslavement, colonization, genocide, and the discourses thereof were formative of self, norms, values, political means and ends. The late nineteenth-century educated elite of Euro-America inhabited an ideological world shaped by the legacy of Cartesian-inspired natural historians, who, in the previous century, had racialized and scientifically ranked the world's cultures and peoples.[3]

This sociocultural project culminated in another (partially overlapping and intersecting) set of binary oppositions: dynamic vs. stagnant, active vs. passive, reason vs. passion, culture vs. nature, civil vs. savage, progressive vs. backward, ethnic vs. tribal, normal vs. pathological, etc. The rising authority of science legitimated "race" as a meaningful categorization of our species. Members of a race share traits with one another that they do not share with members of other races. Natural historians related races to one another via a natural hierarchy, which in turn explained the behaviors of members of specific races. To the extent that these alleged differences (e.g., moral, spiritual, intellectual) warrant differential treatment, race taxonomies provided a foundation for modern racism.

As part of the dominant discourse of the late nineteenth century, race science became a language of common sense that compelled the domination of lesser peoples. Victorian imperialism invented the Dark Continent, the dominant racist construction of Africa that created a continent and peoples requiring the disciplining presence of European morality, science, and religion. Hence the meanings of "Africa," "African," and "blackness" are contested among Africans and non-Africans alike. As E. Frances White observes, "the meaning of Africa—the ideological sign Africa—is contested on discursive terrain."[4]

3. See George L. Mosse, *Toward the Final Solution: A History of European Racism* (New York: Howard Fertig, 1978); Cornel West, *Prophesy Deliverance! An Afro-American Revolutionary Christianity* (Philadelphia: Westminster Press, 1982); and Lucius Outlaw, "Toward a Critical Theory of 'Race,'" in *The Anatomy of Racism*, ed. David T. Goldberg (Minneapolis: University of Minnesota Press, 1990), 58–82.

4. E. Frances White, "Africa on My Mind: Gender, Counter Discourse, and African American Nationalism," *Journal of Women's History* 2, no. 1 (1990): 80.

The curious coincidence Harding documents is the similarity between some feminist and Africanist worldviews. Each is an oppositional discourse created by those whose daily experiences challenge the dominant ideologies of sexism and racism. She specifically addresses the writing of black economist Vernon Dixon,[5] who explores the recurrent tendency in neoclassical economics to construct African-Americans as fundamentally pathological and thus unable to compete effectively in existing capitalist economies.[6]

Dixon's argument is that this tendency is linked to the Euro-American cultural origins of "economic man." *Homo economicus* is the offspring of a separative worldview that understands the nonself and self as totally independent. The perceptual space between the self and the nonself facilitates Cartesian observation and objectivity. Events, things, other human beings, and nature exist apart from the self; they are to be acted upon, controlled, and/or measured: "The phenomenal world becomes an entity considered as totally independent of the self. Events or phenomena are treated as external to the self rather than as affected by one's feelings or reflections."[7] This ontology is consistent with the objectification and domination of other people and of the natural world. Moreover, it generates truncated notions of collectivity and responsibility to institutions or communities.

According to Dixon, the African worldview substantially reduces the distance between self and the phenomenal world; the latter is so close to the former that it compels a response and is accorded a life of its own. Therefore, Africans pursue harmony with rather than domination of nature. The phenomenal world is neither static nor dead. Rather, it is formative of a dynamic and powerful universe. Community is intrinsic to being—the individual without a communal home is not a human being. In contrast to the Euro-American individualist who is morally at liberty to refuse to act in any capacity, Africans must act on behalf of others when asked.

Hence the contours of the curious coincidence begin to unfold. Feminist critiques of the separative androcentric self parallel Dixon's Africanist characterization of Europeans. Men and Europeans view themselves as highly individuated and autonomous selves existing apart from other similarly isolated individuals. Their ethics stress rule-governed negotiation of competing claims between self-interested and autonomous subjects, and their epistemological systems affirm the separation of the knowing subject from the scrutinized ob-

5. Vernon J. Dixon, "World Views and Research Methodology," in *African Philosophy: Assumptions and Paradigms for Research on Black Persons*, ed. L. M. King, V. Dixon, and W. W. Nobles (Los Angeles: Fanon Center, Charles Drew Postgraduate Medical Center, 1976).

6. African-American economists Glen Loury and Thomas Sowell joined the chorus of 1980s voices that explained black poverty and unemployment as a consequence of pervasive cultural pathology. For an interdisciplinary response to their work, see *Praxis International* (July 1987). I recommend Robert Gooding-Williams's "Black Neoconservatism: A Critical Introduction," which contextualizes subsequent essays by Cornel West, Rhonda M. Williams, Lorenzo Simpson, and William Darity, Jr.

7. Dixon, "World Views and Research Methodology," 54–55.

ject. Moreover, variants of both feminist and Africanist/Afrocentric thought characterize Africans and women as relational in orientation and identify self-interest with the well-being of others. They espouse ethics that accord primacy to responsibility, and their epistemologies assert that the knowledge-seeker is affected by and continuous with the phenomenal world.

Although compelling, these broad schemata remain vulnerable to by now well documented parallel criticisms. For example, African cultural nationalists (e.g., Léopold Senghor and Aimé Césaire) depended on a spiritual/material dichotomy—Africans as the creators of the essential spiritual culture—to articulate the meaning of blackness. As White and others have noted, this turns the nineteenth-century colonial discourse, which compelled domination, on its head, albeit in the process of building a political unity that enabled anticolonial and nationalist liberation movements. Moreover, it both obscures differences grounded in the social relations of class and gender, and attributes an ahistoricity and rigidity to African cultures challenged by an extensive literature. As a counterdiscourse, nationalist inventions of Africa run the risk of accepting the terms of racist ideologues, even as they interrupt hegemonic mappings of Africa.

In a parallel analysis, Harding observes,

> Once we recognize that gender differences are socially created, we notice that only within the cultural projects of masculine-dominated societies does it become important . . . to insist on the fundamental sameness of women in every culture . . . to focus on women's world view or the feminine world view, paradoxically supports a masculinist conceptual scheme.[8]

Thus to articulate "women's" self-understanding homogenizes the ways of being and knowing of !Kung San gatherers, Japanese peasants of the Meiji restoration, working-class Chicanas in electronics factories in the Maquiladoras zone, and professional black lesbians in Washington, D.C.

Harding's reading of the coincidence leads her to several observations. First, she suggests that we look to projects of domination for the origins of race and gender contrast schema. Second, these schema overemphasize some differences at the expense of others, yet, third, they simultaneously suppress intragroup differences. It is Harding's last observation that is of particular interest:

> Where the Africanists find important differences between the world views of peoples of African and European descent, and feminists find important differences between the world views of women and men within Western cultures, neither acknowledges the other's dichotomy within its own conceptual scheme.[9]

8. Harding, *The Science Question in Feminism*, 173.
9. Ibid., 177.

In other words, Dixon's Africanism suppresses differences in self-understanding between men and women in the African diaspora while those who speak of a feminine standpoint presume a shared worldview among women of varying nationalities, sexualities, race-ethnicities, and cultures.

No two persons belong to exactly the same set of socially defined groups. Thus "counter discourse struggles against both dominant and competing oppositional discourses." [10] In their quests for principled alliances with male nationalists and white feminists, feminists of color have been in the vanguard of writers and/or activists articulating the interstices and contradictions of liberation movements and oppositional discourses. Black feminists, for example, have reminded their white sisters that race, nationality, sexuality, etc., construct the meaning/experience of gender—there is no unifying "woman". Simultaneously, we struggle with black male nationalists to articulate a vision of liberation that resists (hetero)sexism. [11]

For the purposes of my comments, analysis of the "curious coincidence" suggests the dangers of false universalizations in advancing our feminist economic theories. If some men reject the epistemology and ontology of the separative self, and women's experiences and self-understandings remain mediated by class, nationality, race, etc., our feminist endeavors must engage these complexities constructively or they will run the real and present danger of remaining woefully incomplete.

Let me make my case by exploring the consequences of failing to embrace this challenge. Nelson affirms the importance of reasoning beyond logic. She advocates an imaginative rationality that will break the association of gender with value. She calls for the making of a better, more "human" science that draws from both "masculine" and "feminine" approaches and that attends to the provisioning of human life. Yet Nelson's discussion speaks from unified and stable conceptualizations of masculinity, femininity, and humanity. The separative self is not simply masculinist, even in a Western and modern context. The masculinist voice of which she speaks is not universal but race and class specific.

Indeed, we cannot fully account for the historical emergence of race science unless we racially deconstruct the "masculine" voices that separate themselves from both subordinate men and women of their own communities. As the architects of natural history, European male scientists have constructed *black* males as distinctly devoid of intellectual capacity. Moreover, racialist science of the Victorian era actively embraced and spoke through very gendered metaphors. Nancy Stepan explains how nineteenth-century race sci-

10. White, "Africa on My Mind," 80.
11. Heterosexism is the institutionalized privileging of heterosexual love and sex in social relations, ideologies, and discourse.

ences analogically linked males of the "the lower races" to European women via comparisons of brain size, prognathism, and head shape.[12]

Stepan's analysis of European male phrenology (the science of skull and brain measurement) complements Nelson and McCloskey's theses on metaphors and analogy: metaphors construct new knowledge by constructing similarities. For the nineteenth-century race and gender scientists, the lower races represented the "female" type of the human species, and females the "lower race" of gender. Such metaphors inform the very modes of seeing: "it is the metaphor that permits us to see similarities that the metaphor itself helps constitute."[13]

Stepan's essay demonstrates the importance of deconstructing our discourses on gender and cautions those working to establish a dialogue between feminist theory and economics. Insofar as we fail to deconstruct our discourses, we suppress the effects of differences at work within the binary oppositions of gender. McCloskey, for example, asserts that

> for some reason men and women at present think rather differently, especially about society. The assertion is no more controversial than an assertion that Japanese and Americans at present think rather differently, especially about society. Yet women often think and act in ways that we stereotypically associate with men, and vice versa. Characteristics of women and men, Americans and Japanese, overlap in body weights and lengths of hair. We are mainly human beings, not women or Japanese.

McCloskey's assertion hides and renders irrelevant the differences on each side of his binaries. Which women and men think differently about society— Jeanne Kirkpatrick and Henry Kissinger? And which women think similarly—Phyllis Schlafly and Alice Walker?

McCloskey's struggle to move beyond simple dualisms by asserting a common humanity does not solve his problem. Rather, it sacrifices the specificity of male and female diversity, returning us to the world where the story of "mankind" hides women behind a veil of silence. He does not sustain his humanist impulse throughout the chapter, but repeatedly returns to discussions of "feminine eyes" and girls who stress community and solidarity. In calling for a more humanized economics, both Nelson and McCloskey presume an unarticulated consensus on a universal and coherent human essence.

---

12. Nancy L. Stepan, "Race and Gender: The Role of Analogy in Science," in *The Anatomy of Racism*, 38–57. Two points of clarification are warranted. First, race scientists studied facial angles—i.e., the protrusion of jaws. Prognathism is the state of having a protruding jaw. Second, the analogical science of intelligence (but not, of course, the sciences of sexuality) could ignore women of the "lower races" because of the discovery of similarities between males and females of these races.

13. Ibid., 45.

Yet hierarchies of gender, nationality, sexuality, class, race, etc. continue to trouble the waters of consensus and disrupt agreement on what it means to be fully human.

Of course neoclassical economics long ago answered the question of what it means to be human. William Milberg's deconstruction of neoclassical theory explains why:

> In the neoclassical conception, the individual agent (the text's subject) is naturally, as opposed to socially, constructed. . . . Because the individual agent's preferences are purely subjective [and, recalling England, unchanged], theory poses as value free. By presenting the subject as innocent and noncontradictory, neoclassical discourse is ideological. Deconstructing the neoclassical text uncovers this ideology, that is, its particularity, under its veil of objectivity and generality.[14]

In other words, it is not simply that the language of neoclassical economics is gendered and metaphorical; it is ideological in the sense that it naturalizes the outcomes of exchange relations and thereby naturalizes power in the political economy. Nelson and McCloskey's avoidance of a direct confrontation with the ideological component of neoclassical theory may explain their somewhat optimistic calls for a conjective and more human economics.

Strassmann's chapter speaks more directly to the issues of ideology and power. She chastises choice theorists for failing to recognize the partial truth of self-interested individualism and, in so doing, narrowing the range of explanations in the disciplines. Orthodox theory posits maximizing economic man as a good approximation of humankind across time and space—he is, in other words, universal. Proponents of *homo economicus* pursue their (albeit incomplete) professional hegemony by wielding institutionalized power to marginalize and/or exclude those who do not proceed from the foundational metaphors. Strassmann's discussion also concretizes choice theory's naturalization of power and sociopolitically constructed hierarchies. For example, class- and race-linked wealth differentials appear as "natural" endowments.

Strassmann ends her chapter by speculating that the entry of more women into the discipline may lead to changes that fit within the existing framework. And, of course, her speculation makes sense. The mere presence of women per se may be necessary, but it is hardly sufficient to generate a feminist transformation of neoclassical economics. Ergo, the importance of distinguishing between "feminine" and "feminist" voices.

Jennings's formulation of two types of nineteenth-century dualistic individualism is a provocative demonstration of the intellectual potential of a feminist perspective within institutional economics. Each tradition includes cri-

14. William Milberg, "Marxism, Poststructuralism, and the Discourse of Economists," *Rethinking Marxism*, no. 2 (1991): 96.

tiques of the cultural prioritizing of economic and Cartesian conceptual dualisms. Her feminist-institutionalist analysis posits pecuniary culture as both dualistic and gendered. Jennings concludes that gender is anchored in dualistic constructions of economy and family: "it is the association of women with the family and of men with the market economy, and their dualistic separation, that has been the main foundation of gender distinction since the nineteenth century."

Though Jennings's assertion of a "main foundation" for two hundred years of gender distinctions needs further elaboration, her discussion of gender propriety and true womanhood again confirms the need to advance a feminist economic theory that conceptualizes gender as racially constituted. In the United States, the liberal state clearly did not grant nineteenth-century European immigrant women full rights in the polity or civil society. They were politically "completed" by their husbands and male kin, existing as members of households but not as rights-bearing possessors of a civil personality.

As Jennings correctly observes, the cult of true womanhood was an animating myth of nineteenth-century U.S. culture, although men's and women's activities often transgressed the boundaries between spheres. As ideology, the cult was a very race-specific discourse: it affirmed immigrant women's roles as wives and mothers but did not do so for African-Americans, Chinese-Americans, or women indigenous to the Americas. Settler-colonists viewed these women as either expendable or as a potential source for cheap labor. As Bonnie Thornton Dill explains:

> During the eighteenth and nineteenth centuries, American society accorded considerable importance to the development and sustenance of European immigrant families. As primary laborers in the reproduction and maintenance of family life, women were acknowledged and accorded the privileges and protections deemed socially appropriate to their family roles. . . . The recognition of women's reproductive labor as an essential building block of the family, combined with a view of the family as the cornerstone of the nation, distinguished the experiences of the white, dominant culture from those of racial ethnics.[15]

Consider the experiences of African-American women and their families. For Black women, white majority denial of support for their work as wives and mothers began under enslavement. Chattel slavery denied black familial autonomy, and white men's use of rape as a weapon of terror undermined black women's integrity, forcefully demonstrating the absence of a patriarchally protected "private sphere" for black families. After emancipation, whites criticized black women who removed themselves from fieldwork, accusing them of aspiring to inappropriate norms of womanhood.

15. Bonnie Thornton Dill, "Our Mothers' Grief: Racial Ethnic Women and the Maintenance of Families," *Journal of Family History* 13, no. 4 (1988): 418.

Thus the economy/family dualism anchors gender, but in a racialized fashion. The animating gender mythology of public vs. private spheres suppresses the ideological and material racialization of gender. For most of this nation's history, institutionalized and personally violent white racism has truncated the private sphere of black family life in particular and that of people of color more generally. For Native American and Puerto Rican communities, state welfare and judicial policies have historically threatened rather than supported the creation of autonomous private life.

Folbre's contribution also speaks to the construction of gender-articulated dualisms, only this time from within the socialist and Marxist traditions. She challenges Marx and Engels's definitions of scientific and utopian socialism, arguing that nineteenth-century socialists were both scientific and feminist in their assessments of male altruism in the home, the domestic division of labor, and contraception. Folbre also reminds us of Marx and Engels's determinist tendency to theorize male domination as an epiphenomenon of class conflict.

Folbre's chapter is an important reminder of the substance of socialist feminist thought marginalized by Marx and Engels. Her suggestion that Marx and Engels pushed aside feminist concerns in order to affirm their work as scientific is provocative. Although her argument needs further development, Folbre challenges us to address Marxist claims about the nature of science. She contends that William Thompson and Anna Wheeler contributed to the development of a *science* of political economy by exposing the inconsistencies in the theory of paternal benevolence and by explaining the tension between competitive individualism in the market and altruism at home. She does not explicitly define "science," although her discussion suggests the primacy of reasoned analysis and of a well-defined boundary between science and nonscience. In other words, Folbre seems to accept as unproblematic a definition of political economy as science, which presumes a well-defined "objective" set of external social relations.

Like most Marxist and non-Marxist radical economists to date, Folbre keeps her distance from the deconstructionist view that denies absolute sources of meaning/truth and asserts the ideological nature of all discourse. Deconstruction poses particular challenges to radical economists. The argument that knowledge and being are inseparable from representation both contradicts the notion that radical/Marxist theory offers a better description of "reality" than neoclassical economics (Milberg 1991) and disrupts Engels's neat separation of "scientific" and "utopian" socialism.

Folbre's chapter suggests common ground between some feminist and Marxist projects. This essay has argued that even as the authors in this volume have deconstructed the gendered particularity of meaning in much of economic theory, they sometimes reuniversalize gender, rendering it cultureless and raceless, unintentionally reinventing the timeless human or uncomplicated feminine perspectives. Nonetheless, the authors argue for social constructionist interpretations of gender, subjectivity, and economic relations. Herein lies common ground with those Marxists who reject simple economic determinism and argue that economic relations are anything but "natural." Each literature offers a counterdiscourse, yet both must resist the historical willingness of their traditions to suppress race in thinking and theorizing class and gender.

Robert M. Solow

Feminist Theory, Women's Experience, and Economics

What am I doing here? Anyone who reads the papers in this collection will realize that they are high-tension stuff. Feelings run deep. Instinct tells me, as a man and a part-time neoclassical economist, that I should keep my head down. As it happens, I agree with quite a lot that is said in this book. That is probably why I am here, after all. In particular I think Ferber and Nelson are right to be suspicious of the domination of the profession by men, and I agree with them that this brute fact leads mainstream economics to look away from certain areas of economic life and certain facets of economic behavior.

Women are underrepresented in academic economics. Women are also underrepresented among inside linebackers and among bank presidents, for quite different reasons. You would have to be pretty naive to fail to realize that the case of economics is a lot more like bankers than like linebackers. This situation is changing, but slowly. The pace of change may have something to do with gender differences in intellectual style, as some of the authors in this volume have emphasized. I am not sure about that, because I have doubts about those cognitive differences and their basis. What is true, I think, is that until very recently, and maybe even now, there has been a tendency for male economists to patronize women, and that is just as damaging as keeping them out of the club.

It would be a miracle if this numerical imbalance were not reflected in the profession's choices about what is interesting and what is not. It would take another miracle to avoid bias in the standard treatment of those economic functions and institutions that are assigned primarily to women in our society. Anyone old enough to read these pages is too old to believe in the tooth fairy. Miracles do not happen. Let us go on from there.

I do not agree with everything I have read in these papers, however. In particular, the sweeping gender interpretation of science and cognition sounds forced and fragile to me. I am reminded of a political joke from my childhood. The novice sportswriter for the *Daily Worker* turns in his first story about yesterday's baseball game. The editor hands it back with the injunction to "class-angle the box score." Gender-angle the cost curve. The parallel runs deeper. The first few times you see social phenomena through the prism of class you see things you had never noticed before. After a while, however, a steady diet gets boring and turns into a substitute for thinking. I can feel the same thing happening with gender.

England and Jennings—others, too—think that there is something specifically masculine about "science." It has to do with the mind-set that says: here is a piece of nature and there is a scientist, not outside of nature, of course, but separate from that particular piece of nature. He pokes and prods, shines lights, measures, thinks about what he has seen and about what other scientists have said. Finally he writes up his results. The published paper embodies two hopes or beliefs: that it says something new about this particular piece of nature and that another scientist, somewhere else, looking at the same piece of nature, will come up with similar results. The specifically masculine thing about all this is not just the fact that most scientists have been men, though there may be a connection. It is the notion of the separateness of the investigator and the thing investigated.

Women are different. They are somehow more embedded in the world around them, more focused on their relations with other people and with the rest of nature. (This is, of course, a cultural fact, not a biological imperative.) I am not sure I believe this general assertion, but, like a stereotypical male, I am willing to try out the assumption and see where it leads. Suppose that science were a feminine domain. Or better still, suppose that science were gender-free, with no automatic disposition to adopt masculine or feminine attitudes and habits. It might be impossible to imagine *just* this one change from the way things are, but try. How would science be different? The atmosphere around the lab or the office might be more relaxed, or less; and progress might be faster, or slower. But would the substance of immunology or astrophysics or organic chemistry be any different? (I will come to economics in a minute.) It does not seem to me that it would. I realize that feminists deny explicitly that they are proposing a "female science." But that may reflect their latent common sense resisting the logic of their own arguments.

I put the next point as a question, because it is not something I have thought about a lot. Is it possible that the felt separateness of the investigator from the object of investigation, and from other investigators, too, is part of the intrinsic price of scientific progress? Any other stance might be inimical to the process of investigation. If science were routinely women's work, would female scientists evolve the same habits, even the habit of seeing "objectivity" where others might see "social construction"? Even if the answer to both questions were "yes," it would not trivialize the question of feminist science. It would leave, for instance, the question of the exclusion of women from preferment; it would leave the question of the mode of argument among scientists, as emphasized by McCloskey; and it would leave the question of the choice of problems to be defined as "interesting."

It seems obvious that economics is at least a little different from biology and chemistry, partly because there is no poking or prodding, just passive observing, and partly because the economist, in thinking about the economy, is inevitably thinking about herself or himself. Introspection plays no part in the framing of hypotheses about chemistry or molecular biology, but I do not see how it can be wholly avoided in framing hypotheses about economic behavior. It would be crazy not to ask: what would I do in those circumstances? Even in the economic context, however, I am skeptical about imputing specifically masculine or feminine characteristics.

McCloskey does not feel so constrained. He goes so far as to ascribe a preference for dictatorial government as a masculine taste. "Dictatorship has been the man's model of society since Plato, or for that matter since the caves." Take that, James Madison. Take that, Thomas Jefferson. Sorry, we have no record of a reservation in the name of Peter Kropotkin. It does no credit to Rosa Luxemburg to say that she saw through Leninism because she was a woman. I admired her for being clear-sighted and brave. Apart from this extravagance, much of what McCloskey says strikes me as true. It is mostly about the manner of conducting argument, not so much about conducting research. But there is one place where he—as well as Ferber and Nelson—does get at the content of economics, and there I think he is right on.

Mainstream economics likes to get as far as it can by assuming that greed and rationality characterize behavior. It is not a bad idea, and not only for Occamesque reasons. Capitalist society approves of greed and rationality in the economic sphere. You could almost define the economic sphere that way. Like any such characterization, however, this one needs to be looked at critically. Feminists point out quite rightly that official doctrine supposes greed and rationality to rule absolutely outside the family and not to rule at all inside the family. In fact, the tenderness of one is supposed to offset and even justify the harshness of the other. Feminists are properly suspicious of this extreme characterization. They think they are being handed the dirty end of the stick both times.

One of the goals of economics since Adam Smith has been to show how order can arise out of an apparent recipe for chaos in a decentralized economy. In carrying out that program, the less one has to appeal to mutuality the better. There is an important element of sheer daredevil athleticism in the attachment of economists, male and female, to the model of greed and rationality. "Show me anything, anything, and I will produce a model that derives it from greed and rationality." That can be a useful exercise until it gets in its own way.

I think you could make a case—as several of the authors do—that women are more involved than men in forms of activity that involve solidarity, volunteerism, gift exchange, empathy in an essential way. They may therefore see more clearly the role of those factors in social and economic life. This is one way in which gender roles can have an influence on the content as well as the style of economic research. There may be other ways, but they are not much discussed.

It bothers me that the papers in this volume say almost nothing about the nuts and bolts of economic analysis: demand and supply elasticities, the cyclical behavior of real and nominal wages, you name it. The ideological content of economics attracts attention, but were it not for the nuts and bolts, the market for economics would clear at a very low level. When it comes to the nuts and bolts, however, economics is more like chemistry. In those areas, the effects of feminizing the discipline would be seen mainly in atmosphere rather than in substance. (But not always—women might have a genuinely different perspective on wage determination in the business cycle, for instance.)

I would like to dissent, mildly but firmly, from a detectable mood of formalism-bashing in these papers. Formal argument has its place in economics as it does in most sciences. It is sometimes worth knowing if A implies Q, and formal logic or mathematics is by far the most reliable way to find out. No doubt formalism is easily carried too far. You can find rash claims that some piece of pure mathematical modeling tells you something about the real world. I suspect that you can find just as many rash claims that the result of some piece of data-free informal thought tells you something about the real world. It may even be that formalism helps you to avoid this trap by making it more visible. People who enjoy abstract thought will do it anyway. Taking away mathematics will only cause them to do it less well.

It is a genuine advantage to know of a promising theoretical argument that it is logically consistent. McCloskey quotes Emerson on that subject and I have two bones to pick. Bone one: My recollection is that Waldo described a foolish consistency as the hobgoblin of little minds. That takes quite a lot of the sting away from the remark. There are few defenders of foolish consistency. Bone two: I offer the guess that Waldo was not promoting logical inconsistency. He would not have thought that any virtue resided in maintaining simultaneously the truth of two contradictory propositions. I have always supposed that Emerson was expressing disapproval of the mind-set that resists abandoning old beliefs in the face of new findings. That is a very different meaning of "consistency." It is a mistake not to give formalism its due. What is bad is unwillingness to entertain any other form of argument.

It is possible that theories based on greed and rationality may be especially well adapted to formal treatment, for obvious reasons. But I suspect that alternative models could be better formalized than they are, and they should be. Formal treatment would clarify them in the usual way and would enhance their ability to compete for hearts and minds. There should be more female formalists, too; feminism shoots itself in the foot if it discourages talented women from using those methods.

Formalism has its dark side, of course. The most obvious is that it can be an instrument of intellectual terrorism: how can you be a serious economist when you do not even know the Phragmen-Lindelöf theorem? (Answer: it's easy.) Less obvious but more sinister is the fact that the notion that all serious argument is formal argument can be a way of dodging serious discussion of the choice of a model. That sort of discussion is almost never formal. Even econometric formalism can be dysfunctional at this stage because it tends to limit the range of data that gets considered.

Strassmann has a lot of interesting things to say about how ideas get established and entrenched. Goodness of fit is certainly one advantage, but it is not the only advantage that counts. The "marketplace of ideas" is imperfectly competitive, as she insists. The mainstream certainly feels most comfortable with ideas that fit neatly in the going paradigm, and other stories do not always get a fair shake. But sometimes she seems to verge on the thought that all ideas are equal. Some of her remarks about exclusion from the marketplace of ideas would sound perfectly apropos coming from an astrologer or a chiropractor. That should give one pause, but only pause. "Anything goes" is not a satisfactory alternative to monopolization of the marketplace of ideas. I would support any proposal that offered a fair shake for nonmainstream models and ideas, but it had better include some mechanism for separating wheat from chaff.

The feminine perspective offers legitimate challenges to some of the hoariest assumptions of mainstream economics. But I think the challenge sometimes takes the wrong form. There is a tendency to treat the conventional behavioral assumptions as if they were psychological in character, about people. I think those assumptions are better understood as being sociological in character, describing socially approved and legitimated behavior. Strassmann says that "economic man is the Western romantic hero," whereas I think it more likely that economic man simply embodies what people (men, alas) making business decisions are *supposed* to do. That does not mean it is always so, but it suggests a different way of criticizing the standard model.

Here is one final thought. Some of what I have read here, taken literally, seems to suggest that there is a male economics and a female economics. As things stand, female economics is relegated to a ghetto, where it plots revolution. Suppose the revolution were to succeed: what would that imply? Separate but equal? That does not sound so good to me, and it is certainly not what the authors of these papers stand for. My worry is that their arguments about gender differences in cognition and their apparently unqualified belief in the socially constructed character of (all?) knowledge lead in that direction. I think that this unsatisfactory outcome arises from an excessively simple view of the way science (small "s") evolves. Yes, it is socially constructed, but subject to constraint. (When Strassmann says that "economists are indeed aware that constraints will theoretically influence outcomes," that is surely the understatement of the year.) There really is a lot of economic life to be explained, much of it reasonably "objective." The experience of women suggests hypotheses and ideas that are worth trying out. If they do the job, then they need to be absorbed into common theory and practice, not because they are feminine but because they do the job. "Doing the job" is socially constructed but not only. If the experience of women, economists and others, leads them to reject the "not only," then we are back to the box score.

Helen E. Longino
Economics for Whom?

As someone with a limited but long past academic exposure to the discipline of economics who still attends to the debates of policy-oriented economists, I found the preceding essays unnerving reading for their descriptions of the foundations upon which the debaters must rest. As a philosopher of science, I found them fascinating for the variety of substantive and methodological challenges they pose to the mainstream of the discipline. As a feminist, I found their outline of a discipline self-constructed in images of masculinity equally compelling. *Homo economicus* comes under fire in his several interrelated aspects: the definition, assumptions, and subject matter of the field. In my remarks I want to focus on several of the themes that run through the essays, note some of their convergences and divergences, and finally articulate some further questions that they raise.

What Is Economics?

A number of the contributors note and protest a recent tendency to define economic theory as rational choice theory, a mathematical theory of rational decision by certain sorts of agents. The objections to this account of what the field is range from a critique of the influence of the otherwise unmo-

I wish to thank the director of the School of Justice Studies at Arizona State University, Professor Rita Mae Kelly, for the hospitality extended to me while I was preparing this essay.

tivated mathematization this imposes on economics, to choice theory's empirical shortcomings, to the unacceptable constriction of the field or object of
inquiry. By object of inquiry I mean what a field takes itself to be describing
and explaining.

Julie Nelson and Ann Jennings, from the vantage points of differing theoretical traditions in economics, urge redefinitions of the field in ways more
closely related to some of its ostensible concerns in the nineteenth century.
Jennings's essay alludes to the struggle of economics to define itself as a science, a struggle paralleling the emergence of a set of productive and commer-
cial relations distinct from political and other social relations. Industrialization, by removing production from land and dependence on large
landholdings, meant that the creation of wealth became to that extent independent of political relations; by removing production from the household, it
meant that the creation of wealth was to that extent independent of domestic
relations. In the effort to delineate the economic as a realm separate from
politics and domestic life, economics in England and the United States set
itself on a course that led to the present narrow view of its subject matter. The
simultaneous redefinition of the household as women's place made the economy masculine.

Nelson remarks on the constriction of the subject matter, how economics'
object of inquiry has been reduced from the panoply of phenomena associated
with the production and distribution of goods and services to one way in
which these phenomena can be understood, "the economic approach." She
also points out that, contrary to appearances, the extension of the economic
approach back to the household (as in the "new home economics") is not an
expansion of the discipline recognizing the continuing, if different, role of
households in the economy, but an application of rational choice models to
the family that obscure male power in the home as much as they obscure male
power outside the home.

Jennings sees the solution in institutional economics, a tradition that insists
on the location of economic relations in history and culture and on the impossibility of adequately understanding them outside of those contexts. Nelson
urges a refocusing on and a redefinition of the object of inquiry. She endorses
Georgescu-Roegen's view that the objective of economic activity is the self-
preservation of the human species, but she gives it a more precise formulation
as the generation of commodities and processes necessary to human survival.
Economic relations so understood exist in markets, but also within and among
households, governments, and other forms of organization. Such a definition
of economics, as the study of provisioning, rather than as the study of market
behavior, would make topics previously relegated to "the sociological"—
power, poverty, health care, and education—legitimate subjects for economists.

Strassmann, too, focuses on problems of defining economics. The problem, according to her diagnosis, lies in the "stories" or metaphors around which economics defines itself. To do economics is to elaborate these narratives in an economic setting. Her analysis, then, is similar to Nelson's: economics suffers by defining itself as an approach rather than as a subject matter. Although Strassmann forcefully criticizes the four stories she describes, she seems more cautious than Nelson about the prospects for change.

McCloskey argues that the focus on the internal coherence of mathematical models, that is, their assessment on purely logical and formal grounds, diverts attention from what he describes as their metaphoric and literary dimensions. This focus also renders less visible the narrowing of the subject matter to "masculine tales." A conjective (not conjectural but socially put together) economics would be more conscious of its stories and metaphors and would be unable to carry on with its boys' narratives. But McCloskey thinks that knowledge, including economic knowledge, *is* conjective, that it *is* a matter of conversation and mutual interrogation. Economists, like most other scientists, are just too wedded to the individualist model of knowledge production to acknowledge the social dimensions of that production. What seems to be required, then, is a self-consciousness about the relevance of the conversations, as well as of the proofs, to the construction of knowledge. This, suggests McCloskey, would make discussion of the "intuition behind the model" as central as discussion of its formal adequacy (i.e., internal coherence, consistency and completeness of axioms, deducibility of theorems).

But would McCloskey's approach really make economics less masculine? And is discussion of the intuitions behind the formalisms a literary matter? The other contributions give negative answers to both questions. It matters *who* participates in the conversation: what lies behind the masculine tales are masculine minds and ideals. And feminine minds—really feminine minds— are created to reflect and to defer to the masculine, so they won't bring about much change.[1] Genuinely different voices must be heard around the seminar tables—voices that take women's stories seriously. The debate is not about the literary merits of the models but about their representative adequacy— their historical, psychological, and sociological adequacy. The methodological issue for economics is not modulating mathematical sophistication with literary finesse, but introducing empirical standards to match the mathematical rigor.

Nelson and McCloskey both attribute the preeminence of mathematical modeling to its congruence with a particular image of masculinity, one created in the gender structure of the dualisms by which our culture teaches us to

1. It's worth underlining here that "masculine" and "feminine" minds are not natural kinds. One of the achievements of feminist scholarship is the distinction between sex and gender. In distinguishing gender from sex, feminist scholars have shown that masculinity and femininity exist as historically and culturally variable ideals, that they operate as power gradients, and that individual humans must learn to exemplify them.

understand our experience: hard/soft, fact/story, logic/metaphor, cognitive/intuitive, rational/emotive, objective/subjective, and so on. But surely there must be some attraction other than emotional fit. Why, after all, do economists get paid so much more than other social scientists? One of the points of mathematization in the sciences is the consequent ability to increase the scope and precision of predictions. Successful testing of the accuracy of those predictions through experiment justifies our reliance on the equations and assumptions that generate them when extrapolating to "real life" conditions—for example, planning exploratory space voyages. One would therefore expect that mathematical modeling in economics makes prediction possible and that prediction of certain phenomena is valued by those who make economics possible. So modeling must (or must be hoped to) result in predictions that are good enough, enough of the time.

The essays I have just discussed, which focus on the definition of economics as an intellectual discipline, suggest that the potential subject matter (and value) of economics is not exhausted by prediction. Indeed, one might even infer from some of them that prediction, to the extent that it must satisfy empirical standards, may be an unwelcome demand. Other essays in the volume take issue with the representations of economic relations that are both implicit and explicit in the models. By so doing they also question the adequacy of setting prediction as a goal of economic science and raise the question of how good, good enough is. Let me turn now to some of the particular issues they address concerning the representation of women and women's place in households and concerning the representation of economic agents, and then return to this question of modeling, prediction, and why and for whom economics is done.

Women and the Household

Two criticisms are voiced repeatedly in this book. One is that the treatment of women's work in the household as "outside of production" negates the contributions of female domestic labor to the economy. The facts that the raising of children is necessary to the production of "human capital" and that domestic labor makes it possible for those deemed economic agents to sally forth into the marketplace day after day are ignored. Traditional women's work in maintaining the work force is invisible because not compensated. The true costs of production are thus grossly underestimated. Estimates of national productivity, if understood as a measure of productive activity, are distorted and policy for a society based on such estimates is likely to be unsatisfactory to substantial segments of that society.

This treatment of women's domestic labor is both an effect and an engine of sexism. As Jennings shows in her discussion of the public/private distinc-

tion, family and household always end up on the disprivileged side of dichotomies. The emergence of the production and distribution of goods and services as a set of relations distinct from the political required carving out a
sphere of the private distinct from the domestic. The latter, already subordinated to the public in significance, also became subordinated to the world of
production for exchange and profit. Strassmann sees the effect of that subordination in the "Woman of Leisure" story, which treats women's domestic
work as chosen and unburdensome: women are dependent on the benevolent
patriarch's success in the market; care for, and reproduction of, the patriarch
are not conceptualized as work. Nancy Folbre sees the effect in the history of
socialist theory—in the dismissal of socialist thinking that incorporated feminist issues as utopian. Marx and Engels, like the classical and neoclassical
economists, both reasoned under the influence of sexism and perpetuated it by
treating the work socially assigned to women as trivial and beneath serious
notice. In all three of these economic traditions, the inclusion of women's
domestic work in the calculation of production and productivity, while possible, considerably complicates the resulting picture, if only because it requires new methods of measuring production.

And what of the new attention in neoclassical economics to the family? The
contributors are unanimous in seeing the new home economics as grossly dis-
torting domestic relations and women's experience both in and out of the
household. Ferber and Nelson point out the circularity of arguing that women
earn less in the market because of their household responsibilities and then
arguing that women specialize in household maintenance rather than other
forms of work because their expected return from wage labor is lower. They
question the worth of such explanations when women are socialized to expect
little, or at least less than the men with whom they grew up. England, in
addition, cites research showing that the less women earn outside the family
the less power they exercise in decision-making within the family. If women
are economic agents, then it is not possible to assume that all agents operate
under the same constraints, or maximize the same sorts of utilities. Nor does
gender operate in any simple way. One might ask, for example, how the new
home economics would treat the economic behavior of women and men who,
like members of many inner-city African-American families, confront situations in which the usual gender asymmetry of job opportunities is reversed.[2]

Men's role in the household is no better represented. The assumption of
male altruism within the family obscures male power and the role it plays in
family decisions. Strassmann points out that the benevolent patriarch assumption enables the economist to treat the family as an individual unit. Obviously,
this can be useful for measuring gross or aggregate consumption rates. The
assumption, however, flies in the face of documented inequities in distribution

2. This is not to say that African-American women have the same opportunities as white men,
but that sexism operates differentially in a context of social and institutional racism.

within the family (as indicated by rates of malnourishment, morbidity, mortality, and physical abuse). It results in bad description and bad policy, as Strassmann, relying on the work of Amartya Sen and others, shows.

The failures here are errors of fact, errors at the periphery of the discipline as currently constituted that could be corrected without challenging the overall frameworks within which these biased and mistaken assumptions are deployed. Disaggregating consumption within the family, and recognizing the unequal distribution of power and decision-making within the family, can be accomplished without major theoretical adjustments. Institutionalists need only open their eyes, since, according to Jennings, their theoretical framework is already congenial to feminist insights about power. Socialists have their misnamed utopian tradition to draw on. Neoclassicists might have to revise their calculations, perhaps beat a strategic retreat from intractable territory. But the second major criticism voiced in this book focuses on a more central aspect of economic theorizing, namely the characterization of those recognized as economic agents and of the conditions under which they make decisions.

Economic Agents

The new neoclassical definition of economics as the theory of rational choice means that economists must make a number of assumptions about the nature of the agents in economic interactions. Most of the contributors try to articulate what these assumptions are, how they reflect sexist bias, and how they reflect distorted pictures of reality.[3] There are, however, some interesting divergences in their views.

Paula England draws our attention to three assumptions associated with what she calls the separative self. The entity making rational choices in the market is conceived as independent from other choosing entities in a number of crucial ways.[4] As England points out, this conception of the economic agent is remarkably similar to the stereotype of ideal masculinity that has been culturally powerful in the modern West. Independence of decision-making is

3. Feminist philosophers have also been developing a critique of traditional conceptions of rationality and reason, which complements the more specifically economic critiques. See especially Elizabeth Anderson, "Some Problems in the Normative Theory of Rational Choice with Consequences for Empirical Research," presented at the meetings of the Public Choice Society, New Orleans, 1992 (available from the author, Department of Philosophy, University of Michigan); Genevieve Lloyd, *The Man of Reason: "Male" and "Female" in Western Philosophy* (Minneapolis: University of Minnesota Press, 1984); and Phyllis Rooney, "Gendered Reason: Sex Metaphor and Conceptions of Reason," *Hypatia* 6(2): 77–103.

4. I say "entity" rather than person, because it's not clear to what extent the assumptions are intended to ascribe psychological characteristics to human individuals. England's discussion can be taken to show that when the decision-making entities in a system *are* human individuals, the assumptions fail to characterize the system adequately.

expressed in the assumptions (1) that utilities are interpersonally incommensurable (i.e., it is not possible to establish whether my enjoyment of x is greater or less than your enjoyment of x), (2) that preferences ("tastes") are unchanging and created outside the market (hence, unaffected by interactions that occur within the market), and (3) that utilities are interpersonally independent (i.e., my satisfaction does not depend on your happiness or unhappiness—or, agents are selfish).

The first assumption has the consequence that it is not theoretically legitimate to assert that S_1 is worse off than S_2, whether S_1 and S_2 are individuals or groups. This deprives programs for alleviating poverty of any economic rationale. England argues that if we assume a connected, empathic self rather than a separative self, then utilities could be interpersonally commensurable. Why assume agents are one way or the other? Implicit in England's chapter is the answer that only a masculinist ideal of the economic person leads one to treat an assumption of the noncomparability of utilities as realistic.

England also argues that the second and third assumptions are false. Individuals' tastes do change as a consequence of economic interactions, so they cannot function as the unmoved mover of economic activity. Tastes, or preferences, would be more correctly understood as in dynamic interaction with those activities. This shift would be analogous to the shift away from the Central Dogma in molecular biology. Once biologists treated DNA as an unmoved mover; now the genetic material in cells is understood to change (for example, through transposition) in response to cytoplasmic and other changes. Similarly, the assumption of uniform selfishness in the market is not supported by observations of all market behaviors. Solidarity and collective action do characterize some market interactions (and might well characterize more, were the market not structured to discourage them). In particular, male solidarity (as expressed, for example, in hiring practices) at times overrides pure selfishness (or rational self interest) in the labor market. One might add that white solidarity operates similarly. Women in the academy also experience the adverse effects of male solidarity in the citation patterns reported by Ferber and Nelson.

England seems to think that models of rational choice could simply be amended to acknowledge variation in separation and connectedness in single individuals over time and among individuals, and that the only loss might be in ease of prediction or of calculation. It's not clear to me that such amended models would much resemble the originals, nor whether such amendment, radical as it is, would be sufficient for England's purposes (whether, for example, it could deal with the policy questions that get swept aside under the separative model). The feminist critiques on which England relies require that we rethink our very conception of rationality. Models of rational choice, if such constructs are to survive, are likely to look very different under different conceptions of rationality.

Issues raised by the other contributors also suggest that change will not come easily. Diana Strassmann notes that the assumption that the economic agent is a self-contained individual making choices is central to the self-understanding of economics. She argues at the end of her paper that assumptions at the core of economic theory will be relinquished much more reluctantly than those at the periphery. The neglect of dependence and interdependence is fostered by the field's very conception of itself. And this means that, for some at least, change does not mean modification, it means disappearance.

Jennings and Nelson draw our attention to another consequence of reliance on models of rational choice. They argue that the constraints of the neoclassical focus on choice obscure the important distinction between wants and needs. If we can't distinguish between luxury yachts and a diet meeting the minimum daily requirements for nutrients, we can't have a science of provisioning. It may not be possible to compare the utility of a yacht to me with its utility to you, but we both need food, clothing, a place to sleep, and so forth. Thus, further discussion of the interpersonal comparison of utilities seems warranted. Jennings's and Nelson's alternatives require a redefinition of the discipline, a redefinition that treats the phenomena of production and distribution of goods and services, which economics was originally developed to explain, as the proper subject matter of the field. Such redefinition would draw on subject matter rather than on method.

McCloskey, too, sees the centrality to economics of certain stories and metaphors, but diagnoses the problem as a preference for a "masculine" style of argument. In his view, the inclusion of those halves of the gender dualisms that are currently excluded from permissible economic argument would greatly improve the discipline.

One of the fascinating features of McCloskey's essay is its moving back and forth between economics and the economy. Outlining aspects of a conjective economics, he invokes *Femina economica,* an agent who acts out of solidarity with others, does the neighborly thing. In a "feminine economy," one populated by such individuals, people's needs would be taken into account by their neighbors (echoing England, persons' utilities would be interdependent). But when he claims that conjective economics would take solidarity seriously, it's not clear whether McCloskey is recommending that economists should take current instances of solidarity seriously or that they should take the possibility that solidarity could be an organizing relationship among economic agents seriously (as one that would replace self-interested competitiveness, say). The first is a recommendation for economics, the second a recommendation for the economy. In either case, *Femina economica* may be the wrong model. In the first instance, as England shows, the examples of solidarity that current economics ignores concern the kind of male solidarity that harms women. In the second instance, while the idealization of stereotypical feminine or motherly traits is an understandable reaction to the overvaluation of stereotypical masculine traits, neither offers a good model for solidarity. The person who acts selfishly can harm me, but the person who acts out of empathy with me often acts on her/his (incorrect) assumption that we have the same desires or interests. What might be needed is not a feminine economy but, to use McCloskey's own term, a conjective economy, that is, one we create together.

McCloskey's invocation of a different economy in the context of challenging economics raises a question about the relation of the discipline to its subject matter. Would a differently organized economy require different stories and metaphors? If so, the models of economics are models not of economic behavior generally but of the economic behavior of agents in an economy organized in a particular way. This raises a further question: whether the models themselves do not have a subtly prescriptive effect, encouraging economic agents to conform to them because, after all, that's how, according to economic theory, everyone else behaves, and we know how dove strategies fare against hawk strategies. One of the difficulties in doing social science is that the least units of analysis—humans—deliberate and act on the basis of (changing and always incomplete) understandings of themselves and their social worlds. In this respect they are unlike the least units of natural science (elementary particles, molecules, etc.), which have no self-understandings that affect their behavior. However this difference is theorized, it cannot be ignored. These reflections raise issues both of partiality and of normativity.

Conclusion

As noted earlier in this commentary, and by a number of contributors, one of the intrinsic features of models is their partiality. Partiality, therefore, is not in and of itself a defect. A model of a process highlights some features of the process and suppresses others in an attempt to concentrate attention on what are taken by the modeler to be its significant or interesting aspects. When a process is not amenable to direct observation, as most complex processes are not, one test of the adequacy of a model of it is its ability to predict the phenomena we can observe with whatever constancy and degree of accuracy are sufficient to our purposes. Thus, the rational choice models of neoclassical economics might be considered useful to the extent that they make forecasts of various economic phenomena possible.

Prediction, of course, is not explanation, and the role a model has played in successful prediction is not a guarantee that it has represented all the causally relevant phenomena or the relations between them. I can predict rain on the basis of the barometer's behavior, but the barometer's falling does not explain the rain. One could say in defense of the rational choice models that they enable us to make predictions, and one could add that of course no one intends them to be taken as literal descriptions of what happens in the real world. But this defense would not do. The chapters in this book show time and again that substantive assumptions within the models are used as the basis for policy formation. Here the models are being read literally. Their partiality and selectivity are ignored.

Models can be partial in a number of ways: by leaving out interactors in a process, by leaving out interactions in a process, and by modeling only one of many possible alternatives. This collection has shown that the models of economic theory are partial in all three ways. Calculating production on the basis of monetarily compensated goods and services leaves out uncompensated domestic labor. Hence, it makes one class of interactors, homemakers (who are predominantly women), invisible. Assuming fixed preferences and independence of utilities reduces the number of the interactions that must be considered. This simplification, however, renders invisible certain interactions and relations that disadvantage women when they participate in economic relations that are included in the model. The partiality of these models is not benign.

The third kind of partiality, the representation of only one or several of the possible kinds of process that can underlie the observable phenomena, may be even more vicious. A noneconomic example of this kind of partiality is to be found in evolutionary theory. Natural selection is only one of the processes that can underlie a change in gene frequencies in a population. Neutral mutations and random drift are other processes. And, of course, there is artificial selection, which has given us the great variety of domesticated plants and animals designed for different purposes: food production, fiber production, transportation, and so on. Models of natural selection are partial in that they do not exhaust the possibilities of accounting for genetic change. Just so, market models laden with all the limiting assumptions discussed in the chapters above may represent only one of the possible kinds of process underlying the production and distribution of goods and services. McCloskey's allusion to a differently organized economy raises the possibility of this kind of partiality. So, of course, do the alternative traditions within economics discussed by Jennings and Folbre. Here, as suggested above, "partiality" takes on a double meaning: incomplete treatment and preferential treatment.

Several of the contributors have referred to my ideas about scientific knowledge in their essays. I have argued that scientific inquiry is social in character—that criticism of data, hypotheses, models, and background assumptions is an integral dimension of knowledge construction in the sciences. For such criticism to be effective in promoting objectivity or knowledge rather than the world view of a privileged class, inquiring communities must grant equality of intellectual authority to all qualified participants in the dialogue. They must ensure that potentially critical perspectives are well enough developed to be a source both of informed criticism and of genuinely alternative models. One argument for this account of inquiry is the multiple partiality of models. Only through wide-ranging critical dialogue can their specific partialities be revealed and assessed.

Effective critique requires mastery of a discipline and an understanding of its relation to its broader social context. Transformative critique requires the elaboration of alternative models and alternative practices of inquiry that satisfy both traditional cognitive values and the alternative values motivating the critique. Further development of the challenge begun in this volume will require that feminist economists consider a number of additional questions, among them the following.

1. What are the normative effects of the assumptions of mainstream economics in the United States? How do they constrain the behavior of individuals? How do they limit our perception of what is possible, and thereby of what we dare to construct?

2. What purposes are served by the research programs of mainstream economics? What counts as success, and what is its value? What values are not served? What are the costs—scientific, social, and political—of ignoring them?

3. What would models, theories, and research programs look like that more fully represent the work and the interests of those historically excluded from the development of economic knowledge? With what other groups ought feminist economists build solidarity? What would models that more fully represent the causal interactions of interest to feminists look like? How would they differ from those currently employed by the mainstream? And what would be required for their incorporation into the center of economic thought?

The essays in this volume constitute an important first step in creating a dialogue that could deeply transform economics. Their overwhelming message is a demand not for the inclusion of an alternative or feminine "way of knowing" in economics but for the inclusion of the perspectives of those historically excluded from the construction of economic knowledge into the critical dialogues of the field. When analyzed, the social and cultural experiences of those so excluded provide a vantage point from which to develop hardheaded critiques of mainstream assumptions. In other sciences, particularly biology, researchers relying on their collectively analyzed social experiences as women have shown the background assumptions of their sciences to reflect the social experiences of (middle-class) men. The feminist economists represented in this volume are doing the same for their discipline. As can be seen already in the preceding chapters, feminist critiques need not speak with one voice, and they may overlap with critiques from other excluded perspectives. If economists thinking as feminists can develop alternative models to join to their critiques, we will be on the way to a reconstruction of economic science.

Biographies of the Contributors

REBECCA M. BLANK is assistant professor in the department of economics and the School of Education and Social Policy at Northwestern University, and holds a research faculty appointment in Northwestern's Center for Urban Affairs and Policy Research. She has published a wide variety of academic articles on various aspects of the behavior and well-being of low-income individuals and the operation of the labor market, the macroeconomy, and public assistance programs.

PAULA ENGLAND is professor of sociology at the University of Arizona. She is coauthor, with George Farkas, of *Households, Employment, and Gender: A Social, Economic, and Demographic View* (1986), and author of *Comparable Worth: Theories and Evidence* (1992), and "The Failure of Human Capital Theory to Explain Occupational Sex Segregation," *Journal of Human Resources* (1982).

MARIANNE A. FERBER is professor of economics and director of women's studies at the University of Illinois, Urbana-Champaign. Her research has focused particularly on the standing of women in academia, the interface of work and family, and international comparisons of the position of women. She has published in a variety of scholarly journals and is coauthor, with Francine D. Blau, of *The Economics of Women and Work* (2d ed., 1992) as well as author of *Women and Work, Paid and Unpaid* (1987), an annotated bibliography.

NANCY FOLBRE is professor of economics at the University of Massachusetts. She has written widely on the relationship between feminist theory and political economy, publishing in journals that include the *Journal of Development Economics, World Development, Signs, Feminist Studies, Cambridge Journal of Economics,* and the *Review of Radical Political Economics.* She is currently at work on a book about the history of economic thought, entitled *Self-Love, the Mainspring: Feminism and Political Economy, 1750–1990*.

ANN L. JENNINGS is assistant professor of economics at the University of Wisconsin at Green Bay. She is a board member of the Association for Institutionalist Thought (AFIT) and contributes regularly to the *Journal of Economic Issues*. Her recent research focuses on the cultural articulation of race, class, and gender distinctions.

HELEN E. LONGINO teaches philosophy at Rice University. She is author of *Science as Social Knowledge: Values and Objectivity in Scientific Inquiry* (1990) and of numerous articles in feminist philosophy and the philosophy of science.

DONALD N. MCCLOSKEY is John F. Murray Professor of Economics and professor of history at the University of Iowa. He has published widely in economic history and methodology. He is author of ten books, among them *The Applied Theory of Price* (1985), *The Rhetoric of Economics* (1985), *If You're So Smart: The Narrative of Economic Expertise* (1990), and *Knowledge and Persuasion in Economics*.

JULIE A. NELSON is assistant professor of economics at the University of California, Davis. Her writings on feminist theory have appeared in *Economics and Philosophy, Journal of Economic Studies, History of Political Economy,* and *Hypatia*. She also works in the area of household demand analysis, publishing in journals including *Econometrica, Review of Economics and Statistics,* and *American Journal of Agricultural Economics*.

ROBERT M. SOLOW is Institute Professor at the Massachusetts Institute of Technology. His main publications are *Linear Programming and Economic Analysis* (with R. Dorfman and P. Samuelson, 1958), *Capital Theory and the Rate of Return* (1969), *Growth Theory, An Exposition* (1970), and *The Labor Market as a Social Institution* (1990). He is a past president of the American Economics Association and was recipient of the Nobel Prize in Economic Science in 1987.

DIANA STRASSMANN is senior research fellow in the Center for Cultural Studies, Rice University. Her current research interests include feminist economic theory, economic narrative and rhetoric, the history of economic thought, and industrial organization. She has published articles in the *Review of Economics and Statistics,* the *Journal of Public Economics,* and other journals.

Rhonda M. Williams is assistant professor of Afro-American studies and economics at the University of Maryland in College Park. She is an affiliate faculty member of the women's studies program and a member of the editorial board for *Feminist Studies* as well as a reviewer for the *Review of Black Political Economy*. Her publications address theories of competition and discrimination, culture and poverty, and the evolution of race and gender employment hierarchies in capitalist economies.

INDEX